A Conversation Analysis Approach to French L2 Learning

This book offers a critical examination of second language (L2) learning outside institutional contexts, with a focus on the way second language learners introduce, close, and manage conversational topics in everyday settings. König adopts a conversation analysis for second language acquisition (CA-SLA) approach in analyzing oral data from a longitudinal study of L2 learners of French with au pairs in Swiss families over several years. With this approach, the author presents insights into how L2 learners introduce and close conversational topics in ongoing conversations and how these strategies evolve over time, setting the stage for future research on this little-documented process in SLA. This volume contributes toward a greater understanding of L2 learning "in the wild," making this key reading for students and researchers in SLA, applied linguistics, and French language learning and teaching.

Clelia König is a postdoctoral research assistant at the German University of Koblenz-Landau. She works at the Institute of German Language at the Campus in Landau and teaches several bachelor of arts–level courses for teacher students in the domains of general linguistics, semantics and pragmatics, conversation analysis, and SLA.

Routledge Advances in Second Language Studies
Edited by John Hellermann and Søren Wind Eskildsen

Racialized Identity in Second Language Learning
Speaking Blackness in Brazil
Uju Anya

Teaching and Testing L2 Interactional Competence
Bridging Theory and Practice
Edited by M. Rafaiel Salaberry and Silvia Kunitz

A Conversation Analysis Approach to French L2 Learning
Introducing and Closing Topics in Everyday Interactions
Clelia König

For more information about this series, please visit: www.routledge.com/Routledge-Advances-in-Second-Language-Studies/book-series/RASLS

A Conversation Analysis Approach to French L2 Learning

Introducing and Closing Topics in Everyday Interactions

Clelia König

NEW YORK AND LONDON

First published 2020
by Routledge
52 Vanderbilt Avenue, New York, NY 10017

and by Routledge
2 Park Square, Milton Park, Abingdon, Oxon, OX14 4RN

Routledge is an imprint of the Taylor & Francis Group, an informa business

© 2020 Taylor & Francis

The right of Clelia König to be identified as author of this work has been asserted by her in accordance with sections 77 and 78 of the Copyright, Designs and Patents Act 1988.

All rights reserved. No part of this book may be reprinted or reproduced or utilised in any form or by any electronic, mechanical, or other means, now known or hereafter invented, including photocopying and recording, or in any information storage or retrieval system, without permission in writing from the publishers.

Trademark notice: Product or corporate names may be trademarks or registered trademarks, and are used only for identification and explanation without intent to infringe.

Library of Congress Cataloging-in-Publication Data
Names: König, Clelia, author.
Title: A conversation analysis approach to French L2 learning : introducing and closing topics in everyday interactions / Clelia König.
Description: 1. | New York : Taylor and Francis, 2019. | Series: Routledge advances in second language studies | Includes bibliographical references and index.
Identifiers: LCCN 2019044291 | ISBN 9780367143565 (hardback) | ISBN 9780429031489 (ebook)
Subjects: LCSH: French language—Discourse analysis. | French language—Study and teaching. | Second language acquisition—Research. | Language acquisition—Research. | Discourse analysis.
Classification: LCC PC2434 .K66 2019 | DDC 448.0071—dc23
LC record available at https://lccn.loc.gov/2019044291

ISBN: 978-0-367-14356-5 (hbk)
ISBN: 978-0-429-03148-9 (ebk)

Typeset in Sabon
by Apex CoVantage, LLC

To my family

Contents

Acknowledgments   xi

Introduction   1

1   Data, Methodology, and Research Questions   4

   1.1 *Conversation Analysis: Methodological and Analytical Issues 4*
      1.1.1 *Conversation Analysis's Methodological Way: The Ethnomethods in the Data 4*
      1.1.2 *Participants' Methods and Interactional Phenomena 5*
      1.1.3 *The Investigation of Linguistic Phenomena in Everyday Talk-in-Interaction 7*
   1.2 *The Research Project 9*
   1.3 *The Au Pairs and Their Learning Environment 10*
      1.3.1 *The Chosen Data Sets 10*
      1.3.2 *The Au Pairs' Learning Environment 12*
   1.4 *Research Questions and Contributions of the Present Study 12*
   References 14

2   Topic Analysis in First and Second Languages   17

   2.1 *From the Prague School to Text Linguistics: An Overview 17*
   2.2 *Discourse Analysis 18*
   2.3 *Second Language Acquisition Studies (SLA) 20*
   2.4 *Topics in L1 Interactions 22*
      2.4.1 *Topic Progression 23*

2.4.2 Topical Disjunctions 27
2.4.3 Conversational Topics and Domains of Knowledge 35
References 37

3 L2 Acquisition and Interactional Competence — 43

3.1 Conversation Analysis for Second Language Acquisition (CA-SLA) 43
   3.1.1 Reconceptualizing Learning 46
   3.1.2 Analysis of Competence 47
3.2 The Study of Interactional Competence 48
   3.2.1 The Roots of Interactional Competence 49
   3.2.2 The Investigation of Interactional Competence in the Domain of CA-SLA 51
   3.2.3 L2 Interactional Competence in the Wild 53
3.3 Current Challenges for Longitudinal CA-SLA Investigations 55
   3.3.1 What It Means to Study Change in Talk-in-Interaction: Documenting Learning 55
   3.3.2 Exemplar Longitudinal CA-SLA Studies 56
References 58

4 Topic Management in French L1 and L2 Interactions — 63

4.1 Topic, Reference, and Anaphora in Conversation 63
4.2 Topic Analysis in French Data. From "Objet de discours" to Conversational Process 65
4.3 Topic Management in L2 Talk-in-Interaction 67
   4.3.1 Topic Introduction 70
   4.3.2 Topic Closure 71
References 75

5 Topic Introduction — 79

5.1 Advanced L2 Level: Julie 79
   5.1.1 Topic Introduction at the Beginning of the Stay 80
   5.1.2 Topic Introduction at the Middle of the Stay 83
   5.1.3 Topic Introduction at the End of the Stay 85

5.2 Intermediate L2 Level: Oksana 87
   5.2.1 Topic Introduction at the Beginning of the Stay 88
   5.2.2 Topic Introduction in the Middle of the Stay 90
   5.2.3 Topic Introduction at the End of the Stay 93
5.3 Summary of Findings 96
   5.3.1 The Sequential Environment: Sequence Opening After a Closed Sequence 97
   5.3.2 The Turn Architecture: Linguistic and Prosodic Resources 97
   5.3.3 Difference Between Julie and Oksana: Management of Recipient Design 98
5.4 Topic Shift 99
   5.4.1 Topic Shift Through Reference Shift 100
   5.4.2 Topic Shift Through Pivot-Shifting 102
   5.4.3 Topic Shift Through Multiple Reference 104
5.5 Summary of Findings 106
References 108

6 Topic Closure 110

6.1 Advanced L2 Level: Julie 110
   6.1.1 Topic Closure at the Beginning of the Stay 110
   6.1.2 Topic Closure in the Middle of the Stay 113
   6.1.3 Topic Closure at the End of the Stay 114
6.2 Intermediate L2 Level: Oksana 117
   6.2.1 Topic Closure at the Beginning of the Stay 117
   6.2.2 Topic Closure in the Middle of the Stay 120
   6.2.3 Topic Closure at the End of the Stay 122
6.3 Beginner L2 Level: Christine 124
   6.3.1 Topic Closure at the Beginning of the Stay 125
   6.3.2 Topic Closure in the Middle of the Stay 127
   6.3.3 Topic Closure at the End of the Stay 128
6.4 Summary of Findings 130
   6.4.1 Main Findings Regarding the Participation in Topic Closure 130
   6.4.2 Topic Closure: Longitudinal Observations and Stability Over Time 131
References 132

7 Nature and Development of L2 Interactional Competence 134

7.1 On the Nature of L2 Interactional Competence 134
    7.1.1 L2 Interactional Competence: Not Only Linguistic 135
    7.1.2 L2 Interactional Competence: Local and Shared 136
    7.1.3 L2 Interactional Competence: Many Abilities, One Term 137
7.2 On the Development of L2 Interactional Competence 138
    7.2.1 Topic Introduction: Summary of Findings 139
        7.2.1.1 Topic Introduction 139
        7.2.1.2 Topic Shift 140
        7.2.1.3 Observability of the Development of L2 Interactional Competence 140
    7.2.2 Topic Closure: Summary of Findings 142
        7.2.2.1 Sequential and Linguistic Aspects of Topic Closure 142
        7.2.2.2 Observability of the Development of L2 Interactional Competence 143
7.3 L2 Interactional Competence and Its Development Over Time 143
    7.3.1 L2 Interactional Competence and Topic Introduction 144
    7.3.2 L2 Interactional Competence and Topic Closure 146
References 147

8 Conclusion(s) 150

8.1 Answering the Research Questions 150
8.2 Implications of This Study 152
References 156

Appendix I: Transcription Conventions 160
Index 161

Acknowledgments

I wish to thank John Hellermann and Søren W. Eskildsen for accepting my manuscript in their Routledge series. It has been an intense work, and I have received lots of inspiring and motivating comments on my text. Thank you so much for instructing and guiding me throughout this process. Similarly, I want to thank the Routledge staff (Elysse, Helena, and Allie) for helping me out when I did not know how to make things work and for always being there with an answer to my questions.

My sincere thanks go to my supervisor, Simona Pekarek Doehler, who has introduced me to a new and thrilling research field and who has exercised patience in guiding me during the time of my PhD. Thank you as well to my former colleagues (Evelyne, Simone, Ioana, Virginie D., Etienne, Virginie F., and Cécile) for the nice time we have shared together in Neuchâtel. I also want to thank Anne-Claude Berthoud, Fritjof Sahlström, and Heiko Hausendorff for accepting to be part of the evaluation committee for my doctoral thesis. I have learned so much from your interesting comments and reviews of my thesis after your feedback had already been my first step toward this publication. Thank you!

Finally, I wish to express my gratitude to my family: Philipp and our little children, my parents, and my in-laws. You have always been there for me; you have seen how much work and time I have invested in this project, and you have always supported me in every possible way. Thank you for your time, your help, and the laughter we have shared.

Introduction

Our common-sense knowledge about conversations suggests that when we talk with other people, there is always "something we are talking about." If this is intuitively true, it still also represents a debated aspect in a variety of linguistic, sociolinguistic, and anthropological approaches to the study of language, especially of spoken language. This "something people are talking about" has been labeled in different ways, but it has often been called topic. Depending on the type of data that has been analyzed and given the linguistic approach adopted, a topic can be identified at different levels: it is possible to investigate sentence topic (see Chafe, 1976, 1987; Givón, 1983, 1987) or discourse topic (see van Dijk, 1977), or it is also possible to analyze topic by looking at the information flow of discourses (see Dimroth & Starren, 2003; Lambrecht, 1994). Since the 1960s and the development of the conversation analytic approach, Sacks (1995) also pinpointed the topical nature of everyday talk-in-interaction. His lectures have delivered the basis for the subsequent evolution of conversation analysis (henceforth CA) and he has addressed the complexity of topics and topicality in interaction.

In my study, I sketch different linguistic approaches that have dealt with the concept of topic. Topic has often been defined as the matter (*what*) people are talking about when they are in a dialogue. There are several approaches that operate with this definition of topic, such as text linguistics, discourse analysis, and functionalism. Complementary to these approaches, there is another research field, rooted in the domains of sociology and ethnomethodology, that works with other analytical tools: CA. CA investigates the methods (Garfinkel, 1967) with which conversationalists do what they do when they talk to each other. The concept of topic is redefined in relation to the methods and practices that conversationalists employ for managing topics in interaction: *How* do they introduce a new topic? *How* do they close it? *How* do they go back and forth between topics in an ongoing interaction?

Adopting CA's emic perspective, i.e. investigating the data from an endogenous point of view, I show how topic management is realized in interactions in French as a second language (henceforth L2). I apply CA tools for the conversation analysis for L2 acquisition (CA-SLA): CA-SLA is the research field in which my study is situated. My data stem from everyday family interactions between host family members and au pairs that have spent six to 12 months in the French-speaking part of Switzerland to learn or improve their French L2. The L2 learning process I investigate, then, happens simultaneously with the socialization process in the host families, where the au pairs slowly become members of this new community. As far as the L2 learning process is concerned, my analyses show how the L2 speakers' interactional competence is observable in the data and how it develops (i.e. how the L2 speakers' practices change) over time.

My analysis of topic management is divided into two parts: I investigate separately topic introduction and topic closure, and I compare different examples from different points in time—i.e. a longitudinal design. The research questions guiding my investigations are as follows:

1. How do L2 speakers manage conversational topics in everyday interactions? This first question helps me individuate the methods and practices used by the au pairs for introducing and closing conversational topics.
2. How do the practices for managing topic change over time? Do they all change, or do only some? I show that changes over time are observable for topic introduction, whereas topic closure seems to be a more stable actional microcosm, one that possibly supports reflections on the nature of L2 interactional competence.

Two further sub-questions arise at this point:

3. What do investigations of topic management tell us about the nature of L2 interactional competence?
4. What do longitudinal investigations of topic management suggest about the development of L2 interactional competence?

In Chapter 1, I present the data and the methodology of this study, as well as its more general contributions. An overview of several approaches to the concept of topic is the objective of Chapter 2. Here I concentrate particularly on CA; thus, I introduce both my terminology and the analytical tools I have employed for my investigations. Chapter 3 contains a discussion about the existing literature on CA, CA-SLA, L2 language learning, and the concept of L2 interactional competence. A description of topic management in conversation is the subject of Chapter 4: I review the literature on topic introduction and topic closure for English and French (both L1 and L2) to give a background to the analytical part of the study. Chapter 5 is the first analytical chapter and is concerned with the investigation of topic introduction. Longitudinal comparisons of data from the corpora of two au pairs are presented and discussed. Topic closure is the analytical focus of Chapter 6. Here, the data from the corpora of three au pairs are examined and compared. Chapter 7 discusses the results from Chapters 5 and 6 that relate to the concept of L2 interactional competence. Finally, Chapter 8 proposes some concluding remarks on the utility of my research output for the ongoing debates in the domain of CA-SLA and for the world of practice.

Literature

Chafe, W. L. (1976). Givenness, contrastiveness, definiteness, subjects, topics, and points of view. In C. N. Li (Ed.), *Subject and topic* (pp. 27–55). New York: Academic Press.

Chafe, W. (1987). Cognitive constraints on information flow. In R. Tomlin (Ed.), *Coherence and grounding in discourse* (pp. 21–51). Amsterdam, Philadelphia: John Benjamins Publishing Company.

Dimroth, C., & Starren, M. (Eds.) (2003). *Information structures and the dynamics of language acquisition*. Amsterdam, Philadelphia: John Benjamins Publishing Company.

Garfinkel, H. (1967). *Studies in ethnomethodology*. Englewood Cliffs, N.J.: Prentice-Hall.

Givón, T. (Ed.) (1983). *Topic continuity in discourse*. Amsterdam, Philadelphia: John Benjamins Publishing Company.

Givón, T. (1987). Beyond foreground and background. In R. Tomlin (Ed.), *Coherence and grounding in discourse* (pp. 175–188). Amsterdam: John Benjamins Publishing Company.

Lambrecht, K. (1994). *Information structure and sentence form: Topic, focus, and the mental representation of discourse referents*. Cambridge: Cambridge University Press.

Sacks, H. (1995). *Lectures on conversation*. (Volumes 1 and 2). Oxford: Basil Blackwell.

van Dijk, T. (1977). *Text and context. explorations in the semantics and pragmatics of discourse*. London, New York: Longman.

1 Data, Methodology, and Research Questions

1.1 Conversation Analysis: Methodological and Analytical Issues

The analytical approach of CA is characterized by a detailed focus on specific interactional phenomena. CA investigations are based on transcriptions of naturally occurring interactions as they happen in different everyday contexts. This means that the investigations data are highly dependent on the details of the interactional context in which talk is embedded. CA analyzes interactions as they take place in the interactants' lives, in a panoply of different contexts. The researchers record naturally occurring conversations as they happen every day: in the family, at work, at school, on the street, in a car, with a doctor, on the phone, and so on. Finally, CA focuses on the structural organization of conversation and on the methods that the interactants use when they talk to each other. People, then, are seen not merely as exchanging messages through talk-in-interaction but also as collaboratively accomplishing social actions.

The basic starting point for CA researchers is the question of how interactants do what they do at that specific interactional moment. This question is central to the methods (Garfinkel, 1967)—i.e. the systematic procedures—that interactants employ and develop during social actions with their interlocutors. This attention toward the speakers' methods correlates with CA interest in the language-in-use: the language *as* it is used in specific occasions by specific interactants (cf. ten Have, 2007).

1.1.1 Conversation Analysis's Methodological Way: The Ethnomethods in the Data

CA is based on naturally occurring data, for whose obtainment ethical and formal constraints have to be respected. For example, the participants have to agree to be recorded and to have their data used for scientific purposes. Moreover, the researchers are obligated to anonymize the participants' names and every other piece of information related to the time and place of recordings. The data can be audio-recorded or video-recorded. This depends on the type of data. For example, phone calls are only audio-recorded; it also depends on the willingness of the participants to be video-recorded as well as on the aim of the study. In the next chapter, I present my data: I have audio recordings of family conversations between au pairs and their host family members in the French-speaking part of Switzerland. In this case, the families did not allow the research team to video-record their children.

Once the data is recorded, it is transcribed in a second step. The transcription is already a first data analysis, because it is up to the researcher to decide what to write when something is unclear or when there is a pause. Depending on how an interaction is rendered in the written form and on how many details are included in the transcript, the transcripts vary in their definiteness and precision (for an introduction on how to transcribe talk-in-interaction, see Jenkins, 2011).

If it seems obvious to include as many details as possible, there is a limit to consider: the transcript must be readable and usable. This means that, depending on the phenomena that are being investigated, only the relevant transcription conventions are used. For the present work, the basic reference for preparing the transcript was Gail Jefferson's 1984 paper, in which she presented and discussed a list of transcription conventions (a part of which is included in Appendix I). However, since the focus of the investigation was not exclusively on the prosody of the speech, I have transcribed only in a limited way the prosodic contours of the participants' turns. Instead, I was intrigued by pauses, signs related to turn-taking, and the general organization of the conversation, so I have put these features in the foreground while transcribing.

1.1.2 Participants' Methods and Interactional Phenomena

Using detailed transcriptions as just outlined, CA investigates language as it is employed in people's conversations in different settings. Language, then, is not regarded as a fixed entity that a speaker uses in a right way or a wrong way. On the contrary, it is flexible, adaptable to the practical purposes that the interactants are accomplishing in their conversations. For these reasons, CA analyzes the methods (cf. Garfinkel, 1976: 11) through which interactants accomplish social actions in conversations. Through this approach, the ethnomethodological roots of CA become observable: the "ethnomethods" are the central analytical object of CA research. They are "ethno" because they are endogenous for the interactants themselves, i.e. these methods are known in common in the community that the speakers belong to. A community is not only a regional, political, religious, or linguistic grouping of individuals. Rather it is constituted every time people come together and share a conversation. A community is therefore defined always ad hoc by the participants themselves during the interaction. The interactants do not have to declare their rules for their talk-in-interaction every time they gather. They make the rules each time.

CA investigations are directed either towards members' methods for accomplishing specific actions during interactions—such as repair, (dis)agreement, conversation opening and closing, topic management, (dis)alignment and (dis)affiliation, task opening and closing—toward specific resources (oh, mhm, and), or toward structural principles governing conversational sequences (organization of preference, turn-taking, construction and expansion of adjacency pairs, sequence organization, etc.). The next example illustrates the analytical focus on actions, resources, and structures.

(1) Excerpt 1.2 from ten Have (2007: 4; adapted from Frankel (1984: 153))

```
01   Pt: This chemotherapy (0.2) it won't have any lasting effects on
02       havin' kids, will it?
03   (2.2)
04   Pt: It will?
05   Dr: I'm afraid so.
```

Example 1 stems from a conversation between a doctor and his patient. The patient asks the doctor a question in line 01 and does it by proposing a positive assessment regarding the effects of the chemotherapy she has to undergo. The doctor does not answer this question for a long time (2.2 seconds of pause) to which the patient orients as something that does not align with her positive assessment (Pomerantz, 1984). The pause in line 03, however, gives the patient the possibility of self-selection for another turn. She takes it and reformulates her previous assessment in line 04 in the exact opposite direction, i.e. she "reverses" (ten Have, 2007: 5) her assessment (*It will?*). Now the doctor confirms this in line 05: *I'm afraid so*.

This short example contains several points of interest for CA. First, it shows the action of agreeing/disagreeing. With her first question, the patient projects a response that aligns with the positivity of her stance. The long pause that follows, however, suggests some trouble from the doctor's side to actually align with his patient's stance. With her second question, then, the patient reverses the polarity of her stance, i.e. from a positive (and hopeful) to a negative one. At this point, the doctor can align to her turn. In this case, we see the organization of preference at work: the doctor could have answered the patient's question with a disaligning and disagreeing turn. However, he prefers not to answer in this way and offers the patient the possibility to reformulate her question so that she can answer with an aligning turn. However, no video data are available for this interaction so it could be that some other activities are being carried on by the participants to which we as analysts do not have access.

Second, as far as resources are concerned, ex. 1 illustrates the use of affiliating responses. This example is taken from a doctor–patient consultation, which contains exchanges about private and intimate problems that may arise from a session of chemotherapy. As demonstrated by Selting (1994), Stivers (2008), Stivers et al. (2012), and Steensig (2013), in specific cases, especially at the end of storytelling, the interlocutors are offered a final turn with which they can not only align but also affiliate. An affiliation is observable in the sense that the interactant shows a sort of "empathy" toward the other speaker. In ex. 1, the affiliation of the doctor is seen with his last turn: the doctor does not respond to the patient's first question' instead, he lets her reformulate it so that her next answer is not only aligning but also affiliating. This is observable if one thinks that a merely aligning answer could have been something like "Yes, it will." On the contrary, the doctor proffers a turn that displays empathy toward the difficult and personal topic they are discussing.

Finally, the investigation of conversational structure highlights the organization of preference. Preference is a structural feature of conversation; i.e. when a first pair part is uttered (like the first question in lines 01–02), specific type of second pair part is projected and made conditionally relevant. However, there is not just one possible second pair part that can be delivered (in this case, the second pair part could be the answer to the question or a silence). The second pair part shows the type of alignment its speaker takes toward *the previous turn*. There are essentially two types of alignment: a positive one, i.e. the second speaker structurally aligns to the first pair part of the first speaker (like in question-answer or greeting-greeting), or a negative one, i.e. the second speaker structurally disaligns from the first pair part of the first speaker (e.g. invitation-decline or agreement-disagreement). It is important to state that

> this is not necessarily an alignment with, or distancing from, the *speaker* of the first pair part (although it *may* be that as well) but the project of the first pair part, and the course of action it is designed to implement.
>
> (Schegloff, 2007: 59–60)

1.1.3 The Investigation of Linguistic Phenomena in Everyday Talk-in-Interaction

So far, three underlying features of the study of talk-in-interaction have been addressed: actions, resources, and structure. However, several studies (see among others: Auer, 1996; Couper-Kuhlen, 2004; Ford & Thompson, 1996; Ford et al., 1996, 2001; Lerner, 1991; Selting, 1996; Sorjonen,

8 Data, Methodology, and Research Questions

1996) have concentrated on specific linguistic phenomena in interaction and have the following aim:

> [describe] linguistic phenomena as resources for the construction and organization of practices and actions/activities in interaction.
> (Kern & Selting, 2013: 1)

The attention brought to linguistic resources derives from their being recurrently found in conversation and being strategically used by the speakers in their social actions. This means that interactants can rely on them as resources for achieving a variety of practical purposes during the interaction. Selting and Couper-Kuhlen explain in their introduction to the volume "Studies in interactional linguistics" (2001) that it is worth looking at the linguistic, prosodic, and grammatical resources that the speakers employ in conversation. They support this point of view addressing one of the core machineries of interaction: turn-taking. The authors argue that interactants manage turn-taking on the basis of TCUs (turn constructional units), which are linguistic units, since they can be words, phrases, clauses, or sentences (p. 5). Moreover, the point of completion for TCUs is established in the same way as other linguistic features, namely through their grammatical, prosodic, and pragmatic cues (p. 6). In so doing, they consider that linguistic observations have their rightful place in the research domain of CA and can moreover be helpful in achieving a deeper understanding of the most basic principles and machineries of conversation.

Within this linguistic approach to interactional data, known as interactional linguistics, a specific focus has been on grammar in interaction. In what is arguably the centerpiece in the field of interactional linguistics, Ochs et al. (1996: 3) formulate how

> three genres of inquiry converge here—one grounded in functional approaches to language concerned with its role in communication and cognition, one grounded in linguistic anthropology and the cultural underpinnings of language, and one grounded in conversation analysis and the interactional matrix of language structure and use.

Grammar is no longer seen as a fixed group of rules that can be used in a right way or a wrong way. Instead, grammar in interaction is an open class of rules that the speakers adopt on the spot, i.e. while they are speaking, to adjust their turns and their actional trajectories. The studies in this specific research domain have, for example, challenged the traditional descriptions of syntactic structures in different languages. For French, see especially the works by Horlacher & Pekarek Doehler (2014), Pekarek Doehler et al. (2011), Pekarek Doehler (2011a, 2011b), Pekarek Doehler & Stoenica (2012), and Pekarek Doehler & Horlacher

(2013). Another volume collecting several studies on the emergence of grammar in conversation is Auer & Pfänder (2011). The starting point of these investigations is the relationship between the turn construction and its temporality: since the turn is an in-the-moment production, i.e. it is not defined a priori and delivered in a package. It often happens that an interactant changes their trajectory *while* uttering their turn. Syntactic constructions, then, show their flexible and adaptable nature: they are not fixed entities, but they can be adapted for the ongoing construction of turns at talk.

The studies in the domain of interactional linguistics show that it is possible to analyze the linguistics of interactions (Selting & Couper-Kuhlen, 2001) without neglecting the specificities of the CA research methodology. As I will introduce in Chapter 2, it is central to always adopt the emic perspective of the interactants. In so doing, the analysis of linguistic forms and structures is possible and relevant for a better understanding of interactional mechanisms.

To sum up, the central issue of CA investigations is not to prove one linguistic theory or another but rather to observe the reality and to describe how participants use and orient to linguistic forms in a way that is understandable for the interactants themselves and furthermore in a way that is observable and documentable for researchers and external people (Sidnell, 2010). Because the basis for all CA research is the collection of real-life data, I present in the next section the corpus I have worked on.

1.2 The Research Project

This study arises within the frame of a larger research project financed by the Swiss National Science Foundation (SNF/FNS): Developing interactional competence in a second language. A longitudinal study of actional microcosms (FNS subside n° 100012_126860/1, March 2010–February 2014). The main goal of the project was to document how French L2 speakers develop their interactional competence over time. Using audio recordings made by the participants, the research team set out to depict the developmental trajectories of the L2 speakers by longitudinally analyzing their daily interactions with L1 speakers.

The L2 speakers that participated in the project were au pairs that came to Switzerland for a period of six to ten months and lived with a host family, where they took care of the children. The au pairs also attended a French language course for two hours per week. Before starting this course, they had to pass a test about their French lexical and grammatical skills. Based on the test results, the au pairs were divided into groups with different L2 proficiency levels—in accordance with the Common European Framework of Reference for Languages (CEFRL).[1]

The research group contacted two language schools in two Swiss Cantons (Neuchâtel and Fribourg) where several au pairs volunteered for the project. These au pairs received a questionnaire about their working and living situations and a legal paper concerning the treatment of the audio-recorded data. In our research, ten au pairs contributed data: nine women and one man. Three women were staying in the Canton of Neuchâtel, whereas the other seven were living in the Canton of Fribourg. All the participants received an audio recorder that resembled a little cellular phone from the research team. The host families did not allow for video-recording because of the presence of young children. The participants were all asked to record themselves at least once a week while talking with the host family members, either with the whole family or with only the children. The length of the recordings was not discussed. The complete corpus is made up of about 58 hours of audio-recorded interactions.

The transcriptions were made with the software Transana. All person and place names and possible references that could lead to the identification of the participants have been rendered anonymous. The transcription conventions are inspired by the Jeffersonian conversation analytical conventions from 1984 (see Appendix I), with a few modifications.

1.3 The Au Pairs and Their Learning Environment

1.3.1 The Chosen Data Sets

For this study, the corpora of three participants have been chosen: Julie, Oksana, and Christine. The reasons for this choice are several. First, the chosen participants delivered their recordings at regular intervals over the course of six to nine months, enabling longitudinal analysis. Second, the recordings of the three chosen au pairs have good sound quality. Even though the children of their host families are sometimes loud, only a minimal part of these recordings sounded incomprehensible to the transcribers. Consequently, each of almost all of the databases has been used for the investigations with no loss of data.

Finally, and most importantly for the data comparisons, the chosen au pairs were categorized at the language school as having three different L2 proficiency levels. After an entry-level test, Julie reached a B2 level, Oksana a B1 level, and Christine an A2 level for French L2. For the aim of my study, it is important to consider this initial difference. In the analytical part, in fact, I show that these initial discrepancies are only marginally relevant for discussing the development of the participants' L2 interactional competence. Indeed, the analyses will show that sometimes no actual difference can be found in the actions accomplished by the au pairs, despite their different French L2 starting levels.

In the next table, I briefly show some general information about the three chosen au pairs:

Table 1.1 General information about the au pairs selected for the present study

Au pair	L2 level	Length of stay	Age	L1	Nr. of recordings	Total length
Julie	B2	10 months (Sept. 2009–June 2010)	18	German	20	7h 36min
Oksana	B1	10 months (Sept. 2010–June 2011)	22	Polish	23	3h 17min
Christine	A2	6 months (Sept. 2010–March 2011)	18	Swiss-German	15	2h 55min

As Table 1.1 shows, the data set I have worked with consists of 58 recordings. I have made a further selection within this data set. The au pairs sometimes recorded themselves while playing with the children. Since these conversations have a different structure from those with the host parents or the whole host family, the conversations with the children have not been considered, and the examined interactional context is rather uniform for all the au pairs. The following table shows an overview:

Table 1.2 Overview of the data: Division between au pairs with family and au pairs with children

Au pair	Tot. Rec	Total duration	Rec. with family	Duration	Rec. with children	Duration	Others
Julie	20	7h 30min	10	2h 26min	09	4h 4min	1 accidental rec. (1h)
Oksana	23	3h 17min	08	1h 1min	14	2h 8min	1 rec. with Christine (8min)
Christine	15	2h 55min	14	2h 47min	0	0	1 rec. with Oksana (8min)
TOTAL	58	13h 42min	32	6h 14min	23	6h 12min	3 (1h 16min)

To sum up: the database consists of 58 audio recordings, for a total of 13 hours and 42 minutes of free occurring interactions between the au pairs and their host families. In this study, 32 recordings were investigated (55% of the total data).

1.3.2 The Au Pairs' Learning Environment

The au pairs' experience abroad is characterized by a context specificity that is not found in any other learning environment. In a study of dinner table conversations of the American middle class, Ochs & Taylor (1992) pointed out that families are a political entity, in which there is a hierarchy that concerns the authority for evaluating, criticizing, and managing discourse matters. This aspect must be considered when analyzing the experience of au pairs. On the one hand, au pairs are L2 speakers spending a period abroad to improve the knowledge of their second language. For this reason, they are often categorized as learners by their coparticipants. In so doing, a particular linguistic asymmetry is made locally relevant by the interactants, toward which they mutually orient (e.g. when a repair sequence occurs).

On the other hand, au pairs are also officially employed by the host parents; hence, there is a work contract that involves another class of categories, such as employer/employee or parent/caregiver. These categories come into the foreground in specific interactional moments, such as during storytelling, as shown in Pochon-Berger et al. (2015). This study demonstrates that storytelling is an interactional activity prone to incorporate changes of participant categorization in the course of their progression. Typically, an au pair reports her day with the children to the host parents—and this report happens in the form of a conversational storytelling. During the telling, moments alternate in which either the category of L2 learner or that of caregiver is oriented to by participants. In particular, when it comes to demonstrating one's conduct as a "good caregiver," asymmetries in authority arise, since both the mother and the au pair girl claim to have acted as good caregivers.

A last aspect that needs to be considered in the analyses is the general family setting, in which the L2 learning process takes place. In fact, it is different from institutional contexts like a classroom, because the au pairs participate in the daily activities of their host families. This means that the L2 learning process happens through and while other activities are accomplished, such as preparing lunch or dinner, playing with the children, preparing them for bed, or helping them eat.

1.4 Research Questions and Contributions of the Present Study

During the analytical work on the data, my attention was driven in several directions, which I tried to condense in the form of research questions or leitmotifs for the project. I first directed my investigations to the ways L2 speakers introduce and close conversational topics, and I present these analyses in Chapter 5 (topic introduction) and Chapter 6 (topic closure).

My aim was to identify the linguistic and prosodic resources that the au pairs employ to manage conversational topics. I have analyzed also the turn architecture and the component of recipient design in the au pairs' L2 talk, because these two features are central to participating in conversation (see Sacks et al., 1974) and because they show how the L2 speakers manage conversational topics.

On the basis of a longitudinal study, I have subsequently addressed another aspect of topic management, namely the possibility of documenting change in the methods used by the au pairs for introducing and closing conversational topics. Because the data were collected in regular intervals over six to 12 months for the same au pair, it was possible to compare how an au pair introduces and closes topics from the beginning of their sojourn until the end of it. A differentiation needed to be made, however, because the analysis of topic closure has shown different results from the investigation of topic introduction, especially because topic closure seems to be a more stable action than topic introduction.

My study is inspired by longitudinal CA-SLA studies, a research branch that can be traced back to Brouwer & Wagner (2004). However, my study is also innovative in a number of ways. First, I investigate a language, French, and its learning process, French L2, which are still marginal in the domain of CA-SLA, with the exceptions of the research done by Berthoud, (Pochon-)Berger, Fasel Lauzon, Mondada, Pekarek Doehler, Skogmyr Marian, and me. Second, my study is an investigation of a hybrid learning context, namely everyday conversations where the family is the workplace of an external subject (the au pair). This aspect brings my study in relationship to the study of L2 interactional competence in the wild (cf. Hellermann et al., 2019), i.e. studies that have investigated L2 learning as it happens outside of the classroom. However, in my data, there is always a formal feature in the whole situation, namely the working contract, so I have chosen to label the situation under investigation a "hybrid context." In my analyses, I show what is at stake when institutional and noninstitutional setting features come together.

Finally, the outcomes of my investigations can be considered for starting a more general reflection on the utility and usability of CA-SLA research outputs for the world of practice (Antaki, 2011; Grujicic-Alatriste, 2015, forthcoming; Hellermann, 2008; Wong & Waring, 2010; Salaberry & Kunitz, 2019). I address this matter in the last chapter of the book, and I try to highlight the advantages for the stakeholders (au pairs, host families, recruiting agencies) to discuss and use data like mine. To do this, I also address the actual difficulties that persist in the communication between the world of research and the world of practice. This final chapter closes my study with general reflections and possible future paths both for the research domain and for the collaboration between research units and interested stakeholders.

Note

1. See the complete document here: www.coe.int/t/dg4/linguistic/Source/Framework_EN.pdf

References

Antaki, C. (Ed.) (2011). *Applied conversation analysis: Intervention and change in institutional talk*. London: Palgrave Macmillan.

Auer, P. (1996). On the prosody and syntax of turn continuations. In E. Couper-Kuhlen & M. Selting (Eds.), *Prosody in conversation: Interactional studies* (pp. 57–101). Cambridge: Cambridge University Press.

Auer, P., & Pfänder, S. (2011). *Constructions: Emerging and emergent*. London and New York: Mouton de Gruyter.

Brouwer, C. E., & Wagner, J. (2004). Developmental issues in second language conversation. *Journal of Applied Linguistics, 1*(1), 29–47.

Couper-Kuhlen, E. (2004). Prosody and sequence organization: The case of new beginnings. In E. Couper-Kuhlen & C. Ford (Eds.), *Sound patterns in interaction* (pp. 335–367). Amsterdam: John Benjamins Publishing Company.

Ford, C., Fox, B., & Thompson, S. A. (1996). Practices in the construction of turns: The 'TCU' revisited. *Pragmatics, 6*, 427–454.

Ford, C., Fox, B., & Thompson, S. A. (2001). Constituency and the grammar of turn increments. In C. Ford, B. Fox, & S. A. Thompson (Eds.), *The language of turn and sequence* (pp. 14–38). Oxford: Oxford University Press.

Ford, C., & Thompson, S. A. (1996). Interactional units in conversation: Syntactic, intonational, and pragmatic resources for the management of turns. In E. Ochs, E. A. Schegloff, & S. A. Thompson (Eds.), *Interaction and grammar* (pp. 134–184). Cambridge: Cambridge University Press.

Garfinkel, H. (1967). *Studies in ethnomethodology*. Englewood Cliffs, NJ: Prentice-Hall.

Grujicic-Alatriste, L. (Ed.) (2015). *Linking discourse studies to professional practice*. Bristol: Multilingual Matters.

Grujicic-Alatriste, L. (Ed.) (forthcoming). *Language research in multilingual settings: Doing knowledge dissemination at the sites of practice*. London: Palgrave Macmillan.

Hellermann, J. (2008). *Social Actions for Classroom Language Learning*. Clevedon, UK: Multilingual Matters.

Hellermann, J., Eskildsen, S., Pekarek Doehler, S., & Piirainen-Marsh, A. (Eds.) (2019). *Conversation analytic research on learning-in-action: The complex ecology of second language interaction 'in the wild'*. Berlin: Springer.

Horlacher, A.-S., & Pekarek Doehler, S. (2014). 'Pivotage' in French talk-in-interaction: On the emergent nature of [clause-NP-clause] pivots. *Pragmatics, 24*(3), 593–622.

Jenkins, C. J. (2011). *Transcribing talk and interaction*. Amsterdam and Philadelphia: John Benjamins Publishing Company.

Kern, F., & Selting, M. (2013). Conversation analysis and interactional linguistics. In C. A. Chapelle (Ed.), *The encyclopedia of applied linguistics* (pp. 1–5). Blackwell Publishing. Retrieved from 10.1002/9781405198431.wbeal0203

Lerner, G. (1991). On the syntax of sentences-in-progress. *Language in Society, 20*, 441–458.

Ochs, E., Schegloff, E. A., & Thompson, S. A. (1996). *Interaction and grammar*. Cambridge: Cambridge University Press.

Ochs, E., & Taylor, C. (1992). Family narrative as political activity. *Discourse and Society*, *3*(3), 301–340.

Pekarek Doehler, S. (2011a). Clause-combining and the sequencing of actions: Projector constructions in French conversation. In *Subordination in conversation: a crosslinguistic perspective* (pp. 103–148). Amsterdam and Philadelphia: John Benjamins Publishing Company.

Pekarek Doehler, S. (2011b). Emergent grammar for all practical purposes: The on-line formating of dislocated constructions in French conversation. In P. Auer & S. Pfänder (Eds.), *Constructions: Emerging and emergent* (pp. 46–88). London and New York: Mouton de Gruyter. Retrieved from https://gemma.unine.ch/sites/islc/CLA/Documents%20CLA/Biblioth%C3%A8que%20PDF%20du%20CLA/Pekarek%20Doehler_2011a.pdf

Pekarek Doehler, S., De Stefani, E., & Horlacher, A.-S. (2011). The grammar of closings: The use of dislocated constructions as closing initiators in French talk-in-interaction. *Nottingham French Studies*, *50*(2), 51–76.

Pekarek Doehler, S., & Horlacher, A.-S. (2013). The patching together of pivot-patterns in talk-in-interaction: On 'double dislocations' in French. *Journal of Pragmatics*, *53*, 92–108.

Pekarek Doehler, S., & Stoenica, I.-M. (2012). Emergence, temporalité et grammaire-dans- l'interaction: Disloquée à gauche et nominat ivus pendens en français contemporain. *Langue Française*, *175*, 111–127.

Pochon-Berger, E., Pekarek Doehler, S., & König, C. (2015). Family conversational storytelling at the margins of the workplace: The case of au pair girls. In L. Grujicic-Alatriste (Ed.), *Linking discourse studies to professional practice* (pp. 86–108). Bristol: Multilingual Matters.

Pomerantz, A. (1984). Agreeing and disagreeing with assessments: Some features of preferred and dispreferred turn shapes. In J. M. Atkinson & J. Heritage (Eds.), *Structures of social action* (pp. 57–101). Cambridge: Cambridge University Press.

Sacks, H., Schegloff, E. A., & Jefferson, G. (1974). A simplest systematic for the organization of turn-taking in conversation. *Language*, *50*(4), 696–735.

Salaberry, R. N., & Kunitz, S. (Eds.) (2019). *Teaching and testing L2 interactional competence: Bridging theory and practice*. New York and London: Routledge.

Schegloff, E. A. (2007). *Sequence organization in interaction* (Vol. 1). Cambridge: Cambridge University Press.

Selting, M. (1994). Emphatic speech style: With special focus on the prosodic signaling of heightened emotive involvement in conversation. *Journal of Pragmatics*, *22*(Special Issue: Involvement in Language), 375–408.

Selting, M. (1996). On the interplay of syntax and prosody on the constitution of turn-constructional units and turns in conversation. *Pragmatics*, *6*(3), 357–388.

Selting, M., & Couper-Kuhlen, E. (2001). *Studies in interactional linguistics*. Amsterdam and Philadelphia: John Benjamins Publishing Company.

Sidnell, J. (2010). *Conversation analysis: An introduction*. London: Wiley Blackwell.

Sorjonen, M.-L. (1996). On repeats and responses in Finnish conversation. In E. Ochs, E. A. Schegloff, & S. A. Thompson (Eds.), *Interaction and grammar* (pp. 277–327). Cambridge: Cambridge University Press.

Steensig, J. (2013). Conversation analysis and affiliation and alignment. In C. A. Chapelle (Ed.), *The encyclopedia of applied linguistics* (pp. 1–6). Blackwell Publishing. DOI:10.1002/9781405198431.wbeal0196

Stivers, T. (2008). Stance, alignment, and affiliation during storytelling: When nodding is a token of affiliation. *Research on Language and Social Interaction*, *41*(1), 31–57.

Stivers, T., Mondada, L., & Steensig, J. (2012). Knowledge, morality and affiliation in social interaction. In T. Stivers, L. Mondada, & J. Steensig (Eds.), *The morality of knowledge in conversation* (pp. 3–24). Cambridge: Cambridge University Press.

ten Have, P. (2007). *Doing conversation analysis: A practical guide*. London: Sage Publications.

Wong, J., & Waring, H. Z. (Eds.) (2010). *Conversation analysis and second language pedagogy: A guide for ESL/EFL teachers*. New York and London: Routledge.

2 Topic Analysis in First and Second Languages

This chapter deals with different approaches to the study of topic. The notion of topic itself is characterized by a variety of definitions, and which one is used depends on the approach for the data analysis. In a first step, I present an overview of more traditional studies on topic (2.1), which is followed by a discussion of topic notion in the domain of discourse analysis (2.2). The description of the notion of topic in the domain of second language acquisition (henceforth SLA) follows (2.2). The central part of this chapter is dedicated to topic analysis in conversation and outlines the approach of conversation analysis (2.3).

2.1 From the Prague School to Text Linguistics: An Overview

The researchers in the Prague circle discussed the centrality of the concept of topic with an approach that is based on syntactic and pragmatic cues (Danes, 1974; Firbas, 1992; Jakobson, 1985, 1987; Mathesius, 1975). These researchers defined language as a system and concentrated their analysis on its structure.

Within this framework, the sentence topic was identified as the known information (the theme) and the element with a lower degree of communicative dynamism. The sentence, following a functionalist perspective, was built in a given-before-new fashion (although the researchers noted that exceptions were also possible). The notion of topic emerging from the approach of the Prague School shows two major aspects: on the one hand, the identification of the sentence constituent that coincides with the topic, and on the other hand, the problematization of its dynamic aspect, i.e. the degree to which the topical element can change within a text.

Developing partially from the results of the Prague School, the research in the field of text linguistics also focused mainly on the surface structure of sentences (Halliday, 1967; Hornby, 1971) related to theme and sentence topic (Reinhart, 1981) and on the anaphoric chains in text (Haviland & Clark, 1974; Halliday & Hasan, 1976). The research is concerned with sentence topic (see the studies by Davison [1984] on strong and weak topic NPs, i.e. nominal phrases; Hyman & Zimmer [1976] on the relationship between word order, subject saliency and definiteness and the expression of topic in French sentences; and Pérez de Ayala Becerril [1997] on topic marking at question times in the House of Commons). Sentence topic is generally considered the first element in the sentence and the element about which something is predicated. Studies on French have addressed interlinguistic variation in spoken language, where numerous topic-marking structures were found (Galambos, 1980; Hanson, 1987).

In line with the results of the Prague School, Halliday shares the idea that the theme/rheme organization in the sentence is reflected into a left-to-right sentential construction pattern in which the given information precedes the new one: "the theme is assigned initial position in the clause, and all that follows is the rheme" (Halliday, 1967: 212). Within the approach of text linguistics, the sentence theme identifies a sentence constituent: it generally coincides with the subject. Consequently, what is said about it identifies another sentence constituent: it is generally the verb or the verbal predicate (rheme/comment). Thus, a sentence is generally constructed in a left-to-right fashion, in which old information precedes new information. Three main consequences can be drawn from this observation:

1. The sentence topic coincides with the old information, whereas the comment coincides with the new information.
2. The old information shows the link between a sentence and what was said before in the text.
3. Therefore, the topic is likely to be found in the left periphery of a sentence.

Finally, the sentence topic is what a sentence is about.

2.2 Discourse Analysis

Unlike the two previous approaches, discourse analysis includes both spoken and written texts as data for the analyses (cf. van Dijk, 1977; Brown & Yule, 1983).

The interest in spoken language influences the terminological choice in the field: authors no longer talk about *sentences*, as sentences occur in the written language; rather, they talk about *utterances* as units for spoken language. Moreover, talk is seen as fulfilling two functions: on the one hand, it is a means for transmitting information to another participant (transactional function); on the other hand, talk allows speakers to do something with the language. In this case, Brown & Yule (1983) speak of the interactional function of language, which they relate to the theory of speech acts (Austin, 1962; Searle, 1969). From the approach of textual linguistics, which analyzes "text as a product" (Brown & Yule, 1983: 24), the researchers who follow the discourse analytical approach shift their focus on discourse as a process that brings together a message producer and a message receiver: "The discourse analyst, then, is interested in the function or purpose of a piece of linguistic data and also in how that data is processed, both by the producer and by the receiver" (Brown & Yule, 1983: 25).

The influence that this approach has on the study of topic is multifaceted. A central place is taken by the fact that researchers are focused on interpreting the discourse: their concerns are the message that a speaker sends and how it is received and understood by the hearer. For this reason, discourse is cut into smaller fragments "and the discourse analyst always has to decide where the fragment begins and ends" (Brown & Yule, 1983: 69). This is an external, etic perspective on the data, following which different definitions of discourse topic have arisen.

A first attempt of defining "discourse topic" is made by Ochs-Keenan & Schieffelin (1976). The authors are concerned with language development and analyze the talk produced in mother–child interactions in family settings. They define "discourse topic" as "the proposition (or set of propositions) about which the speaker is either providing or requesting information" (Ochs-Keenan & Schieffelin, 1976: 338; see also Kramsch, 1983). They start from the assumption that for every part of a discourse, there is always an utterance that represents the topic of that piece of talk (cf. Bransford & Johnson, 1973). Moreover, they explain that participants use a part of their conversations for actually formulating the discourse topic, such as via reference to background knowledge, to interactional environment, or to previous discourse. I take the following example:

(2) From Ochs-Keenan & Schieffelin (1976: 339)
```
01 Mother: (trying to put too large diaper on doll, holding
          diaper on) Well we can't hold it on like that. What do we
          need? Hmm? What do we need for the diaper?
02 Allison: Pin?
```

According to Ochs-Keenan & Schieffelin (1976), the discourse topic in ex. 2 is the proposition "we need something for the diaper." This proposition is attended to both in the question and in the answer, so this question–answer pair has a single discourse topic. Consequently, conceiving the discourse as "any sequence of two or more utterances produced by a single speaker or by two or more speakers who are interacting with one another (at some point in time and space)" (Ochs-Keenan & Schieffelin, 1976: 340) will necessarily mean considering how topics are related to one another in the flow of discourse. The researchers have distinguished two types of discourse topic:

1. Collaborating discourse topics when two or more utterances share the same topic (like in the case of question–answer sequences).

2. Incorporating discourse topics when a new utterance develops the presuppositions contained in the previous discourse.

As a consequence, the discourse flow can be seen to be either continuous (when collaborating or incorporating topics are at hand) or discontinuous (when no linkage between topics is made and a speaker disengages herself from the previous discourse).

The concept of topic, then, is not used for describing a fragment of talk but rather for indicating what that fragment is about. It is the analyst who judges the relevance of a speaker's contribution to the talk on the basis of their own knowledge and of the contextual clues of the discourse. The concern is not about defining which sentence element is the topic but about delineating what the topic framework is. This is explained in van Dijk (1977): discourse topic belongs to the macro-structure of discourse and is therefore more difficult to grasp than sentence topic. The analyst can observe whether a speaker talks topically, by looking at the utterances they produce and by determining whether they "fit closely to the most recent elements incorporated in the topic framework" (Brown & Yule, 1983: 84).

Topic in discourse analysis, then, is determined by the analyst, who cuts a conversation in different topically relevant parts and observes the coherence relations present in every fragment. The underlying idea is that the topic is shared between the participants, although sometimes there are also "personal topics" (Brown & Yule, 1983: 87) that a speaker introduces into the talk and that can possibly become shared discourse topics in what follows. To summarize, then, discourse topic is not related to a *sentence* but rather to a spoken *utterance* or a set of utterances; it also is the point of departure for the discourse, what the discourse is about; topic is determined not for an entire discourse, but for its constituent fragments, which are cut by the analyst; and finally, it is a source of coherence for an entire discourse and retrievable through it by means of the existing linkage between parts of subsequent utterances.

2.3 Second Language Acquisition Studies (SLA)

Topic has been studied in SLA, particularly in functionalist approaches (Ariel, 1988; Chafe, 1976, 1987, 1997; Givón, 1976, 1983, 1987; Lambrecht, 1987, 1994; Prince, 1981). A way to analyze L2 language production is to examine how communicative tasks are accomplished verbally by L2 learners. The analytical object, then, becomes the way L2 speakers code information in their utterances, including how they structure new and old information. Consequently, the study of topic coding gains a particular role within this approach. A prominent project in the functionalist approach to study L2 acquisition has been guided by C. Perdue and W. Klein (cf. Klein & Perdue, 1997) in the late 1980s. The research was based mainly on the analysis of the information structure in L2 written texts and oral narratives (from picture stories or film retelling activities). Probably the most prominent result that came out of this project was the idea of the *Basic Variety*, which is a learner language system that in spite of little morpho-syntactic variation has a rich and systematic information structure (Dimroth, 2008).

The analysis of information structure was construed on the assumption that a text is constituted of utterances delivering information as answers to an underlying question (cf. "*quaestio*" Klein & von Stutterheim, 1987; von Stutterheim, 1998). This implicit question represents how a speaker understands a certain communicative task (e.g. they tell a story or explain something).

On the basis of the studies on first languages and taking into account several L1s and L2s, functionalists have widely analyzed the encoding strategies adopted by L2 learners. Particular attention was paid to the verbalization of spatial and temporal relationships (see, among others, Andersen, 1991; Andorno, 2005; Bardovi-Harling, 2000; Benazzo, 2003; Carroll et al., 2008; Dimroth et al., 2003; Klein, 1994; Perdue et al., 2002; Starren & van Hout, 1996).

Topic and topic (dis)continuity in discourse have been studied as well, and "topic" was defined in terms of aboutness (Lambrecht, 1994). Hendriks (2000) studied how French children develop the topic-marking techniques (especially dislocation) in their L1 compared to how this happens with adult Chinese learners of French L2. Hendriks defines a dislocated structure as follows: "Dislocated structures (or detachments) consist of a full NP and a coreferential clitic pronoun. In these constructions, the NP ends up in either initial or final position" (p. 376). The results showed that children first need to learn the pragmatic-discursive functions of dislocation, whereas adult L2 learners already know them but realize them by using non-standard forms. Children thus produce utterances of the type "*Un cheval il court au champs*" (a horse he runs in the field). Here the first full NP ("un cheval" [a horse]) is positioned to the left of the clitic pronoun "il" (he) and is used by children to introduce a new referent into the discourse. Adults, instead, are shown to use dislocation in more complex contexts, such as when coreference occurs. When two referents are available, the L2 adult speaker promotes the most prominent one to the status of topic via a left dislocation, as is shown in the utterance "*et derrière le chat aussi il y a un chien . . . et le chat il est déjà eh. . . à la limite de saisir les oiseaux bébés*" (and behind the cat also there is a dog and the cat he is already um. . . about to catch the bird babies). The coreference exists here between the two full NPs: "the cat" and "a dog." The L2 speaker then promotes the lexeme "the cat" to the topic of the utterance via a left dislocation with the clitic pronoun "*il*" (he).

The study by Hendriks & Watorek (2008) investigated the "universal" nature of the topic-comment structure on the basis of French, English, and Polish L1 data from speakers of different ages. The authors found that age plays a crucial role, because younger children structure their utterances in a different way than older children or adults do. Generally, the topicalized information is found at the beginning of the sentence in French and Polish, whereas in English, it can vary, and it can appear also at the utterance end. A comparison has been drawn up between English and Polish adult learners of French. The results partially have reflected those for the L1: the topic was placed in first place in the utterance, but for the use of more complex structures (like dislocations), a higher L2 developmental level needed to be reached.

The functional research on SLA has shed light on the referential and anaphoric processes in discourse and especially on the encoding strategies adopted by the L2 speakers for referring to a known or an unknown referent. The results align with the studies conducted on the L1s: when an unknown referent is introduced in discourse, it is encoded by means of more linguistic material (e.g. with a full NP) than in a later mention in the same discourse (e.g. with a pronoun or even zero anaphora). More complex and "non-universal" structures like French dislocations appear only at a later L2 developmental stage and need some time to stabilize. However, these studies have neglected what they define as "deviant cases," such as the use of pronouns in long-distance anaphora (cf. under-specification Fox, 1987) or the repetition of a full NP after a short-distance anaphora (cf. over-specification Pekarek, 1999). The existing L2 research on social interactions has shown that topic management in such natural contexts is worth careful attention, because it poses a challenge for L2 users (cf. Pekarek Doehler, 2004).

2.4 Topics in L1 Interactions

Intuitively speaking, it seems clear that interlocutors are talking about something when they talk to each other. The issue addressed by CA researchers is, how do people display that they are talking about something right now? CA is interested in the interactional work done by the participants themselves: when talking to each other, they produce turns in a specific fashion for the purpose of the ongoing conversation. This is all negotiated on a turn-by-turn basis, and this also means that the communicative purpose can be changed locally and adjusted in every moment of the conversation. CA's major concern is to analyze how interlocutors do topic talk. This means considering topic not only at a mere content level but also as a jointly accomplished activity that underlies talk-in-interaction. The question, then, is not *what* but rather *how*: how do interactants manage (i.e. introduce, change, close, shift, and construct) topics in conversation?

Looking globally at a conversation, one has the feeling that turns hang somehow together in a way that make them depend on one another. One possibility for the description of this dependency is to consider it as topical. These sequences can be seen to be topically glued together, or "topically coherent" (Heritage & Sorjonen, 1994: 4), but also to be structured by the action(s) that a speaker is accomplishing. For analyzing the content level of conversations, researchers within the CA approach have generally followed two paths (cf. Seedhouse & Harris, 2011): they have focused either on topic progression, i.e. how topics develop during the conversation and flow almost unremarkably into one another, or on topic boundaries, i.e. moments in which speakers mark the beginning or the end of a topic at hand. I now present an overview of the literature on both phenomena.

2.4.1 Topic Progression

Most of the time, at a certain point in conversation, people talk about something completely different from what they had started with, and they often would not be able to say how this happened. The explanation lies in the inherent conversational feature of topics to develop in a mostly unmarked way. Jefferson (1984), extending the analysis of her 1972 article about side sequences, illustrated a detailed, step-by-step analysis of how speakers overcome troubles by telling in talk without interrupting the conversational flow (see also Jefferson, 1981, 1993). After talking about some difficult matters, a speaker can summarize their point of view (e.g. via a general or final statement) and simultaneously turn to some ancillary matters, i.e. some aspects of the main story that were marginal thus far. These techniques are typical for closing sequences. At this point, the story recipient can topicalize the ancillary matters (with a question like, what is then with X?) in a way that not only invites an answer by the troubles-telling speaker (the answer is conditionally relevant) but provides a slot for the story recipient themselves, who can immediately start their own story on the ancillary matter. This is the case of pivot utterances (see Drew & Holt, 1998; Holt & Drew, 2005), i.e. an utterance that is still "on topic" but that already points toward a different matter. Such an utterance allows for the bridging of two unconnected matters via the collaborative creation of a (new) common starting point.

In a similar way, Maynard (1980) studied the conversational places in which topic changes generally occur. Parallel to Jefferson, he identified different conversational environments in which troubles in speakership transfer are observable. Maynard worked with the concept of topicality, and not of topic, the latter being for him too closely related to the idea of "entity":

> Topicality is an achievement of conversationalists, something organized and made observable in patterned ways that can be described.
> (Maynard, 1980: 263).

24 Topic Analysis

Problems in the transfer of speakership can be identified by a frequent presence of longer inter-turn pauses, as in the following example:

(3) From Maynard (1980: 266, partial transcription of the whole example)

```
01    . . . (talk about a party given by a friend)
02    (1.2)
03    Al: ye::ah
04    (1.0)
05    Al: tch th- that'd be really impressive ya know, just that
          rent out a place heh
06    (1.0)
07    Al: throw a formal party. It- it was kinda fun though
08    (3.0)
09    Al: ye:ah
10    (1.0)
11    Al: y'ever get into sports cars or anything er?
12    Bob: umm I used to be e a mechanic
13    . . . (talk goes far about cars)
```

In ex. 3, Al is talking about a party he went to. When he reaches the end of his story, he tries to solicit a reaction from Bob, but this fails several times: lines 02, 04, 06, 08, and 10. After this series of long pauses, Al changes the topic at hand by introducing a new referent into the conversation: sports cars (line 11). This time he succeeds in transferring the speakership to his interlocutor, who starts talking about his experience with sports cars, and this can be due to the question format of his turn in line 11. A series of pauses can intervene when a story is being closed but the story recipient fails to align or affiliate with the storyteller (cf. Selting, 1994), so that, after several pauses, the story recipient changes the topic. A particular case is represented by topic shift, which Maynard identifies either as the passage from one aspect to another of a same subject in order to occasion a new class of mentionables (in the sense of coclass membership, as introduced by Sacks) or as the passage from a rather general to a rather particularized statement. Finally, topic change can also be engendered because a first topic was just a transitional one: it is introduced in order to keep the turn machinery going but for which no further development is in sight (cf. the case of "weather," Garfinkel & Sacks, 1970).

With a specific focus on topic change, Covelli & Murray (1980) studied how topics are managed in interaction on the basis of data from middle-class, English-speaking North American families. The researchers use the concept of topic line, i.e. an introduced topic that is further developed in the conversation. With the idea of line, the authors present topical talk as a system that develops chronologically on a temporal line and in which "topic change occurs and recurs" (Covelli & Murray, 1980:

384). Through the identification of different cues that participants use for signaling that a topic is vanishing (e.g. by summarizing one's main point, which happens mostly when a speaker is unable to further develop the topic at hand), the authors identify several techniques that the interactants adopt for changing the topic at hand, such as the proposition of different topics or the introduction of a new topic line (more or less related to the preceding one) through the use of "by-the-way information" (Covelli & Murray, 1980: 386; cf. Jefferson, 1984 on ancillary matters). The researchers conclude with a parallelism between topic change and the turn-taking system: "both systems are recursive, and both are at once context-free and context-sensitive" (Covelli & Murray, 1980: 386).

Recalling Maynard & Zimmerman's (1984) study, West & Garcia (1988) studied conversations between unacquainted dyads and highlighted the participants' orientation toward the topical progression of conversation focusing particularly on gender. They identified cases of topic extinction and topic closure in conversations. The former is characterized by a series of pauses and unsuccessful attempts to create topical talk (e.g. only minimal responses were given, and no further turns about the topic were uttered). The latter is related to topic-bounding activities and therefore presents different features, such as concluding remarks or arrangements for future activities together. Their results show the following:

1. men generally change topics more often than women.
2. this influences the course of activity of a conversation.

According to them, these results were because

> [W]hat was achieved through men's unilateral topic changes was the then-and-there determination of activities that would not be pursued and the tellables that would not be told.
> (West & Garcia, 1988: 570)

Finally, topic progression has also been studied in particular institutional contexts, such as meetings of Alcoholics Anonymous (AA) (Arminen, 1996), doctor–patient interactions (Campion & Langdon, 2004), business interactions (Du Babcock, 1999, 2006; Bolden, 2008), and classrooms (Heyman, 1986). In such contexts, different factors were found that influenced the conversational flow, especially asymmetries in authority and knowledge. Arminen (1996) relates the specific organization of turn-taking during AA meetings to how participants occasion topical talk and reintroduce or reformulate a previously discussed topic. Typically, this happens via an idiomatic expression that links two topics also when they are in contrast with each other. Two examples are the use of expressions like "I recognize the reverse of the coin" (Arminen, 1996: 101, ex. 5), which allows a speaker to "acknowledge the prior turn, and give them its own addition even as a reverse of the coin" (Arminen, 1996: 102) and the use of tying techniques (Sacks, 1995) to highlight a stronger link to the previous talk.

During doctor–patient interactions (Campion & Langdon, 2004), several topics are discussed throughout the conversations. However, new topics are introduced mainly by patients via either a pre-announcement like "first of all," which projects more than one "thing" the patient wants to talk about, or via the use of marked "in-situ announcements" of the type "I know it's another thing but" or "and I have another little problem." With a crosslinguistic comparison, Du Babcock (1999) suggested that there are two ways of managing topic in Chinese Cantonese meetings compared to English meetings. In Cantonese meetings, interlocutors follow a more circular and communicative topical line, recurrently coming back to a previous talk, whereas English meetings are characterized by a rather linear topical development. A similar analysis was conducted by Chen (1995) on intra- and intercultural dyads. The author pinpointed different ways for eliciting topical talk and for reacting to context cues depending on the cultural similarity or difference of one's interlocutor.

Investigating the management of topics and agendas in business conversation, Bolden (2008) individuated the role played by the discourse marker "so" at juncture points in conversation: it seems that this marker signals that the upcoming action is introducing the intended topic after a conversation has been opened. Heyman (1986) studied the use of topic formulations in classroom discourse: he argues that formulations are central to this type of conversation insofar as they "fix" the topic (Heyman, 1986: 40). The author proposes an analysis of cases in which topic formulation seems to be problematic, such as when the teacher verbalizes for the class what they intend to do next and for this reason relates to what has been done before. In fact, while one would expect topical talk in the classroom to be rather coherent, it is when formulating topics that troubles may arise:

1. It can be that not all members have the same access to the "stock of knowledge" (ibid.: 53) that is needed for understanding the topic formulation.
2. Asymmetries in authority arise as far as only the teacher seems to have the right to propose particular formulations and glosses.

A critical point may be, however, that it is not always clear what the author means by "topic." In fact, it seems that topic and activity almost always coincide. For example, the formulation "what I wanna do today is continue uh talkin' about why the volumes were different" is analyzed as topic formulation and contributes to the conclusion that classroom conversations differ from everyday conversations because in the latter ones, no such formulations are found.

To sum up, the investigation of topical progression in conversation has highlighted the unstable nature of conversational topics and the collaborative nature of topic progression. It is never just one interlocutor who decides a priori what the topic will be, but rather, it is the continuous adjustment among participants that makes available to the researcher the progression line of a certain topic. In fact, researchers have the traces left by the interactants at their disposal for "reconstructing" a particular topical talk: thanks to linguistic structures, overlapping turns, pauses, and nonverbal communication, topics are collaboratively managed in a way so as not to interrupt the conversational flow and to show acknowledgment for what has been previously said by others.

2.4.2 Topical Disjunctions

Of course, topic transitions do not always occur smoothly. Research on topical disjunctions or on topic boundaries shows how topics are initiated and terminated by the interactants. Most of the research has concentrated mainly on topic introduction, which can be generated with topic initial elicitors, such as the question "what's new?" (Button & Casey, 1984). This resource accomplishes several actions at once:

1. It segments the upcoming talk in three parts (the inquiry, a response to it, and a topicalizer, i.e. an element that invites the interlocutor to tell more about the topic).
2. The interactant using it shows to their interlocutors their own availability for talking about a topic.
3. It provides a ground for a certain domain of talkables.

Topic initial elicitors are typically found after sequence-opening or sequence-closing components and after topic-bounding elements. In this case, "their design is aimed at newsworthy events but without marking them as further for the conversation, and without marking them as immediately current" (Button & Casey, 1984: 174).

However, topics can be introduced also by other resources, such as itemized news inquiries and news announcements (Button & Casey, 1985), each of which is labeled as a topic nomination. In contrast to topic initial elicitors, itemized news inquiries "aim themselves directly at a particular item" (Button & Casey, 1985: 6). An important structural property of itemized news inquiries is that the response that follows need not be exclusively on the item addressed in the inquiry but can be extended to some other related aspects, so more generally, "the [initiated] sequence is designed to begin a topic" (Button & Casey, 1985: 17). News announcements are not used to inquire, but to "report on an activity" (Button & Casey, 1985: 22) that is speaker related, only partially reported on, and presented to show that the speaker is aware of some

28 *Topic Analysis*

recipient's knowledge about it. Finally, topics can be initiated while there is an actual business at hand, i.e. when a particular event is happening or has happened that a speaker wishes to address and to introduce in the conversation. Consequently, interactants are shown to deploy a "topic-sensitive method" (Button & Casey, 1988/1989: 63). This is illustrated in the following example:

(4) MDH:1:8:8: (From Button & Casey, 1988: 64)

```
01   Dr. D:   If we wait tod:ay perhaps tomorrow if we reng
02            Through and see if we can get ah:
03            (0.4)
04       ()   .ts
05   Dr. A:   Yes:
06   Dr. D:   Er:
07            (1.5)
08   Dr. A:   Y eah
09   Dr. D:   w ritt en reports an if we (0.7)^ you know=
10   Dr. A:                                      Mmm
11   Dr. D:   =I: should think (0.8) we should really get full
12            author:ty (.) hhh an if: (1.0) it is alright
13            then we'll go a:head
14            (3.4)
15   Dr. D:   No|w then: hhhh (1.0) Mr. E:llacott
16            (1.4)
17   Dr. A:   He's very well.
```

In ex. 4, two doctors are talking about their patients while the doctors review and complete information in the patients' paper files. The line focused on is line 15: Dr. D. accomplishes the introduction of a new topic by means of, first, a transition marker (*now then*) at turn beginning. The speaker introduces the referent Mr. Ellacott, who cannot be found in the immediately preceding talk. However, this introduction is oriented to by both interactants as non-problematic and understandable at this point in conversation. Dr. A. does not initiate any repair sequence after line 15 but aligns with his colleague and reacts to his topic introduction with a description of Mr. Ellacott's health state.

Ex. 4 shows that under specific conditions, interactants can rely on previous knowledge from the recipient about some specific matters: in this case, the two doctors are going through their files, and it is possible that Mr. Ellacott will at some point be addressed during the conversation. Taking another approach to the generation of topics in conversation, Adato (1980) and Bergmann (1990) investigate the occasionality (Adato, 1980) or the local sensitivity (Bergmann, 1990) of topic introduction. In their studies, the authors shed light on the local and co-constructed nature of topics by showing that they are often related to the context in which conversations are happening; i.e. the real world itself becomes a way of generating topics in conversation.

The analysis and comparison of conversations between acquainted and unacquainted pairs of interlocutors allowed Maynard & Zimmerman (1984) to investigate the methods that speakers use for introducing topics in conversation. Considering three basic factors that influence the accomplishment of topical talk (relevance of the topic as regards previous conversations, reference to what is known/unknown by the interlocutor, and management of interpersonal relationships), the researchers highlighted the strong link between topical talk and the construction of interpersonal relationships:

> conversationalists' relationship is an ongoing accomplishment partly exhibited in those procedures utilized for initiating and pursuing topical talk.
>
> (Maynard & Zimmerman, 1984: 313)

Through the introduction of known referents, the topicalization of previous introduced matters and the continuous adjustment to one another, acquainted speakers "do being acquainted." On the contrary, unacquainted speakers were seen to start their conversations with different types of question–answer sequences, such as with inquiries that help categorize their interlocutors or with questions about the activities related to some specific membership categories (if someone is a student, they might take courses or participate in some campus activities). These conversation-opening sequences accomplish an important pre-topical activity for producing further topical talk, for categorizing one's interlocutor, and for framing what is sayable during the ongoing conversation, thus increasing affiliation.

Topical talk between unacquainted dyads was also investigated by Svennevig (1999), who presented five principles of topical talk, i.e. general organizational "precepts" that involve *production constraints* and *interpretive resources* (Svennevig, 1999: 172) for producing and participating in topical talk: reportability, projectability, local connectedness, progressivity, and procedural information. I now discuss them in detail, supporting the explanations with several examples. Especially the fifth principle will be discussed, because it can be seen also as an underlying feature of human conversations and not only as a specific principle governing topicality.

Topical talk is in the first place reportable; i.e. the interactants presume their talk to be of some interest for their coparticipants, and this is established in the opening sequences, as it is observable in the following example:

(5) "Lecture" (3: 82–88), from Svennevig (1999: 174)[1]

```
01   R:    ... 'oh,
02         ... it was a bit too 'much for me that last
```

Topic Analysis

```
03           ... lecture
04   V:  (0) 'yeah?
05   R:  ... (2.1) <X on the X> go from two till
06           ... ['six, and then]    -
07   V:      [yeah that's . . .] ex'hausting.
08   R:  ... 'very,
```

The interesting turn is in line 04, 'yeah?, which accomplishes a topicalization of R's assessment via rising intonation and precision timing directly after R's turn. A topicalizer, then, "establish[es] the topic proposal interactionally as the joint topical project for the subsequent turns of talk" (Svennevig, 1999: 174). To better understand the collaborative nature of topic reportability, the author illustrates an example of non-topicalization, i.e. a case in which the coparticipant does not topicalize the proposed matter and, in so doing, rejects its reportability. The main aspects of this rejection are to be found in the coparticipant's delayed reaction and in the falling intonation of his minimal response:

(6) "Legendary" (5:866–889) (from Svennevig, 1999: 174–175, partial report of the whole example)

```
01   B:  (0) hm
02           ... (2.5) of course the 'premises are
03           e = legendary
04           or like
05   L:  ... yeah.
06   B:  .. [yeah you know?]
07   L:     [yeah yeah yeah.]
08   B:  ... [[it--]]
09   L:     [[it's]] a 'good 'story [that one.]
10   B:                              [@@@]@@
11           ... 'really.
12           ... (2.0) 'unbe'lievable,
```

A comparison between L's turn in line 5 in the current example and V's turn in line 3 in the previous one shows striking differences. L's first turn in ex. 6 is delayed, and it has a final, falling intonation. Consequently, whereas R in ex. 5 expands his matter and V participates in it via a demonstration of affiliation, in this example B is fishing for L's topicalization in the lines 06, 08, and 10–12. Moreover, L assesses his knowledge of the story that B wishes to talk about by verbalizing it in line 09, thus rejecting the newsworthiness of the story itself.

A second principle is that of projectability: when a topic is proposed, it structures the upcoming talk in a specific way and this needs to be accepted by all participants. A special group of projectors occurs in narratives, as they are prefaced and framed in such a way as to project their main point. Local connectedness is the third principle presented and relates to topic continuity and talk interpretation. Topic continuity is to be assumed if no other techniques are exploited to signal that there is no disruption whatsoever in the ongoing talk (Sacks et al., 1974). Therefore, a turn is seen and interpreted as being related to the preceding one—if the contrary is not clearly signaled. The next example clarifies this point. It stems from my au pairs corpus, and the transcript contains a part of a conversation between Marie, a host mother, and the au pair Julie. They are talking about their ability of speaking languages other than French. The interesting lines for the investigated principle are highlighted in bold.

(7) Julie, 05.02.2010 *anglais* "English"

```
01 Mar: >alors< dans ma lettre je lui ai écrit en allemand, les deux
        well     in  my letter   I her-IND have written in german   the two
02      autre:s (0.6) en anglais.
        others        in  english
        well in my letter I have written to her in German, whereas to the other two I
        have written in English
03 (0.6)
04 Mar: déjà    alors moi au téléphone en anglais +je suis pas sûre que
        already well  me-DIR on the phone in english  I am  not  sure that
05      je (peux) tellement   ((en riant))+
        I  can    really      ((laughing))
        to begin with, on the phone I am not even sure that I can really ((laughing))
06 (0.8)
07 Jul: ouais moi- oh non: en anglais c'est- c'est- (0.3) c'est
        °terrible.°
        yeah  me   oh no  in english   it's   it's         it's
        terrible
        yeah, me too, oh no it's terrible to speak English
08 Mar: >bon toutes< les  ↑trois=↑elles ont dit qu'elles parlaient
        un pe-
        well all-F.pl. the three       they have said that they speak
        a  bi-
09      qu'elles avaient fait un peu de français=[parce que&
        that they had    done a  bit of french   because
        well, all three have said that they have learned a bit of French because
10 Jul:                                         [ah:=(ouais)
                                                 oh   yeah
11 Mar: &ça c'était    un peu  une  condition parce que on veut
        pas quelqu'un
        this-DIR it was a bit  a    condition because   we don't
        want someone
12      qui dit pas  un mot   quelqu'un (x) rien à comprendre
        [°quand même°.
        who say not  one word someone   (x) nothing to understand
        in any case
        this was a sort of condition because we don't want someone who can't speak or
        can't understand a word at least
```

32   Topic Analysis

```
13  Jul: [ou:ais.
              yeah
14  (0.5)
15  Mar: [°c'est quand même      embêtant°.
              it's     anyhow         annoying
         it's really annoying
16  Jul: [.hh
17  Jul: >ouais=MOI< (0.2) j'ai: eh: maintenant   avec les cours
         de ski là à
              yeah   me        I have uh   now    with   the   ski lesson
                                                                         at
18       l'uni?
         the university
         yeah, for me too, now that I'm attending the ski lessons at the university
19  (0.4)
20  Jul: euh  des   fois je parle angl↑ais parce que y a: ce=sont
         qu↑e de:s
              uh    some  times I  speak  english    because  there are it's
              only
         sometimes I speak English because there are only
21       (0.5) [des gens-&
                DET people
                people
22  Mar:       [°des étrangers°.
                DET foreigners
                foreigners/strangers
23  Jul:       [ah:=ouais >des étrangers.<&
                oh   yeah    DET   foreigners
                yeah, foreigners/strangers
24  Mar:       [ouais.
                yeah
25  Jul: &.h et:=euhm (0.9) <o::uais> c'est vraiment (0.8) c'est ↑dure
              and  uhm            yeah       it's    truly          it's   hard
26       de parler anglais parce que .hh maintenant
         to  speak  english   because       now
         and it's really hard to speak English because now (I always speak French)
```

In ex. 7, Marie is explaining to Julie how she goes about searching for the next au pair, and she is saying that one of the girls whom she has contacted wishes to speak to her on the phone in English. Marie's concern is that she might not be that good in speaking English on the phone (lines 04–05), and Julie reacts with an affiliating response (line 07): she admits that speaking English is terrible for her (*c'est terrible*). Marie continues explaining that all the girls had had French courses, because the condition of speaking a little bit of French is essential for her (lines 08–12). After Marie's closing remark (line 15), Julie starts talking about her ski classes at the university (lines 17–18). Julie contextualizes her talk by linking it to herself via the left dislocation *moi je* in line 17 and by introducing the ski classes of the university, but the topical linkage is observable only later in this turn, when she says that she sometimes speaks English during these classes (line 20). After a repair sequence about the word "foreigners/strangers" (lines 20–24), Julie continues, assessing that it's very hard for her to speak English (lines 25–26).

Julie is therefore accomplishing many things at once: her story mirrors Marie's story structure by first delivering facts and then commenting on them, expressing a negative stance. Moreover, Julie's talk remains on topic, although her turn beginning in lines 17–18 could be interpreted as disruptive regarding the preceding talk—but it is not. Finally, Julie tells a story that is structurally aligned to Marie's and herewith allows her to affiliate with Marie's point of view. In conclusion, local connectedness is a multilayered matter that relates not only to the content (or information) level of conversation but also to its linguistic verbalization and its sequential organization.

The fourth principle addressed is progressivity: the possibility of carrying on a topic as long as it is interesting for the participants. Interactants are generally shown to be interested in continuing their activities through the conversation (Stivers & Robinson, 2006). This means that they exploit the structural features of interactions for their purposes: they tend to place a second pair part right next to the first pair part, or the selected speaker takes the floor as soon as possible when they are allowed to do so. In so doing, the conversation can progress while other actions are being carried out, such as answering, (dis)aligning, and affiliating. In the same way, progressivity also concerns topical talk: as long as the interactants orient to one another's turn as not yet being closing implicative, they can add new information or topicalize the actual one: they develop further the topical line of the conversation so far. When it happens that one or more of these four principles are not respected, i.e. when some work is done to indicate that a disruption is coming in, then the fact that they are not respected "gives [the principles] a potential for conveying procedural information" (Svennevig, 1999: 186).

Procedural information is, thus, the fifth principle and, at the same time, also an underlying feature of talk-in-interaction. When a topic is maintained, then progressivity and local connectedness are followed, whereas the establishment of reportability and the related projection appear at work when a new topic is being introduced. Subsequently, when talk off topic is done or a disjunction in the topical talk is coming, the interactants will signal it with some extra interactional work. This does not mean that the interactants will directly address or label their talk as, for instance, off topic. They will do "being off topic" and will employ several means that will be oriented to as off topic by their interlocutors. For this reason, procedural information is an underlying feature of conversations in general: it is always present in interactions since it is created, used, and oriented to by the participants when they mutually collaborated to accomplish social actions.

Finally, Holt (2010) analyses topic terminations and identifies a specific use of laughter at the end of storytelling, although she concentrates on specific types of stories; i.e. no complaint-stories or tragic stories are treated in her paper. She shows that, in this particular conversational environment, both alignment and affiliation are required from the story recipient. When it is delivered, at least two turns contain laughter, which is not a sufficient closing device per se (it is, at most, a closing implicative). However, it indicates the speakers' orientation toward the introduction of a possible new matter. Instead, when affiliation is not achieved, the storyteller tries to expand the topic at hand, thus creating a new opportunity for the recipient to affiliate.

The author is interested in analyzing topic terminations in relation to laughter but subsequently focuses on storytelling, which is an activity that participants accomplish collaboratively. Clearly, a story needs to have a topic, in the sense that a storytelling reports on something newsworthy, i.e. on something mentionable or reportable. For this reason, when a story ends, the topic it was about might also end. However, a story need not necessarily be about only one topic, and any topic from the preceding storytelling might be expanded by a next speaker.

In this chapter, I have presented a variety of approaches that have dealt with the problem of identifying and defining topic as an entity at different analytical levels, such as the clause or sentence, the discourse, the text, and the monological spoken discourse. Moreover, the approach of CA has been presented more in depth because it builds the basis for the data analysis (Chapters 5 and 6). CA researchers have adopted a different concept of topic, for which they do not identify the topic as an entity, i.e. as a static part of language, but rather as a process, i.e. with an unstable nature that evolves through the conversation as it is created and developed by the interactants' turns at talk. My analyses of conversational topics in L2 interactions will show that topic management is an intrinsic feature of everyday interactions as well as of everyday institutional interactions. In fact, the family conversations investigated in this work unify both formal and informal traits because the L2 speakers are au pairs employed by the host families for taking care of children. Therefore, even if the conversations take place in a familiar setting, they show also institutional features, such as when the host parents questions the au pairs about the day with the children, which brings explanations and tellings to light. Moreover, the questioning also reveals the relationship between topics and epistemic access to the conversation. In fact, the host parents and the au pairs have different experiences with the children, and this aspect is uncovered only when directly addressed and talked about (cf. Pochon-Berger et al., 2015). After the first conversations in the new family, which resemble more an interrogation because of the frequent question–answer pairs, the au pairs develop their storytelling more independently and report about the day (e.g. expanding their narrative after responding to the host parents' question) or introduce new conversational topics about their families and lives in the form of a storytelling. In the literature about topics, storytelling is presented as a preferred activity for packaging newsworthy information (see Covelli & Murray, 1980; Holt, 2010; Jefferson, 1981, 1984).

Narratives, however, have also been analyzed under a different light, namely regarding their intrinsic property of structuring the conversation in a specific way. When a speaker starts a narrative, they do so with prefacing work that projects more to come. The other interactants do not claim the floor and become story recipients, whereas the first speaker takes the role of storyteller (cf. Goodwin, 1984). Storytelling is therefore a conversational practice that puts on hold the normal turn-taking machinery and distributes the speakership among the interactants in a different way. Through narratives, knowledge is transmitted, and the storyteller designs their turns to show the newsworthiness of the upcoming talk.

2.4.3 *Conversational Topics and Domains of Knowledge*

Conversations, however, show how knowledge cannot be reduced to the information status of separated bits of text or of discourse. On the contrary, knowledge in interaction is managed by and distributed among conversationalists:

> Each time we take a turn in conversation we indicate what we know and what we think others know. However, knowledge is neither static nor absolute. It is shaped by those we interact with and governed by social norms.
>
> (Stivers et al., 2011, preamble in the first page)

In the domain of CA-SLA, Berger (2017) has investigated the epistemic positioning of an au pair, Julie, reporting to the host mother about the misconduct of her children. The author observes that a narrative offers a privileged place in conversation for delivering such information. Moreover, the epistemic authority of a mother vs. that of an au pair is observable in the evaluations of the children' misconducts: whereas the mother explicitly address the negativity of such conduct, Julie embeds her criticism in direct reported speech, thus in a more indirect way. Finally, Julie and the host mother construct their specific territories of knowledge (see

Heritage, 2012; Raymond & Heritage, 2006) in the sense that each one claims for herself a different type of authority, experience, and knowledge about child education and caregiving. Pochon-Berger et al. (2015) have addressed the issue of epistemic access and primacy in relation to storytelling about the activities that the au pair Julie has accomplished with the children during the day. In this case too, storytelling assumes a central role in the institutional (working) context for exchanging important information between the parents and the caregiving person. In line with CA research on L1, then, narratives are seen as a preferred practice for making observable one's epistemic stance and one's epistemic authority in comparison to other interactants.

Generally speaking, conversational topics embedded in different types of larger sequences such as storytelling have the property of structuring the upcoming talk. In my case, I have investigated this structuring feature when conversational topics are introduced (see Chapter 5). Button & Casey (1984, 1985) and Covelli & Murray (1980) have already addressed that when conversationalists introduce a new topic in the interaction, the coparticipant can topicalize the previous turn and herewith start a new topical sequence or stop the topical talk from the beginning. If the topical sequence is initiated, then the interactant introducing the topic develops it. This is observable especially when a storytelling is initiated the interactional identities of storyteller and story recipient are distributed among the participants.

The research on epistemics in interaction has shown how narratives are related not only to the distribution of identities but also to the distribution of territories of knowledge, i.e. how interactants construct on a turn-by-turn basis their epistemic status and how they claim their primacy about it (Berger 2017; Heritage, 2013; Pochon-Berger et al., 2015; Raymond & Heritage, 2006; Stivers et al., 2012). However, CA and CA-SLA research so far lacks in showing the link between conversational topics and epistemics.

My data on conversational topics, and especially the chapter on topic introduction, will show that conversational topics produce two types of interactional organization: on the one hand, they have the feature of structuring the upcoming talk, and on the other hand, they also influence the distribution of knowledge between participants. When a new conversational topic is introduced, it is generally presented as new or newsworthy for the coparticipants. This aspect concerning the recipient design and the turn design is linked with the speaker's responsibility about the topic they introduce, i.e. about their knowledge about it. Moreover, my investigations into French L2 interactions show that the link between topic management and epistemics in conversation needs not be restricted to L1 conversational data only (see also the analyses in Pochon-Berger et al., 2015; Berger, 2017 for French L2 interactions).

The relation between conversational topics and epistemics highlights that topic management is an underlying feature of every conversation that cannot be ignored when dealing with interactional data. The difficulties in grasping, defining, observing, and analyzing it demonstrate its centrality to conversationalists. It is therefore desirable to mind the existing literature gap and to show in a clearer way that conversational topics and epistemics strongly depend on one another.

I now turn to the second main area of my research, namely the concept of interactional competence and its observation in longitudinal data (Chapter 3). Afterward, before presenting the analytical parts, I focus on the particularity of topic management in French and French L2 talk-in-interaction (Chapter 4).

Note

1. I report only the English translation of this example. The original Finnish transcription can be found in Svennevig (1999: 174).

References

Adato, A. (1980). 'Occasionality' as a constituent feature of the known-in-common character of topics. *Human Studies, 3*, 47–67.

Andersen, R. W. (1991). Developmental sequences: The emergence of aspect marking in second language acquisition. In T. Huebner & C. A. Ferguson (Eds.), *Crosscurrents in second language acquisition and linguistic theories* (pp. 305–324). Amsterdam and Philadelphia: John Benjamins Publishing Company.

Andorno, C. M. (2005). Additive and restrictive particles in Italian as a second language: Embedding in the verbal utterance structure. In H. Hendriks (Ed.), *The structure of learner varieties* (pp. 405–460). Berlin and New York: Mouton de Gruyter.

Ariel, M. (1988). Referring and accessibility. *Journal of Linguistics, 24*(1), 65–87.

Arminen, I. (1996). The construction of topic in the turns of talk at the meetings of alcoholics anonymous. *The International Journal of Sociology and Social Policy, 16*(5/6), 88–130.

Austin, J. L. (1962). *How to do things with words: The William James lectures delivered at Harvard University in 1955.* (J. O. Urmson & M. Sbisà, Eds.). Oxford: Clarendon Press.

Bardovi-Harling, K. (2000). Tense and aspect in second language acquisition: Form, meaning, and use. *Supplement to Language Learning, 50*(Thematic issue).

Benazzo, S. (2003). The interaction between the development of verb morphology and the acquisition of temporal adverb of contrast. In C. Dimroth & M. Starren (Eds.), *Information structure, linguistic structure and the dynamics of language acquisition* (pp. 187–210). Amsterdam: John Benjamins Publishing Company.

Berger, E. (2017). Se plaindre des enfants: positionnements épistémiques et rapports institutionnels dans les récits conversationnels entre au pair et famille d'accueil. *Travaux neuchâtelois de linguistique, 67*, 103–125.

Bergmann, J. R. (1990). On the local sensitivity of conversation. In I. Markovà & K. Foppa (Eds.), *The dynamics of dialogue* (pp. 201–226). New York: Harvester Wheatsheaf.

Bolden, G. B. (2008). 'So what's up?': Using the discourse marker so to launch conversational business. *Research on Language & Social Interaction, 41*(3), 302–337.

Bransford, J. D., & Johnson, M. K. (1973). Considerations of some problems of comprehension. In W. G. Chase (Ed.), *Visual information processing* (pp. 383–438). New York: Academic Press.

Brown, G., & Yule, G. (1983). *Discourse analysis*. Cambridge: Cambridge University Press.

Button, G., & Casey, N. (1984). Generating topic: The use of topic initial elicitors. In J. M. Atkinson & J. Heritage (Eds.), *Structures of social action* (pp. 167–190). Cambridge: Cambridge University Press.

Button, G., & Casey, N. (1985). Topic nomination and topic pursuit. *Human Studies, 8*, 3–55.

Button, G., & Casey, N. (1988). Topic initiation: Business-at-hand. *Research on Language & Social Interaction, 22*, 61–92.

Campion, P., & Langdon, M. (2004). Achieving multiple topic shifts in primary care medical consultations: A conversational analysis study in UK general practice. *Sociology of Health & Illness, 26*(1), 81–101.

Carroll, M., Natale, S., & Starren, M. (2008). Acquisition du marquage du progressif par des apprenants germanophones de l'italien et néerlandophones du francais. *Acquisition et Interaction En Langue Etrangère (AILE), 26*, 31–49.

Chafe, W. L. (1976). Givennes, contrastiveness, definiteness, subjects, topics, and points of view. In C. N. Li (Ed.), *Subject and topic* (pp. 27–55). New York: Academic Press.

Chafe, W. L. (1987). Cognitive constraints on information flow. In R. Tomlin (Ed.), *Coherence and grounding in discourse* (pp. 21–51). Amsterdam and Philadelphia: John Benjamins Publishing Company.

Chafe, W. L. (1997). Polyphonic topic development. In T. Givón (Ed.), *Conversation: Cognitive, communicative and social perspectives*. Amsterdam and Philadelphia: John Benjamins Publishing Company.

Chen, L. (1995). Interaction involvement and patterns of topical talk: A comparison of intercultural and intracultural dyads. *International Journal of Intercultural Relationships, 19*(4), 463–482.

Covelli, L. H., & Murray, S. O. (1980). Accomplishing topic change. *Anthropological Linguistics, 22*(9), 382–389.

Danes, F. (Ed.) (1974). *Papers on functional sentence perspective*. The Hague: Mouton de Gruyter.

Davison, A. (1984). Syntactic markedness and the definition of sentence topic. *Language, 60*(4), 797–846.

Dimroth, C. (2008). Perspectives on second language acquisition at different ages. In J. Philp, R. Oliver, & A. Mackey (Eds.), *Second language acquisition and the younger learner: Child's play?* (pp. 53–79). Amsterdam: John Benjamins.

Dimroth, C., Gretsch, P., Jordens, P., Perdue, C., & Starren, M. (2003). Finiteness in Germanic languages: A stage-model for first and second language development. In C. Dimroth & M. Starren (Eds.), *Information structures and the dynamics of language acquisition* (pp. 65–93). Amsterdam and Philadelphia: John Benjamins Publishing Company.

Drew, P., & Holt, E. (1998). Figures of speech: Figurative expressions and the management of topic transition in conversation. *Language in Society*, 27(4), 495–522.

Du Babcock, B. (1999). Topic management and turn-taking in professional communication. *Management Communication Quarterly*, 12(4), 544–574.

Du Babcock, B. (2006). An analysis of topic management strategies and turn-taking behavior in the Hong Kong bilingual environment. *Journal of Business Communication*, 43(1), 21–42.

Firbas, J. (1992). *Functional sentence perspective in written and spoken communication*. Cambridge: Cambridge University Press.

Fox, B. (1987). Anaphora in popular written English. In R. Tomlin (Ed.), *Coherence and grounding in discourse* (pp. 157–174). Amsterdam: John Benjamins Publishing Company.

Galambos, S. J. (1980). A clarification of the notion of topic: Evidence from popular spoken French. In J. Kreiman & A. E. Ojeda (Eds.), *Papers from the parasession on pronouns and anaphora*. Chicago: The University of Chicago Classics.

Garfinkel, H., & Sacks, H. (1970). On formal structures of practical action. In J. McKinney & E. A. Tiryakian (Eds.), *Theoretical sociology: Perspectives and developments* (pp. 338–366). New York: Appleton-Century-Crofts.

Givón, T. (1976). Topic, pronoun and grammatical agreement. In C. N. Li (Ed.), *Subject and topic* (pp. 149–188). New York, San Francisco and London: Academic Press.

Givón, T. (Ed.) (1983). *Topic continuity in discourse*. Amsterdam and Philadelphia: John Benjamins Publishing Company.

Givón, T. (1987). Beyond foreground and background. In R. Tomlin (Ed.), *Coherence and grounding in discourse* (pp. 175–188). Amsterdam: John Benjamins Publishing Company.

Goodwin, C. (1984). Notes on story structure and the organization of participation. In J. M. Atkinson & J. Heritage (Eds.), *Structures of Social Action: Studies in Conversation Analysis* (pp. 225–246). London: Cambridge University Press.

Halliday, M. A. K. (1967). Notes on transitivity and theme in English: Part 2. *Journal of Linguistics*, 3(2), 199–244.

Halliday, M. A. K., & Hasan, R. (1976). *Cohesion in English*. London: Longman.

Hanson, K. (1987). Topic constructions in spoken French: Some comparisons with Chichewa. *Proceedings of the Thirteenth Annual Meeting of the Berkeley Linguistics Society*, 105–116.

Haviland, S. E., & Clark, H. H. (1974). What's new? Acquiring new information as a process in comprehension. *Journal of Verbal Learning and Verbal Behavior*, (13), 512–521.

Hendriks, H. (2000). The acquisition of topic marking in L1 Chinese and L1 and L2 French. *SSLA*, (22), 369–397.

Hendriks, H., & Watorek, M. (2008). L'organisation de l'information en topique dans les discours descriptifs en L1 et en L2. *Acquisition et Interaction En Langue Etrangère (AILE)*, (26), 149–171.

Heritage, J. (2012). The epistemic engine: Sequence organization and territories of knowledge. *Research on Language and Social Interaction*, 45(1), 30–52.

Heritage, J. (2013). Action formation and its epistemic (and other) backgrounds. *Discourse Studies*, 15(5), 551–578.

Heritage, J., & Sorjonen, M.-L. (1994). Constituting and maintaining activities across sequences: And-prefacing as a feature of question design. *Language in Society*, 23(1), 1–29.

Heyman, R. D. (1986). Formulating topic in the classroom. *Discourse Processes*, (9), 37–55.

Holt, E. (2010). The last laugh: Shared laughter and topic termination. *Journal of Pragmatics*, 42, 1513–1525.

Holt, E., & Drew, P. (2005). Figurative pivots: The use of figurative expressions in pivotal topic transitions. *Research on Language & Social Interaction*, 38(1), 35–61.

Hornby, P. A. (1971). Surface structure and the topic-comment distinction: A developmental study. *Child Development*, (42), 1975–1988.

Hyman, L. M., & Zimmer, K. E. (1976). Embedded topic in French. In C. N. Li (Ed.), *Subject and topic* (pp. 189–211). New York, San Francisco and London: Academic Press.

Jakobson, R. (1985). *Verbal art, verbal sign, verbal time*. Minneapolis: University of Minnesota Press.

Jakobson, R. (1987). *Language in literature*. Cambridge/London: Harvard University Press.

Jefferson, G. (1972). Side sequences. In D. N. Sudnow (Ed.), *Studies in social interaction* (pp. 294–333). New York: New York Free Press.

Jefferson, G. (1981). *On the articulation of topic in conversation*. Final report to the British Social Science Research Council.

Jefferson, G. (1984). On stepwise transition from talk about a trouble to inappropriately next-positioned matters. In J. M. Atkinson & J. Heritage (Eds.), *Structures of social action* (pp. 191–222). Cambridge: Cambridge University Press.

Jefferson, G. (1993). Caveat Speaker: preliminary notes on recipient topic-shift implicature. *Tilburger Papers in Language and Literature*, 30(June 1983), 1–25.

Klein, W. (1994). *Time in language*. London: Routledge.

Klein, W., & Perdue, C. (1997). The basic variety (or: Couldn't natural languages be much simpler?). *Second Language Research*, 13, 301–347.

Klein, W., & von Stutterheim, C. (1987). Quaestio und referentielle Bewegung in Erzählungen. *Linguistische Berichte*, 109, 163–183.

Kramsch, C. J. (1983). Discourse function of grammar rules: Topic construction in German. *The Modern Language Journal*, 67(1), 13–22.

Lambrecht, K. (1987). Sentence focus, information structure, and the thetic-categorial distinction. *BLS*, 13, 366–382.

Lambrecht, K. (1994). *Information structure and sentence form: Topic, focus, and the mental representation of discourse referents*. Cambridge: Cambridge University Press.

Mathesius, V. (1975). *A functional analysis of present day English on a general linguistic basis*. Paris and The Hague: Mouton de Gruyter (original 1909).

Maynard, D. W. (1980). Placement of topic changes in conversation. *Semiotica*, 263–290.
Maynard, D. W., & Zimmerman, D. H. (1984). Topical talk, ritual and the social organization of relationships. *Social Psychology Quarterly, 47*(4), 301–316.
Ochs-Keenan, E., & Schieffelin, B. B. (1976). Topic as a discourse notion: A study of topic in the conversation of children and adults. In C. N. Li (Ed.), *Subject and topic* (pp. 335–384). New York, San Francisco and London: Academic Press.
Pekarek Doehler, S. (1999). Linguistic forms and social interaction: Why do we specify referents more than is necessary for their identification?. In J. Verschueren (Ed.) *Pragmatics in 1998*. (Vol. 2, pp. 427–447). Antwerp: International Pragmatics Association.
Perdue, C., Benazzo, S., & Giuliano, P. (2002). When finiteness gets marked: The relation between morphosyntactic development and use of scopal items in adult language acquisition. *Linguistics, 40*, 849–890.
Pérez de Ayala Becerril, S. (1997). Topic management at question time: Contextual constraints. *Estudios Ingleses de La Universidad Complutense*, (5), 169–183.
Pochon-Berger, E., Pekarek Doehler, S., & König, C. (2015). Family conversational storytelling at the margins of the workplace: The case of au pair girls. In L. Grujicic-Alatriste (Ed.), *Linking discourse studies to professional practice* (pp. 86–108). Bristol: Multilingual Matters.
Prince, E. F. (1981). Toward a taxonomy of given-new information. In P. Cole (Ed.), *Radical pragmatics* (pp. 223–255). New York: Academic Press.
Raymond, G., & Heritage, J. (2006). The epistemics of social relations: Owning grandchildren. *Language in Society, 35*, 677–705.
Reinhart, T. (1981). Pragmatics and linguistics: An analysis of sentence topic. *Philosophica, 27*(1), 53–94.
Sacks, H. (1995). *Lectures on conversation* (Vol. 1 & 2). Oxford: Basil Blackwell.
Sacks, H., Schegloff, E. A., & Jefferson, G. (1974). A simplest systematic for the organization of turn-taking in conversation. *Language, 50*(4), 696–735.
Searle, J. (1969). *Speech acts: An essay in the philosophy of language*. London: Cambridge University Press.
Seedhouse, P., & Harris, A. (2011). Topic development in the IELTS speaking test. *IELTS Research Report, 12*, 1–50.
Selting, M. (1994). Emphatic speech style: With special focus on the prosodic signalling of heightened emotive involvement in conversation. *Journal of Pragmatics, 22*(Special Issue: Involvement in Language), 375–408.
Starren, M., & van Hout, R. (1996). Temporality in learner discourse: What temporal adverbials can and what they cannot express. *Zeitschrift Für Literaturwissenschaft Und Linguistik, 104*, 35–50.
Stivers, T., & Robinson, J. D. (2006). A preference for progressivity in interaction. *Language in Society, 35*, 367–392. DOI: 10.10170S0047404506060179
Stivers, T., Mondada, L., & Steensig, J. (Eds.) (2011). *The morality of knowledge in conversation*. Cambridge: Cambridge University Press.
Stivers, T., Mondada, L., & Steensig, J. (2011). Knowledge, morality and affiliation in social interaction. In T. Stivers, L. Mondada, & J. Steensig (Eds.), *The morality of knowledge in conversation* (pp. 3–24). Cambridge: Cambridge University Press.

Svennevig, J. (1999). *Getting acquainted in conversation*. Amsterdam and Philadelphia: John Benjamins Publishing Company.

van Dijk, T. (1977). *Text and context: Explorations in the semantics and pragmatics of discourse*. London and New York: Longman.

von Stutterheim, C. (1998). Global principles of information organisation in texts of L2 speakers. *Information Organization in Texts*, 89–111.

West, C., & Garcia, A. (1988). Conversational shift work: A study of topical transitions between women and men. *Social Problems*, 35(5), 551–575.

3 L2 Acquisition and Interactional Competence

The previous chapter discussed different approaches to the concept of topic and its relationship to the acquisition of an L2. CA-SLA research in particular deals with the L2 learning process by looking at how the same action is accomplished by different L2 speakers or how the same action is accomplished by the same L2 speaker at different moments in time. In this chapter, I discuss the application of CA for the analysis of L2 talk-in-interaction; i.e. I present the main features of CA-SLA (3.1), which are reconceptualizing learning (3.1.1) and the analysis of competence (3.1.2). Subsequently, the concept and definition of interactional competence is discussed (3.2), which is central to CA-SLA analyses. The roots of interactional competence are briefly presented (3.2.1), the use of this term with the domain of CA-SLA is then depicted (3.2.2), and finally, some studies on interactional competence "in the wild" are reviewed (3.2.3). I close this chapter with a section on L2 interactional competence and its development over time (3.3), specifically addressing the challenge represented by longitudinal studies for the domain of CA-SLA.

3.1 Conversation Analysis for Second Language Acquisition (CA-SLA)

I begin with an example from my data to illustrate how CA investigates language in everyday talk-in-interaction. It shows a conversation between the au pair girl Oksana (L1 Polish) and her host father Pierre. At the time of recording, Oksana has been living with the host family for about one month. Oksana and Pierre are talking about the possibility of getting a new mixer.

(8) Oksana, 28.09.2010 *mixer* "food processor"

```
01   Pie:   .h jeu↑di >moi demain< j'irai   en acheter un au[tre   ].
            on thursday  me tomorrow  I will go  to buy of it    another one
            on thursday I will buy another one of these
02   Oks:                                                      [°°°oui]
                                                                  yes

                   OK°°°.
                   OK
```

```
03    (.)
04    Pie:  °effectivement°°.
            indeed
05    Oks:  >ouais c'est bon ↑et la même (.) mixer ou::: plus grande?
            yeah   that's good and the-F.sg. same  mixer-M.sg. or  bigger
            yeah, alright, and the same mixer or a bigger one?
06    (...)
07    Oks:  c'est:- parce que c'est (.) c'est mixer le nom de cette
            chose?
            it's-    because    it's       it's  mixer the name of this
            thing
            because is it mixer the name of this thing?
08    (..)
09    Pie:  oui s- c'est- s::: c'est un mixer normal, ↑toi ce que tu
            penses
            yes i- it's  i     it's  a normal mixer      you what you think
            about
10          c'est le robot.
            it's   the food processor
            yes, a normal mixer. what you are thinking about is the food processor.
11    Oks:  o- oui parce que s- c'est bon pour gâteau?
            y- yes because   i- it's  good for  cake
            yes, because it's good for baking a cake
12    (..)
13    Oks:  [(x)-
14    Pie:  [mh=oui.=
             mh yes
15    Oks:  =↑ah ↑OK.
             oh  OK
16    (..)
17    Pie:  tu penses  c'est nécessaire u:n plus grand?
            you think  it's  necessary   a  bigger one
            do you think that a bigger one is necessary?
18    (...)
19    Oks:  mh PAS POUR ÇA: mais pour gâteau: normalement avec les
            yeux:=et
            mh not for this but  for  cake    usually      with the
            *eyes and
20          avec les far↑ine peut-être ↑mais pour ça?
            with the-pl. flour-sg. maybe   but  for  this
            no not for doing this, but usually when you bake a cake with eggs and
            flour maybe it helps but not for this
21    (..)
22    Pie:  je le regarde (lui) qu'est-ce qu'il y a demain.
            I look at it-M.sg. (it-M.sg.) what     is there    tomorrow
            I will see tomorrow what I find
```

A first look at this example draws one's attention to the non-standard vocabulary and grammatical items employed by Oksana. For example, in line 05, she uses *la même mixer* ("the same mixer": article *the* in feminine) instead of *le même mixer* (article *the* in masculine); in line 11, she uses the construction *c'est bon pour gateau* ("it's good for cake") instead of *c'est bon pour faire un gateau* ("it's good for making a cake") or *c'est bon pour les gâteaux* ("it's good for cakes"); and she uses the term *yeux* ("eyes") in line 19 instead of *oeufs* ("eggs").

However, Pierre does not address any of these non-standard items and shows herewith his orientation toward the conversation progression. Pierre can identify the sense of Oksana's turns, probably drawing on environmental and co-textual information related to the interactional setting. In the ecology of this interaction, no negotiation of linguistic forms takes place about the non-standard items used by Oksana. Only in line 07 does Oksana ask for a clarification concerning the name of the object that they are talking about: *c'est mixer le nom de cette chose?* ("it's mixer the name of this thing?") and Pierre answers this question in line 09, explaining that it is indeed a mixer they are talking about, which is different from a bigger food processor.

Drawing on CA analytical tools, I first observe that Oksana is able to convey the information she wants to (a new mixer should be bought, and the ingredients for a cake), and she is also capable of asking for clarifications (line 07) despite some difficulties in the production of her turns. Moreover, both interlocutors are collaborating to achieve mutual comprehension and are helped not only by their respective knowledge in the domain of baking cakes but also by the ecology of their interaction.

This example shows how the interactants create and maintain intersubjectivity during the conversation. Comprehension is achieved on a turn-by-turn basis and how the L1 and the L2 speakers adjust their turns to each other in order to accomplish a larger joint activity (the next day's organization). Neither of them is behaving like merely a learner (Oksana) or an expert (Pierre) of French. Their identities are negotiated as the conversational flow progresses. Oksana and Pierre work together on a turn-by-turn mutual understanding: this is a basic constraint for the conversation to progress and it is observable for the researcher in "the way parties in interaction rely on what has been or is accountably present in the interaction" (Emanuelsson & Sahlström, 2008: 206).

The just-mentioned observations indicate how from a CA-SLA perspective, L2 learning cannot be reduced to the development of vocabulary or grammatical skills in a second language. L2 learning happens mostly through the use of the second language in a panoply of contexts in one's everyday life (in the bakery, in a bank, at the hospital, at school, with friends or unknown people, etc.). To observe and trace learning, it is important to consider the interactions that take place in all these environments in a second language. And it is also important to investigate how L2 speakers participate in these conversations. Looking at the diversity of resources and practices that L2 speakers employ for locally relevant purposes sets the basis for the analysis of their L2 interactional competence. This is a multilayered competence that cannot be reduced to only vocabulary or grammar. L2 interactional competence incorporates other aspects that are related to the construction and maintenance of intersubjectivity, i.e. "the ongoing work people carry out through visible conduct to ensure a common understanding of what is currently happening in interaction" (Eskildsen & Majlesi, 2018: 4). This interactional work consists, for example, of how speakers position themselves in relationship to their interlocutors or how they open or close a conversation (Hellermann, 2008). The inclusion of these features in the analysis of the L2 learning process is needed in order to understand what changes take place in the L2 speaker's interactional competence.

3.1.1 Reconceptualizing Learning

Not focusing on individuals' cognitive processes in isolation, CA-SLA looks at L2 learning as it happens through naturally occurring interactions in a wide range of environments—including the classroom, the workplace, and family conversations. A substantial change in the conceptualization of learning is advanced:

> CA-SLA views learning processes as contingent upon (and observable within) the micro-details of social interaction, and as socially distributed.
>
> (Pekarek Doehler, 2013: 1)

This is to say that L2 learning is not observed in terms of comparing L2 use to a priori defined patterns of language development (cf. for instance the concept of interlanguage) but is seen as taking place in everyday conversations. These interactions represent occasions in which L2 speakers collaboratively construct mutual understanding with their interlocutors. L2 learning is therefore not reduced to the mere movement of a learner's lexis and grammar toward a standard language norm, nor is it conceived of as language transfer from the L1 into the L2. L2 learning is observable in how L2 speakers participate in conversation with the resources they have available. The central point is the joint work between the participants to achieve mutual understanding and make sense of their coordinated social actions:

> A more emically based perspective would allow the authors to explicate the competencies through which the participants conjointly accomplish meaningful communication with the resources—however seemingly *imperfect*—at their disposal.
>
> (Firth & Wagner, 1997: 290, my emphasis)

The emic perspective adopted in CA and CA-SLA studies is a key analytical tool for investigating everyday talk-in-interaction as it happens, like in example 8 earlier. If we were to assume an exogenous perspective on this excerpt, then we would list all the errors that Oksana produces while talking to Pierre. In so doing, however, we would approach the data with a "learner-as-defective-communicator mindset" (Firth & Wagner, 1997: 290), which would lead us to highlight only the non-standard language forms in Oksana's turns. Instead, CA-SLA research distances itself from the expectations regarding linguistic norms and standard expressions in a second language. The resources employed by the L2 speakers are observed to be purposefully exploited for enhancing the possibility of establishing and maintaining intersubjectivity during the interaction.

3.1.2 Analysis of Competence

Under the impact of a growing body of CA-SLA studies, an important analytical shift is taking place, which is also accompanied by a terminological one: the analytical object has become the L2 speaker's ability to participate in social interactions (Firth & Wagner, 1997; cf. also Sfard, 1998 on learning as participation as a new, emergent concept of learning in applied sciences). According to a CA-SLA perspective, participation is understood to be the accomplishment of actions through the unfolding of turns at talk. The interactants are observed achieving the opening or the closing of a conversation; the introduction, shift, or closure of a conversational topic; the deployment of (dis)agreements with their interlocutors; the initiation and accomplishment of repair; and so on.

The performance of these specific actions displays the interactional competence of a speaker. Since the decontextualized language structure is no more the primary analytical object, different issues are addressed that altogether feed into the concept of competence, specifically of interactional competence. Pekarek Doehler (2005) pinpoints the collective nature of competence in interaction. In fact, she states that interactional competence is built in relation to sense-making activities, to the creation of context and to the establishment of intersubjectivity between the participants (p. 49). The idea of competence is no longer restricted to the mind of one speaker but involves the collaborative nature of interactions, i.e. competence is observable *because* it is shared between (or among) the interactants. For example, the establishment and the management of intersubjectivity is a continuous ongoing conversational activity, through which the interlocutors position themselves in mutually observable ways that help them in the production of turns that are designed for the recipient (i.e. adapted to the recipient) and topically relevant (i.e. related to the matter so far). For instance, Berger (2017) shows how an au pair and the host mother construct their respective territories of knowledge (Heritage, 2013) in the ongoing conversation regarding the children's misconduct. The construction of these territories, for which each speaker claims epistemic primacy (Stivers et al., 2012), is achieved turn after turn so as not to affect the interpersonal or the working relationship between the participants. The L2 speaker's interactional competence is observable in the ways she positions herself in comparison to the host mother claiming a minor or indirect right to overtly sanction a child's misconduct.

L2 interactional competence is analyzed as being situated, constructed, and activated within a specific interactional ecology, not as being universally valid, present, and active.

> la compétence (en langue, mais aussi tout autre compétence) est *contingente* (*nonautonome*) par rapport à d'autres compétences, dans la mesure où sa mobilisation et son développement se font dans le cadre d'interprétations des activités d'autrui, des contraintes situationnelles, des valeurs et légitimités mises en pratique et du choix des façons appropriées, opérationnelles, légitimes d'agir et de dire.
> (Pekarek Doehler, 2006: 39, emphasis in the original)

> Competence (language competence as any other competence) is contingent (non-autonomous) on other competences as far as its mobilization and its development are done within the interpretation of someone else's actions, of situational constraints, of practiced values and entitlements, and of the choice of appropriate, operational, and legitimate ways of acting and speaking.
> (my English translation)

Pekarek Doehler stresses the dependence of language competence on the situation in which this competence is activated. That is to say that a linguistic competence (as well as any other competence) is defined in conversation when a speaker interprets what others have said and done so far in the conversation, under the specific circumstances in which the exchange takes place. Consequently, the speaker's competence is distributed among the participants, as is the learning process. Learning takes place thanks to the collaborative nature of conversations, i.e. in a way that all the participants are part of the process, not only the L2 speaker.

3.2 The Study of Interactional Competence

The concept and the definition of interactional competence are recent achievements in the domain of CA-SLA. In the first volume entirely dedicated to L2 interactional competence, Hall and Pekarek Doehler define this competence as follows:

> IC [interactional competence], that is the context-specific constellations of expectations and dispositions about our social worlds that we draw on to navigate our way through our interactions with others, implies the ability to mutually coordinate our actions.
> (Hall et al., 2011: 1–2)

This is only a part of their precise definition, containing many analytical levels that concern all the actions accomplished by the interactants during a conversation. The authors address the issue of context specificity, which is central to the study of conversations, since every conversation represents a specific non-repeatable instance and needs to be investigated as such. Hall and Pekarek Doehler mention *our social worlds*, which include the establishment and maintenance of interpersonal relationships, through the creation and maintenance of intersubjectivity.

However, interactional competence is not limited to the linguistic level of an exchange between interactants: the authors state that such exchanges imply the ability of a mutual *action coordination* between participants. The focus of this definition is on the *action level* of conversations, which broadly contains verbal and nonverbal actions as well as activities related to the interactional context (e.g. storytelling). Moreover, interactional competence is not described as an ability that a speaker transfers from the L1 to the L2 simply because they can already accomplish specific actions like disagreeing with their L1. Interactional competence is instead composed of an ensemble of abilities that a speaker learns and develops through their participation in L2 talk-in-interaction. The precise interdependency of speakers' interactional competence in their L1 and L2 remain a point that merits investigation (Pekarek Doehler & Pochon-Berger, 2015).

This definition of interactional competence is the result of a system of describing the L2 speaker's competence(s), which started with Hymes's definition of communicative competence. I now sketch the historical roots of interactional competence (3.2.1) and then concentrate on more recent investigations into it (3.2.2), especially on the study of interactional competence and its development over time.

3.2.1 The Roots of Interactional Competence

Hymes conceptualized the idea of communicative competence. In one of his first works (Hymes, 1962) in the domain of linguistic anthropology, stating the centrality of actions and activities to the investigation of speech, his main concern was not the language per se but rather the functioning of human behavior. For this reason, he describes the *ethnography of speaking* (p. 3) as an area that links studies on language (especially on grammar) to studies in the ethnographic domain. From the beginning, he concentrated on the active participation of speakers such as children or foreigners in conversation. Hymes identified an analytical object that is not described only in linguistic terms:

> this is a question of what a child internalizes about speaking . . . while becoming a full-fledged member of its speech community. Or, it is a question of what a foreigner must learn about a group's verbal

behavior in order to participate appropriately and effectively in its activities.

(Hymes, 2008 [1962]: 3)

Hymes's description sheds light on the centrality of socialization through interaction. In this sense, children and foreigners undergo the same process: they have to learn the rules of the linguistic and cultural community that they are going to be part of, and they do this through their participation in community discourses. The result is, normally, their inclusion as "fully fledged members" of the community. At the same time, Hymes characterized the children' and foreigners' participation as appropriate and effective. This is the actual challenge of the language-learning process that children and foreigners have to face, i.e. participate effectively with limited resources at their disposal. Finally, he emphasizes the word "activities," which children and foreigners contribute to and manage in cooperation with their interlocutors. Not only language-related activities but also social activities such as the creation and maintenance of relationships or the general face-to-face work (Goffman, 1955) with one's interlocutor are meant.

In a later paper, Hymes put forward that one can analyze competence either "from the standpoint of a system *per se* or from the standpoint of persons" (Hymes, 1972: 282). Communicative competence can be grasped only through a multilayered analysis that includes the following:

1. The means a speaker uses in order to understand what is feasible for them.
2. The contextual constraints for understanding what is appropriate.
3. The speaker's performance, which enlightens what is done and what is at stake while performing (Hymes, 1972: 281).

However, at the beginning of the 1990s, some researchers focused eminently on interactions and socialization-related matters. Hall published several papers on the sociocultural aspects of interactions related to SLA. In her 1993 paper, she discusses the concept of oral practice, which she defines as follows:

Oral practices are culturally-mediated moments of face-to-face interaction whereby a group of people come together to create and recreate their everyday social lives.

(Hall, 1993: 145)

The emphasis of this definition is on the cultural side of people's encounters. In fact, culture can be seen to be constructed, modified, and adapted in every situation where interactants come together and share their lives, beliefs, and social rules for a certain span of time. Moreover, they create, recreate, and adapt their social and interpersonal context during interaction, in order to create group cohesion and membership.

Hall (1995) describes the concept of interactive practice in relation to interactional competence:

> Interactive practices are recurring episodes of purposeful, goal-directed talk which are significant to the establishment and maintenance of a group or community.
>
> (Hall, 1995: 39)

For the author, the creation of a group or a community depends on the realization of talk aimed at achieving a specific purpose. The achievement of a purpose, i.e. the existence of a goal and of goal-directed talk, structures the community through the unfolding of conversation. The more an interlocutor participates in the activities of a community, the more they learn what is appropriate for that community. Hence, they learn to participate in a competent way in the community life through their use of the community language to cooperate in community activities. Consequently, Hall's definition of interactive practice is strongly related to the inherent goal-oriented nature of community conversation. One aspect of interactive practices concerns particularly the development and management of topical issues in "practice-relevant ways" (Hall, 1995: 39). Topical issues can be analyzed at two different, though intertwined, levels. On the one hand, a topical relation is present at the utterance level, i.e. when "a locally relevant utterance is lexically linked to the prior utterance" (Hall, 1995: 39). On the other hand, topics are managed more extensively when they are embedded in a larger course of action, such as in storytelling.[1]

3.2.2 The Investigation of Interactional Competence in the Domain of CA-SLA

Within CA-SLA, interactional competence is defined "in terms of participants' methods for accomplishing L2 talk-in-interaction" (Hall & Pekarek Doehler, 2011: 7). This presupposes considering L2 acquisition not merely as acquisition of linguistic items and syntactic structures but also as a process through which an L2 speaker is socialized into the L2. Studying the development of L2 interactional competence implies the consideration of at least two aspects.

First, a reconsideration of the importance of L2 daily use for participating in conversations. This is the way through which L2 speakers learn to mutually collaborate during interactions for co-constructing the context(s) with their interlocutor(s). Kasper & Wagner (2011) state that interactional competence is a distributed competence; i.e. it is available between (or among) the participants. In this sense, interactional competence becomes also a procedural competence, because L2 speakers have to learn interactional practices (e.g. turn-taking, disagreeing, or introducing and closing a conversational topic) for participating in conversation. If interactional competence is built up of a panoply of procedures that L2 speakers need to develop, then it is arguable that interactional competence is a "condition for and a means of learning" (Kasper & Wagner, 2011: 119).

Second, the analysis of L2 talk-in-interaction needs to include a broader range of resources that are employed during conversations: not only linguistic (grammar and vocabulary), but also prosodic, sequential, and multimodal ones. In fact, our social worlds are not constructed only through language but also through actions that are finely tuned among the participants (Hall & Pekarek Doehler, 2011). Interactional context(s) are continuously reshaped by the interactants through every turn and action that they accomplish. In the same way, the focus of attention is constantly shifted toward different contextual and interactional aspects that are made relevant on a turn-by-turn basis by the participants. For example, Mori (2004) has shown how the focus of attention of Japanese L2 speakers shifts from accomplishing an assigned task to a linguistic problem while accomplishing that task. The participant's orientation converges at the boundaries of repair sequences, where code-switching is purposefully used to address the linguistic problem at hand and then to close the repair sequence once the problem has been solved.

L2 interactional competence has been studied also in relation to study abroad contexts (for an overview, see Kinginger, 2013), which have some common features with the learning context under investigation (work in a family abroad). Three significant investigations concern Japanese learning. Masuda (2011) traces the development of interactional competence in a group of English-speaking Japanese learners by analyzing their use of the Japanese aligning particle *ne*. The author compares two sets of data, namely first interactions between the JFL learners and Japanese peers at the beginning of their stay and interactions between the same participants during the fifth week of their stay. The development of identity as it is observable via the analysis of stance-taking resources in Japanese conversation is the research object of Cook (2014). Finally, Taguchi (2015) investigates the experience abroad of intermediate Japanese L2 learners. She focuses on speech styles in peer-to-peer interactions, and her results show an increased L2 speakers' ability to shift from polite style to plain style when talking to a peer, the markedness of these shifts, and the speakers' increased participation in meaning-constructing exchanges.

These studies show the difference between L2 interactional competence development and linguistic L2 development. The development of L2 interactional competence is in fact visible in the adaptation of existing resources to mutating interactional contexts (Brouwer & Wagner, 2004; Markee, 2008), whereas L2 linguistic development points mainly to the acquisition of new linguistic items. In a recent paper, however, Hall

(2018) rehashes the use of the term competence for referring to interactional competence. Her point is that, considering the growing number of studies on this aspect of L2 talk-in-interaction, there is the risk that two meanings cannot be separated anymore. On the one hand, there is the competence as analytical object per se, because it is investigated in different linguistic and sociological research areas. (It suffices to think of Chomsky's definition of a universal language competence and to compare Sacks's idea of a universally functioning structure of interactions through which interactional competence can be observed [cf. Hall, 2018].) On the other hand, and more empirically, the enacted competence of L2 speakers is composed of all the semiotic resources that they employ in conversation to create meaning and manage intersubjectivity. For this reason, Hall suggests introducing a new term that allows for a better distinction between the theoretical and the more empirical term. For the former, interactional competence can be maintained, whereas for the latter, interactional repertoires would be more appropriate. For my study, I use the term "interactional competence" for both cases. However, I find the proposed distinction interesting and useful, especially in relation to the possibility of spreading CA and CA-SLA research into the world of practice, and I therefore return to this discussion in the concluding chapter.

Now I turn to a less investigated context in which L2 learning takes place on a daily basis and in a rather informal way, namely the informal context (family, friends, and everyday activities like buying food, a bus ticket, and so on). This type of context is relevant to my study because it characterizes the language immersion situation of au pairs. In fact, even though they are employed by the host families to take care of their children and hence receive a regular work contract, which makes their stay in some sense formal, they also live with their host families, share daily routines with them, and perform all sorts of everyday activities with the children. In this sense, their lives during their sojourns are lived in informal contexts, so their learning occurs in the wild.

3.2.3. L2 Interactional Competence in the Wild

The movement to scrutinize L2 learning in the wild comes from the previously mentioned observation that people learn their L2 through everyday encounters and socialization and is driven epistemologically by a sociological understanding of L2 learning (Wagner, 2015, 2019).

The expression "in the wild" was first used by Hutchins (1995) for talking about experiences in "real life" as opposed to experiments in prepared settings. Hutchins shows the "nature of real cognitive practices" (1995: xiv) by analyzing a navigation experience. His aim was to clarify "that the study of cognition in the wild may reveal a different sort of task world that permits a different conception of what people do with their minds" (ibid.: 371).

Within the domain of CA-SLA, "L2 learning in the wild" has modified Hutchin meaning:

> we use the term to bring out the fundamental difference for L2 speakers between navigating in the real world of everyday activities involving other people, sometimes strangers, in the target language community and the safer world of the classroom where L2 speakers engage in tasks orchestrated and scaffolded by a teacher behind closed doors.
> (Eskildsen & Theodórsdóttir, 2017: 145; see also Eskildsen et al., 2019)

The difference between the classroom context and the wild resides in the less structured, more spontaneous, and unpredictable nature of talk in the latter contexts. For pedagogical purposes, it is therefore crucial to start investigating such informal contexts, in which L2 learning takes place on a daily basis, because such investigations will permit a critical comparison with the many SLA investigations that have concentrated only on classroom contexts and that have shaped our understanding of language learning for decades.

A CA-SLA investigation of L2 interactional competence as it is observable in noninstitutional contexts has addressed different interactional aspects. On the one hand, central features of conversations, such as the creation and maintenance of intersubjectivity, have been illustrated in several studies. Thedórsdóttir & Eskildsen (2011), for instance, show the function of language switching in everyday interactions, presenting the investigation of data from a Canadian L2 learner of Icelandic and focusing on interactions in the wild, such as buying a hotdog or retelling a personal experience. The switch to English here accomplishes primarily the function of maintaining intersubjectivity, and only secondarily does it aim at starting a word-search sequence (cf. Brouwer, 2013). But also word-search sequences can function to reach intersubjectivity or manage conversational problems (Eskildsen, 2018 on L2 Danish). The analysis of these sequences highlights the L2 speakers' orientation toward learning as a socially accountable activity. Majlesi & Broth (2012) have shown how this happens: the speakers' turns are presented and oriented to as learnables and teachables, and the speakers overtly address their activities as part of learning.

L2 learning in the wild has also been shown through the lens of a specific action, such as topical backlinking (König, 2014) or storytelling (Berger & Pekarek Doehler, 2018). The papers stress the particular conditions of French L2 learning in a family context and highlight the relevance of the ongoing socialization process for the L2 learning process. Another investigated action is repairing: Theodórsdóttir (2018) shows how the essential part of "doing repair" in the wild is the interactants' mutual orientations toward the same problematic issue. The author remarks that repairs in the wild happens mostly because of a "lack of response on the part of the L2 speaker as a last part of a repair/correction sequence" (Theodórsdóttir, 2018: 41). In this sense, the article shows the intrinsic social nature of L2 learning through the lens of repair practices in everyday informal conversations. The analysis of a French L2 speaking au pair and of how she deals with language problems is the focus of König (2018). In this paper, the author discusses the nature of repair sequences as they happen in interactions between the au pair and the L1-speaking children. It is shown that the underlying didactic contract is somehow reversed, bringing the older, authority-holding au pair in the position of nonexpert, whereas the children are addressed as language experts. Similarly, Eskildsen & Theodórsdóttir (2017) compare the creation of learning space as it happens in naturalistic L2 Icelandic conversations and English L2 classroom conversations. The authors conclude by stating that

> The construction of the vast learning space in conversation with an L1 speaking guest in the classroom, the richness of potential learning moments, and the participants' public agreements that they were engaged in learning something new signals the importance of breaking down the barriers between *the classroom* and *the wild*.
> (Eskildsen & Theodórsdóttir, 2017: 160, emphasis in the original)

In several papers investigating L2 learning in the wild, the wish has been addressed to integrate more of the research outcome into the world of classrooms. I discuss this aspect in more detail in Chapter 8. Now I turn to the last crucial feature of L2 interactional competence: the longitudinal documentation of L2 interactional competence and its development over time.

3.3 Current Challenges for Longitudinal CA-SLA Investigations

3.3.1 What It Means to Study Change in Talk-in-Interaction: Documenting Learning

The study of L2 interactional competence development forces the researcher to focus on the process of L2 acquisition rather than on its products, and this puts forward the importance of longitudinal studies. These studies observe

> interactional practices [that] are locally accomplished . . . as part of mutually coordinated actions, and the change that the document in these practices over time is part of how members elaborate and continuously adapt the sense-making procedures by means of which they treat their own and other's actions as recognizable and accountable.
> (Wagner et al., 2018: 20)

The organization of a longitudinal study for documenting change in the speakers' practices needs to face several methodological challenges. If a study has to show some kind of learning, and if learning is seen as a process and not only as a result, then we need to search for regularities in the data. According to Koschmann, "to recognize that a change has occurred requires a judgment of regularity. To study learning, therefore, is to plunge into an investigation of regularities" (Koschmann, 2013: 1038).

This type of investigation is possible through data comparability. Hence, comparability is one of the aforementioned challenges for longitudinal studies. Comparability is assured when the same interactants are recorded over a longer period of time as they converse with each other in the same contexts and speech exchange system. For example, for the present study, the same au pair was recorded for a minimum of six months, at least once a week, while interacting with her host family during mealtimes. On a second step, it is necessary to build collections of cases to show to what extent there has been change in the performance of the same action over time. The difficulty herein is that, unlike traditional CA collections, collections built for documenting change over time need to be organized around the same speakers and the same contexts, since it is crucial to know "*who* produced a particular practice and *when*" (Koschmann, 2013: 1041, emphasis in the original). Finally, it is important to discuss and interpret the change observed in the data in CA's emic perspective. Wagner et al. (2018) also discuss this aspect, and recalling a passage from Garfinkel & Sacks (1970), they pinpoint that "from an emic perspective, conduct is competent when it is analyzable and recognizable for what it is by coparticipants, that is, when it provides no ground for comment or repair" (Wagner et al., 2018: 27). Interpreting change in the data, then, does not mean to subjectively interpret what is in the data—since every researcher can obtain a different result—but it means to highlight the co-constructed nature of talk, since it is possible to document what the coparticipants' responses are to an interactant's turn (cf. Schegloff, 2007 on next turn proof procedure).

Despite a number of methodological challenges, several longitudinal studies have been undertaken in the domain of CA-SLA, which are sketched in the next chapter.

3.3.2 Exemplar Longitudinal CA-SLA Studies

Conversation analytical investigations are conducted with suitable analytical tools for "uncovering details involved in the development of interactional competence in a language" (Hellermann, 2011: 167), because they focus on a specific phenomenon that is comparable either longitudinally or cross-sectionally. Moreover, this research area facilitates accounting for developments in terms of changes in the way of performing the same action at different points in time (Hellermann, 2007). It is, then, possible to apply the same methodology also when L2 speakers' contributions are analyzed.

CA-SLA studies have gone in mainly three directions:

1. Studies that traced specific words and utterances as part of interactional competence.
2. Studies that traced social practices and how they were accomplished over time.
3. Studies that showed the role of social relations in L2 interactional competence development.

In all cases, the documentation of changes in the practices for performing an action accounts for learning through interactions in a second language. Language learning is addressed as a social activity that happens collaboratively for speakers in a variety of contexts: the classroom, work settings, and informal settings (such as among family and friends).

The way researchers trace linguistic forms or utterances shows great variety. Filipi (2018) illustrates for instance the developmental trajectory of yes as response in second-turn position in conversations between family members. Investigating how L2 Swedish-speaking children develop methods for taking the floor in the classroom while speaking with their peers, Cekaite (2007) shows a learning trajectory for a specific interactional practice. With the analysis of several activities related to classroom and dyadic tasks, Hellermann (2008, 2011, 2018) highlights the ways participants change their methods in the same community of practice.

The investigation of topic introduction in French L2 family conversation was the focus of König (2013), who points out that introductions become smoother over time; i.e. the L2 speaker engages in a more complex interactional work for preparing upcoming talk. Similarly, discussing the changes in the ways two Japanese boys learning L2 English initiate topics with their English tutor, Kim (2017) shows the importance of a growing acquaintance between the parties, which leads to the building of common knowledge over time (see also Nguyen, 2011 for L1).

More recently, Pekarek Doehler & Pochon-Berger (2015) offered an overview on the existing literature about longitudinal development of L2 interactional competence. The authors compared the results of existing studies on turn-taking, sequence organization, repair organization, and preference organization. They also presented analyses of their own collected data on French L2. The authors were able to outline some central principles that help make sense of how L2 interactional competence develops over time. Specifically, changes are seen in the resources employed by L2 speakers. The authors state that L2 speakers begin with more rudimental techniques for taking turns or starting a repair. However, these resources become more diversified when time passes so that interactants participate more effectively to conversations. The diversification is observable both at a sequential and at a linguistic level. Generally, then, L2 speakers increase their ability to design their turns for the recipient, i.e. to adapt their turns to their interlocutor so as to respect the principle of preference organization in conversation. As far as language is concerned, the authors observe that, indeed, linguistic resources built an important part of a speaker's interactional competence. What develops over time is the way these resources are employed, i.e. the purposes for which they are locally used in conversation.[2]

To sum up, the argument of the present study is based on a concept of learning that derives from CA and theories of language socialization. I consider L2 learning as visible changes in the participation in a community of practice (Lave & Wenger, 1991; Hellermann, 2008; Pekarek Doehler et al., 2018). To discuss eventual changes in my data, I adopt the concept of L2 interactional competence (Hall et al., 2011) and investigate topic management in the forms of topic introduction (Chapter 5) and topic closure (Chapter 6). My analyses show how French L2 speakers introduce and then close conversational topics and if and how their practices change over time. This allows me to show to what extent L2 interactional competence goes beyond mere L2 linguistic knowledge, how it is distributed among participants, and if and how it observably changes over time. My results integrate ongoing debates on the concept of learning within the field of CA-SLA pinpointing two major aspects. First, they derive from a longitudinal study, which is a choice that needs to be opted for more often in the CA-SLA domain. Second, through the lens of two specific actional microcosms, it is possible to show how these are at the same time *objects of* and *ways for* learning how to participate in L2 talk-in-interaction.

In the next chapter (Chapter 4), I review the literature about topic management, specifically topic introduction and topic closure, and the studies about topics and anaphora on French data. This review is useful in that it prepares the field for Chapters 5 and 6, which deal with the investigations of topic introduction and of topic closure respectively.

Notes

1. As I have already noted, the boundary between story(telling) and topic is rather unclear, and storytelling or "topic under discussion" tends to be superimposed.
2. Literature overviews on longitudinal studies in CA and CA-SLA are offered in Lee & Hellermann (2014), Pekarek Doehler et al. (2017), Skogmyr Marian et al. (2017), Skogmyr Marian & Balaman (2018).

References

Berger, E. (2017). Se plaindre des enfants: positionnements épistémiques et rapports institutionnels dans les récits conversationnels entre au pair et famille d'accueil. *TRANEL Travaux neuchâtelois de linguistique*, 67, 103–125.

Berger, E., & Pekarek Doehler, S. (2018). Tracking change over time in second language talk-in-interaction: A longitudinal case study of storytelling organization.

In S. Pekarek Doehler, E. González-Martínez, & J. Wagner (Eds.), *Longitudinal Studies on the Organization of Social Interaction*. (pp. 67–102). Basinkstoke: Palgrave Macmillan.

Brouwer, C. E. (2013). Conversation analysis methodology in second language studies. In C. A. Chapelle (Ed.), *The encyclopedia of applied linguistics* (pp. 1055–1061). Chichester: Wiley-Blackwell Publishing.

Brouwer, C. E., & Wagner, J. (2004). Developmental issues in second language conversation. *Journal of Applied Linguistics*, 1(1), 29–47.

Cekaite, A. (2007). A child's development of interactional competence in a Swedish L2 classroom. *The Modern Language Journal*, 91, 45–62.

Cook, H. M. (2014). Language socialization and stance-taking practices. In A. Duranti, E. Ochs, & B. B. Schieffelin (Eds.), *The handbook of language socialization* (pp. 296–321). Malden and Oxford: Wiley-Blackwell.

Emanuelsson, J., & Sahlström, F. (2008). The price of participation: Teacher control versus student participation in classroom interaction. *Scandinavian Journal of Educational Research*, 52(2), 205–223. http://dx.doi.org/10.1080/00313830801915853

Eskildsen, S. W. (2018). 'We're learning a lot of new words': Encountering new L2 vocabulary outside of class. *The Modern Language Journal*, 102(Supplement 2018), 46–63. DOI:10.1111/modl.124510026-7902/18/46-63.

Eskildsen, S. W., & Majlesi (2018). Learnables and teachables in second language talk: Advancing a social reconceptualization of central SLA tenets: Introduction to the special issue. *The Modern Language Journal*, 102(Supplement 2018), 3–10. DOI:10.1111/modl.124620026-7902/18/3-10

Eskildsen, S., Pekarek Doehler, S., Piirainen-Marsh, A., & Hellermann, J. (2019). Introduction: On the complex ecology of language learning "in the wild." In J. Hellermann, S. Eskildsen, S. Pekarek Doehler, & A. Piirainen-Marsh (Eds.), *Conversation analytic research on learning-in-action: The complex ecology of L2 interaction in the wild* (pp. 1–1). Berlin: Springer.

Eskildsen, S. W., & Theodórsdóttir, G. (2017). Constructing L2 learning spaces: Ways to achieve learning inside and outside the classroom. *Applied Linguistics*, 38(2), 143–164. DOI:10.1093/applin/amv010

Filipi, A. (2018). Making knowing visible: Tracking the development of the response token yes in second turn position. In S. Pekarek Doehler, E. González-Martínez, & J. Wagner (Eds.), *Longitudinal studies on the organization of social interaction* (pp. 39–66). Basinkstoke: Palgrave Macmillan.

Firth, A., & Wagner, J. (1997). On discourse, communication and some fundamental concepts in SLA research. *The Modern Language Journal*, 81(3), 285–300.

Garfinkel, H., & Sacks, H. (1970). On formal structures of practical action. In J. C. McKinney & E. A. Tiryakian (Eds.), *Theoretical sociology: Perspectives and developments* (pp. 338–366). New York: Appleton-Century-Crofts.

Goffman, E. (1955). On face-work. *Psychiatry*, 18(3), 213–231. http://doi.org/10.1521/00332747.1955.11023008

Hall, J. K. (1993). The role of oral practices in the accomplishment of our everyday lives: The sociocultural dimension of interaction with implications for the learning of another language. *Applied Linguistics*, 14(2), 145–166.

Hall, J. K. (1995). 'Aw, man, where you goin'?': Classroom interaction and the development of L2 interactional competence. *Issues in Applied Linguistics*, 6(2), 37–62.

Hall, J. K. (2018). From L2 interactional competence to L2 interactional repertoires: Reconceptualising the objects of L2 learning. *Classroom Discourse*, 9(1), 25–39. DOI:10.1080/19463014.2018.1433050

Hall, J. K., & Pekarek Doehler, S. (2011). L2 interactional competence and development. In *L2 interactional competence and development* (pp. 1–18). Clevedon: Multilingual Matters.

Hellermann, J. (2007). The development of practices for action in classroom dyadic interaction: Focus on task openings. *The Modern Language Journal*, 91(1), 83–96.

Hellermann, J. (2008). *Social actions for classroom language learning*. Clevedon: Multilingual Matters.

Hellermann, J. (2011). Members methods, members' competencies: Looking for evidence of language learning in longitudinal investigations of other-initiated repair. In J. Hall, J. Hellermann, & S. Pekarek Doehler (Eds.), *L2 interactional competence and development* (pp. 147–172). Tonawanda, NY: Multilingual Matters.

Hellermann, J. (2018). Talking about reading: changing practices for literacy event. In S. Pekarek Doehler, E. González-Martínez, & J. Wagner (Eds.) *Longitudinal Studies on the Organization of Social Interaction*. (pp. 105-142). Basingstoke: Palgrave Macmillan.

Heritage, J. (2013). Action formation and its epistemic (and other) backgrounds. *Discourse Studies*, 15(5), 551–578.

Hutchins, E. (1995). *Cognition in the wild*. Cambridge and London: The MIT Press.

Hymes, D. (1962). The ethnography of speaking. In T. Gladwin & W. C. Sturtevant (Eds.), *Anthropology and Human Behavior* (pp. 99–138). Washington, DC: Anthropological Society of Washington.

Hymes, D. (1972). On communicative competence. In J. B. Pride & Janet Holmes (Eds.), *Sociolinguistics, Selected readings* (pp. 269–293). Harmondsworth: Penguin Books.

Hymes, D. (2008). The ethnography of speaking. In I. Hutchby (Ed.), *Methods in language and social interaction* (Vol. 2, pp. 1–39). Los Angeles, London, New Delhi and Singapore: Sage Publications.

Kasper, G., & Wagner, J. (2011). A conversation-analytic approach to second language acquisition. In D. Atkinson (Ed.), *Alternative approaches to second language acquisition* (pp. 117–142). London and New York: Routledge.

Kim, Y. (2017). Topic initiation in conversation-for-learning: Developmental and pedagogical perspectives. *English Teaching*, 72(1), 73–103. DOI:10.15858/engtea.72.1.201703.73

Kinginger, C. (Ed.) (2013). *Social and cultural aspects of language learning in study abroad*. Amsterdam: John Benjamins.

König, C. (2013). *Topic management in French L2: A longitudinal conversation analytic approach* (pp. 226–250). EUROSLA Yearbook 13. Amsterdam/Philadelphia: John Benjamins Publishing Company.

König, C. (2014). Competenza interazionale in francese L2: l'esempio della 'parola ripresa' nella conversazione familiare. *Linguistica e Filologia*, 34, 135–165.

König, C. (2018). Französischlernen mit Kindern. Reparatursequenzen im Alltagsleben von Au pair Mädchen. In G. Albert & S. Diao-Klaeger (Hgs.), *Mündlicher Sprachgebrauch zwischen Normorientierung und pragmatischen Spielräumen* (pp. 45–64). Stauffenburg Verlag.

Koschmann, T. (2013). Conversation analysis and learning in interaction. In C. A. Chapelle (Ed.), *The encyclopedia of applied linguistics* (pp. 1038–1043). Oxford: Wiley-Blackwell.

Lave, J., & Wenger, E. (1991). *Situated learning: Legitimate peripheral participation*. Cambridge: Cambridge University Press.

Lee, Y.-A., & Hellermann, J. (2014). Tracing developmental changes through conversation analysis. *TESOL Quarterly*, 48(4), 763–788.

Majlesi, A. R., & Broth, M. (2012). Emergent learnables in second language classroom interaction. *Learning, Culture and Social Interaction*, 1, 193–207.

Markee, N. (2008). Toward a learning behavior tracking methodology for CA-for-SLA. *Applied Linguistics*, 29(3), 404–427.

Masuda, K. (2011). Acquiring interactional competence in a study abroad context: Japanese language learners' use of the interactional particle ne. *The Modern Language Journal*, 95(4), 519–540.

Mori, J. (2004). Negotiating sequential boundaries and learning opportunities: A case from a Japanese language classroom. *The Modern Language Journal*, 88(4), 536–550.

Nguyen, H. T. (2011). Achieving recipient design longitudinally: Evidence from a pharmacy intern in patient consultations. In J. K. Hall, J. Hellermann, & S. Pekarek Doehler (Eds.), *L2 interactional competence and development* (pp. 173–205). Clevedon: Multilingual Matters.

Pekarek Doehler, S. (2005). De la nature située des compétences en langue. In J. P. Bronckart, E. Bulea, & M. Puliot (Eds.), *Repenser l'eneseignement des langues: Comment identifier et exploiter les compétences* (pp. 41–68). Villeneuve d'Arc: Presses Universitaires du Septentrion. Retrieved from https://gemma.unine.ch/sites/islc/CLA/Documents%20CLA/Biblioth%C3%A8que%20PDF%20du%20CLA/Pekarek%20Doehler_2005a.pdf

Pekarek Doehler, S. (2006). Compétence et langage en action. *Bulletin Suisse de Linguistique Appliquée*, 84, 9–45.

Pekarek Doehler, S. (2013). Conversation analysis and second language acquisition. In C. A. Chapelle (Ed.), *The encyclopedia of applied linguistics* (pp. 1–8). Blackwell Publishing. DOI:10.1002/9781405198431.wbeal0217

Pekarek Doehler, S., & Pochon-Berger, E. (2015). The development of L2 interactional competence: Evidence from turn-taking organization, sequence organization, repair organization and preference organization. In T. Cadierno & S. Eskildsen (Eds.), *Usage-based perspectives on second language learning* (pp. 233–267). Berlin: Mouton de Gruyter.

Pekarek Doehler, S., Wagner, J., & González-Martínez, E. (Eds.) (2017). *Longitudinal studies on the organization of social interaction*. Basingstoke: Palgrave Macmillan.

Schegloff, E. A. (2007). *Sequence organization in interaction. A primer in conversation analysis* (vol. 1). Cambridge: Cambridge University Press.

Sfard, A. (1998). On two metaphors for learning and the danger of choosing just one. *Educational Researcher*, March 1998, 4–13.

Skogmyr Marian, K., & Balaman, U. (2018). Second language interactional competence and its development: An overview of conversation analytic research on interactional change over time. *Lang Linguist Compass*, 1–16. DOI:10.1111/lnc3.12285

Skogmyr Marian, K., Petitjean, C., & Pekarek Doehler, S. (2017). Le développement de la compétence d'interaction en langue seconde: état des lieux et illustrations empiriques. *Revue française de linguistique appliquée, 22*(2), 127–145.

Stivers, T., Mondada, L., & Steensig, J. (2012). Knowledge, morality and affiliation in social interaction. In T. Stivers, L. Mondada, & J. Steensig (Eds.), *The morality of knowledge in conversation* (pp. 3–24). Cambridge: Cambridge University Press.

Taguchi, N. (2015). *Developing interactional competence in a Japanese study abroad context*. Bristol: Multilingual Matters.

Thedórsdóttir, G., & Eskildsen, S. W. (2011). The use of English in everyday Icelandic as a second language. *Nordand 6, 2,* 59–85.

Theodórsdóttir, G. (2018). L2 teaching in the wild: A closer look at correction and explanation practices in everyday L2 interaction. *Modern Language Journal, 102*(Supplement 2018), 30–45.

Wagner, J. (2015). Designing for language learning in the wild: Creating social infrastructures for second language learning. In T. Cadierno & S. W. Eskildsen (Eds.), *Usage-based perspectives on second language learning* (pp. 75–104). Berlin/Boston: Mouton de Gruyter.

Wagner, J., Pekarek Doehler, S., & González-Martínez, E. (2018). Longitudinal research on the organization of social interaction: Current developments and methodological challenges. In S. Pekarek Doehler, E. González-Martínez, & J. Wagner (Eds.), *Longitudinal studies on the organization of social interaction* (pp. 3–35). Basingstoke: Palgrave Macmillan.

Wagner, J. (2019). Towards an epistemology of second language learning in the Wild. In J. Hellermann, S. W. Eskildsen, S. Pekarek Doehler, & A. Piirainen-Marsh (Eds.), *Conversation analytic research on learning-in-action: The complex ecology of second language interaction 'in the wild'*. Dordrecht: Springer.

4 Topic Management in French L1 and L2 Interactions

The aim of this chapter is to explain what topic management is, how it works in everyday interactions, and how it is possible to analyze and document it with the methodological tools of CA. To do this, I now turn to two particular foci of interest in my research. I first discuss the existing literature about the linguistic features of conversational topic (4.1). Subsequently, I present an overview of the basic studies about topic in French (L1/L2) (4.2). This subsection shows how the research has concentrated on the "topic matter," especially in the 1990s, and how the approach changed from a more discursive to a more conversation-analytic one. Finally, the literature on topic introduction (4.3) and topic closure (4.4) is reviewed, marking especially the differences between the studies of these two actions.

4.1 Topic, Reference, and Anaphora in Conversation

Studies of reference focused particularly on the strategies for encoding referents in L1 and L2 productions. The most significant result of these studies is a scale that fixes the coding possibilities that the speakers draw on (Givón, 1983). However, conversations function differently from monologues or written texts in the sense that the activities carried on during conversations are always collaborative. As soon as more than one speaker is involved, particular methods and practices are required to ensure that everyone understand the various referents. Thus, a question arises: what happens with reference, anaphora, and deixis when more than one person is concerned? How do interactants establish and stabilize the referents they are talking about?

Two preferences for establishing the mutual understanding of personal reference have been illustrated by Sacks & Schegloff (1979). A preference for recognitionals, i.e. definite expressions that make a referent available to the recipient within a specific discourse, and a preference for single form references, i.e. the use of minimal reference forms for referring to certain items/people/events. Usually, reference "is done *en passant*" Auer (1984: 628, emphasis in the original), which means that whenever speakers describe their interactions, they say that they were telling something or complaining about something—but they will never say that they were establishing reference (cf. Perrault & Cohen, 1981; Quasthoff, 1984). However, moments can be found in conversations where repairs concern reference, and reference can be addressed in conversation as a source of trouble in different ways, such as through an other-initiated repair. Using speakers' preparatory questions at turn beginning like "Do you know X?" the recipient also has methods available for completing the reference recognitional work: back-channeling devices or agreement tokens indicate that the reference has been recognized. Deictic expressions (Auer, 1988) and topic management also play a crucial role in the establishment of references in conversation. CA studies by Bolden (2008) and Betz (2011) have addressed the linguistic resources related to this action. Bolden (2008) has investigated the use of the marker "so" for entering the first conversational topic of an interaction, whereas Betz (2011) has concentrated on the use of the adverb "now" in a variant of German.

With regard to French (L1/L2), studies have been conducted on different ways of dealing with the establishment of reference. When a referent is over-specified (Pekarek Doehler, 1999), such as when a speaker uses an NP when a pronoun would theoretically be enough, this may achieve other interactional functions beyond the mere accessibility of the referents. Specifically, over-specification is shown to structure discourse and the speaker's argumentation. Referential over-coding with a full NP where a pronoun would be possible can be used as a way of reappropriating (or multiply re-categorizing) the referent in question. Finally, the use of a left dislocation also topicalizes the element and shifts the attention of the interlocutor to it. On the argumentative level, the over-specification sustains the action of disagreeing with the interlocutor, marking two contrastive stands. In conclusion, over-specification is not just a "deviant case" with respect to the accessibility scales (Ariel, 1988). Rather, it is a referential process that reflects possibilities for a speaker to modify the discourse and to structure social actions.

Over-specification, i.e. the phenomenon of encoding too many referents in discourse relates to anaphora, left dislocation, and sequence organization. Pekarek Doehler (2000b) discusses the use of this phenomenon in French conversations and shows that information structure alone cannot account for over-encoding referents. The author shows that left dislocation is a resource that plays a crucial role in the organization of preference and the management of disagreement in conversation. In the next example, the same referent is anaphorically linked to with a left dislocation at turn beginning event though it was mentioned just earlier in the preceding turn. Following the rules of information structure (cf. Givón, 1983), if a referent was nominated previously, then it should be encoded with less linguistic material. Pekarek Doehler shows, then, that the over-specification has to do not only with the information structure but also with the functional organization of the ongoing conversation:

(9) 2 MH/LA, ent., i. (from Pekarek Doehler, 2000b: 188, my English translation)

```
P: mais si on aime eh un langue c'est plus facile .. je crois
   but  if we love  uh  a language it's   easier      I believe
   but I believe that it's easier, if we love a language

   la motivation est très importante
   the-det.F.sg. motivation is very important-det.F.sg.
   motivation is very important

S: la motivation c'est importante mais aussi eh . le talent.
   the-det.F.sg motivation it's important-det.F.sg. but also uh  the talent
   motivation is important but so is the talent

   je veux dire . la: disposition à apprendre une langue eh . (...)
   I want to say the-det.F.sg disposition  for learning  a language  uh
   I mean the disposition to learn a language
```

This example shows how the preference for agreement leads S to construct his turn in two parts: a first part partially repeating P's last TCU, i.e. turn construction unit, (*la motivation est importante*). It is only a partial repetition, though, because S transforms this utterance with a left dislocation (*la motivation c'est importante*). The over-specification signals to the interlocutor that a possible deviation from the preference structure is ongoing: in fact, after this first agreement, a disagreement follows (*mais aussi le talent*). Similar results are also presented in Pekarek Doehler (2001), where the author investigates the use of left dislocations in disagreement sequences in which a referent is promoted to the status of topic. Pekarek Doehler (2000a) focuses on long-distance anaphora in conversation. Recalling Fox's study (1987) on return pops, the author addresses the question of how a referent can remain activated across several turns at talk (long referential distance). The data suggests that not only inference or precoding mention but also (and foremost, in conversation) the sequence organization and progression in conversation and the participants' orientation toward a specific activity type influence the understanding of reference, specifically and more generally the development of conversational topics.

4.2 Topic Analysis in French Data. From "Objet de discours" to Conversational Process

In research on French (L1/L2), a series of studies on topics has addressed several aspects of this complex notion. On the one hand, the unstable nature of conversational topics has been illustrated. Berthoud & Mondada

(1993, 1994) have discussed the topic's procedural nature that depends on the discourse. Because the topic is not considered a fixed entity but rather a process and, consequently, can be constantly rearranged and reformulated, it has to be addressed through the lens of procedural information. In so doing, its changes and its transitions can be seen to be locally relevant and orderly accomplished by the interactants themselves, i.e. in a way that is observable for all the parties in the conversation. The authors highlight the contrast between a notion of topic as a fixed entity and a notion of topic as a process, which they use for their analysis. Hence, the topic is not fixed once a conversation starts and kept invariable during the conversational flow; rather, it is constantly changed and adapted during the conversation. Investigating topics as entities *en devenir* (Mondada, 1995) implies that all participants can shape their form. Therefore, topics can be proposed by one interlocutor via a question or an assessment, but they constantly change in conversation through other participants' turns. Interactional topics are a collaborative matter, which means that interactants can make use of different strategies to implement their topical line. In some cases, the turns are seen to strongly connect, so that even if the topic is still stabilizing (but not yet totally stabilized), the interactants are following the same topical line. On the contrary, other cases show that participants' topical developments are competing.

On the other hand, formal aspects of interactional topics can be addressed, such as marking strategies. With a comparison between topic introduction strategies in children French L1 and adult French L2 conversations, Berthoud & Mondada (1992) show that children tend to use deictic means for introducing new referents and that their discourse is often characterized by several topical ruptures. Instead, adult L2 speakers' discourse does not show so many ruptures, but the topics are introduced with different means, such as without phatic markers (cf. Berthoud, 1991; Berthoud & Mondada, 1995). Marking a topic in discourse is also seen as a way of thematizing it (Berthoud, 1996), and the investigation of topic introduction, change, and closure shows their evolution in the moment and the participants' collaboration to these changes (cf. also Grobet, 2002). Instead of crystallizing the topic as an independent entity, the analyst should look at conversations in order to detect the pragmatic operations accomplished by the interlocutors. Berthoud's analysis concentrates mainly on topic introduction in conversation. The author presents an investigation of the different possibilities for introducing a topic in conversation, such as through existential markers, (un)determined NPs, deixis, and so on. An extra chapter is devoted to the *thématisation*, i.e. to the operation of topic introduction, which is accomplished mainly through right and left dislocations.

Finally, structural aspects also help in analyzing the co-construction of conversational topics. For example, first topics in conversations are shown to be placed in the so-called anchor position (Schegloff, 1986) and to identify the "reason for calling." A look at the endings of phone calls, however, also helps show how topic introduction and topic closure are related to each other. With a study on topic introduction after opening sequences and in pre-closing environments in phone calls, Mondada (2003) shows that, normally, a pre-closing sequence signals the end of a previous topic, and this frees a new slot either for starting the closure or for introducing a new topic. Topics that appear in this position are, however, marked by misplacement markers or are introduced in a fashion that shows to the coparticipant that they are dislocated as regards what preceded (bad news, afterthoughts).

The studies presented so far lead to the conclusions that interactional topics need to be analyzed in a way that takes into account different, intertwined aspects:

1. Their introduction and identification are created in the moment through the turns that interactants produce in the conversation.
2. Their organization is sensitive to other systems working in conversation, like turn-taking.
3. The stabilization and the development of a topic are collaborative accomplishments, which means that participants have to orient themselves to others' turns in order to contribute in a coherent way to the topic at hand, or when this is not the case, they need to account for going off topic.

To conclude, topic management in conversation can be analyzed by concentrating on two different aspects, starting either from the forms or from the sequence organization and action organization. However, it is clear that as the topic is at the crossroads of these two levels, both must be taken into account when investigating conversational topics. I now turn to the (fewer) studies about topic management in a second language.

4.3 Topic Management in L2 Talk-in-Interaction

In recent years, the field of SLA has seen a change in the approaches adopted to investigate how learners of a language actually use it in everyday life. A major change has occurred with a stronger orientation toward the sociocultural aspects of the process of L2 learning and the application of CA methods to shed light on widely neglected characteristics of L2 learning (cf. Pekarek Doehler, 2013 on CA-SLA).

The studies addressing the issue of topic in a second language in the research domain of CA-SLA are few and can be categorized on the basis of the research design (longitudinal or not). Non-longitudinal studies have investigated topic change (Morris-Adam, 2014, 2016), the use of left dislocation for topic introduction (Pekarek Doehler, 2004) and topical backlinking (König, 2014). With a collection of classroom data,

Pekarek Doehler (2004) presents an investigation of left-dislocated constructions by advanced French L2 speakers. A quantitative analysis shows that L2 speakers' use of left dislocation is generally rarer than its use by L1 speakers and that sometimes the left-dislocated constructions display non-standard features, such as the dislocation of an indefinite NP. However, the functions accomplished by the left dislocations are very differentiated—such as when a referent is promoted to topic status, as shown in the following example:

(10) en3cII, 1–12 (from Pekarek Doehler, 2004: 19–20)[1]

>1P: mesdames messieurs bonjour nous avons lu avant Pentecôte le reste
>de notre texte . avant de: avant d'approcher certains problèmes plus
>particulièrement d'abord un petit résumé peut-être: pour nous
>remettre un petit peu en forme monsieur M s'il-vous-plaît
>((voix basse))
>
>ladies and gentlemen good morning before Pentecost we read the rest
>of our text before before approaching certain problems more
>precisely let's start with a little summary maybe to bring us
>back in shape mister M if you like ((low voice))
>
>2H: eh . .
>uh
>
>3P: bon alors qu'est-ce qui se passe.
>well then what happens
>
>4H: eh
>uh
>
>5P: qu'est-ce qui se passe à la fin de ce scénario . .
>what happens at the end of this scenario
>
>6H: alors **Pierre . eh il entre dans le hangar** . et là il rencontre ses
>amis les conspirateurs . et: . il veut les convaincre .
>ehm il veut
>les aider qu'ils
>
>well Pierre uh enters the hangar and there he meets his
>friends the conspirators and he wants to convince them uhm he wants
>to help them so that they

In this case, Pierre is the protagonist of a book that the students have read, so it is an inferable referent, which has not yet been activated, however. Through the left dislocation "Pierre—il," the referent becomes the topic at hand. Other cases show that left dislocations are used by the L2 speakers to reorient the discourse, namely when a former topic has been abandoned and is reintroduced later on via a dislocated construction. The author concludes that despite some structural and lexical differences in the realization of left dislocations by French L2 speakers as compared to French L1 speakers, the functions of the left dislocations used by L2 speakers conform to the pragmatic constraints found in the use by L1 speakers, especially concerning topic management. The analysis of interactional data has allowed the author to relate the use of left dislocation not only to the level of information structure but also to the issues of turn-taking and interaction management in collaboration with other interlocutors.

A single case analysis of topical backlinking in the data of an au pair with low-intermediate French L2 level (König, 2014) indicates how the speaker manages not only conversational topics but also other parallel conversational activities. Specifically, the au pair is able to deliver an answer to an interlocutor maintaining the topic he proposed, and she can recall a referent that she had introduced previously in the conversation with only a pronoun while continuing her answer and bringing forward the story she started. The L2 speaker, then, shows her orientation toward the content level of the conversation and toward the other activities that structure the conversation.

An analysis of small group works in a Hong Kong school illustrate how ESL students (i.e. students of English as a Second Language) of different proficiency levels negotiate topics (Gan et al., 2008). The students started their interactions with typical transitional/first topics, such as short comments on the movie (they previously saw *Forrest Gump*). During the interaction, the participants' orientation was made mutually observable both toward the task to accomplish (through many formulations and reformulations of it) and toward new topics or topic shifts, as the participants overtly address the next matter to be discussed at turn beginning. In conclusion, the students were able to manage the task they were assigned and, in so doing, also to collaboratively create, change, and eventually close the topics they proposed. As the authors say (p. 330), "Such instances of either 'marked' topic shift or 'stepwise' topic movement . . . display characteristics of emergent topical development in conversation."

On the other hand, longitudinal investigations have addressed change within the performance of the same action at different points in time. For instance, a French L2 speaking au pair has shown constant change in the ways she introduces conversational topics in everyday interactions with her host family (König, 2013). At the beginning, introductions are rather abrupt, without a real contextualization of the introduced referent and with almost no preliminary work (cf. Gan et al., 2008) in "preparing the ground" for the upcoming talk. Over time, however, the au pair shows an increasing ability to introduce new topics in a smoother way, using misplacement markers for announcing a disjoint, upcoming talk.

Finally, conversation-for-learning settings offered the possibility for studying topic initiation between two Japanese brothers and their English-language tutor (Kim, 2017). This investigation points out the changes in doing topic initiation work by the Japanese learners. In the beginning, conversational topics are initiated only by the English L1 speaker, whereas over time, the Japanese speakers become more confident and, depending on the growing common knowledge between them and the tutor, introduce more other-attentive conversational topics; i.e. they ask about matters that are of interest to their tutor and not necessarily to them (what he did on the weekend, how the courses at the university are, and so on).

4.3.1 Topic Introduction

As explained in Chapter 2, one possibility for analyzing conversational topics is to focus on the moments in which a topical disjunction is made relevant by the participants themselves, i.e. when they address and make mutually comprehensible topic boundaries. The studies of Button & Casey (1984, 1985) on topic initiation are particularly relevant, because they illustrate two strategies for proposing a new topic, i.e. through topic initial elicitors (Button & Casey, 1984), such as news inquiries, or through topic nominations (Button & Casey, 1985), such as news announcements.

How a topic is routinely introduced in conversation differs in relation to the interactional context. Knowledge asymmetry, power relationships, and institutional expectations might influence the turn-taking system of an interaction when they relate to an agenda of points or issues that are known to only one party. This is the case of classroom interactions, for example, (Heyman, 1986; Seedhouse & Harris, 2011; van Compernolle, 2011) or doctor–patient consultations (Stivers & Heritage, 2001).

In contrast, in everyday interactions outside the classroom and in a family context, the participation patterns are different to some extent. First, no pre-established unilateral agenda appears normally in everyday talk. For instance, the question–answer pattern is often absent in everyday interactional data. Second, the interaction does not aim at a precise purpose, such as collecting or delivering specific information. Third, other extra-linguistic constraints are normally found in everyday interactional data; for example, the lack of institutional expectations is reflected in a different participation mechanism, in which overlapping occurs more often than it would in a more controlled conversation. Especially at home, people interact with each other while accomplishing other activities (such as watching TV, cooking, or playing). The participants' focus of attention can thus be on different aspects of the same interaction and of the same context simultaneously. This divergence is occasionally made relevant by the interactants themselves throughout the conversation, such as when they explicitly address a lack of response by their interlocutor.

Particularly in everyday talk, topical progression has been seen to unfold in a rather seamless way (Sacks, 1995). Typically, speakers talk about a subject, and at the end of their conversation, they are talking about something completely different without having made any marked breaks in the conversational flow. In contrast to this, there are cases where a speaker introduces a completely new conversational topic or interrupts the topic at hand by changing it. In these cases, the speaker has to do further conversational work to show their interlocutor(s) that they are going to introduce or change the conversational topic. This extra work produces a break in the conversational progression and marks topic boundaries (see Sacks, 1995: 352 on "marked topics'; see also Jefferson (1984) on "disjunctive topics"). Research has shown that disjunctions in conversation are normally made visible through discourse markers used as misplacement markers (cf. Bolden, 2008 for an overview; cf. Auer, 1988 on "displaced language"), with the aim of signaling a change in the topical progression in the ongoing conversation. Typically, such markers are placed at turn-beginning positions to project a change in what follows, and pauses, hesitation markers (*uhms*, *uhs*), and changes in communicative projects (Sacks & Schegloff, 1973) often characterize the upcoming talk.

All this information derives from studies on L1 interactions undertaken mostly in English. In my study, I focus on French L2 conversations and am interested in showing how L2 speakers manage to introduce a new conversational topic in an ongoing interaction, which is a rather rare action, given that topics generally flow from one to the other without marked disjunctions. However, this analytical object allows me to pinpoint clear occasions in which the L2 speaker overtly orients to topic boundaries. Moreover, I identify a recurring pattern in this microcosm from two features: first, its sequential position in conversation—i.e. the topic that is introduced after a previous sequence and topic have been closed—and, second, the first turn's architecture, e.g. the use of discourse markers, pauses, and hesitation markers.

4.3.2 Topic Closure

Although conversational topics are typically seen to flow into one another, i.e. to progress in a rather seamless way, much attention has been paid to the moments in conversation when interactants mark a disjunction at the topical level, such as when a new topic is introduced. This is related to the fact that, generally, speakers need to do some extra interactional work to make their interlocutors aware that they are introducing a new conversational topic. Thus, speakers need to show where and how the disjunction happens and if and what kind of relationship their next turn has with the preceding talk. All this has been shown in the preceding chapter.

On the contrary, the analysis of topic closure is not as broad and deep. I begin by reporting on studies about L1 conversations that concentrate mainly on conversational closure in general, but not specifically on topic closure. This allows me to better explain what the specificities of topic closing are as compared to conversational closings. Conversational closure is shown to be initiated (or proposed) by one speaker, and the other(s) have the possibility to align with that turn. In what follows, three possibilities for investigating closing sequences are discussed.

The first analytical possibility focuses on the sequential structure of closing sequences: the starting point is the minimal closing sequence, as proposed by Sacks & Schegloff (1973). This study does not concentrate at all on topic-related issues. Rather, the authors individuate a minimal sequence that regularly happens at the end of phone calls. This minimal sequence is built up of two adjacency pairs: a first pair, in which a speaker proposes a closure and in response the interlocutor accepts it, i.e. aligning with the previous turn, and a second pair, containing final greetings. Later on, Button (1987) defined this simplest type of closing as "archetype closing" (p. 102) and propose a further analysis of closing sequences in this paper and in his later paper, in 1990. He identifies different types of closing sequences, which differ mainly on the sequential level: the actual closing can be delayed if other turns are proffered after the first turn of proposing the closure. For instance, if something in the turn initiating the closure is not clear, then a repair sequence occurs; or if an arrangement is still to be made, then the closing implicative environment is made relevant, but the actual closing is delayed and is reinitiated later on in the conversation.[2]

The second possibility for investigating conversational closure is to orient toward the management of intersubjectivity during closing sequences. "Leave-taking serves to project possible future encounters and is, thereby, a practice for maintaining a continuous relationship across periods of separation," as Bolden (2008) describes it. Therefore, managing the relationship assumes a more important role within a closing implicative environment, since it rules the time in which the interactants will not be together. In her paper, Bolden shows the importance of relationship management in the closing sequences of Russian phone calls. Her analyses highlight the link between the introduction of a new matter in the closing sequences and the orientation of the speaker introducing it to her addressee. In fact, the author observes that only matters that concern the addressee are introduced in the closing sequences and that the person introducing these is the one who initiated the closing. Holt (2010) analyzes the way speakers terminate stories in conversation. She highlights the importance of joint laughter: laughter per se is not closing but is often found in relation to a "potentially termination-relevant" context (p. 1520), i.e. when a possible closing is approaching. When joint laughter has been reached, the interactants are seen to treat that moment in conversation as suitable for introducing a new matter. The main challenge with Holt's article is that it is not always clear where the terminological boundaries of sequence, topic, and story are. These three levels are deeply intertwined in conversation and are all concerned when a closure is collaboratively accomplished by the speakers. However, since it is in their nature to be linked to each other, it is even more important to clearly state at the beginning which aspect one is orienting to in the analysis.

The third possibility is to discuss sequence closing *and* topic closing. Jefferson (1984) has shown how topics progress in a stepwise fashion. For her analyses, she has concentrated on unmarked boundaries in conversation when speakers gently shift from one topic to a following matter. After a troubles-telling, this happens at best when an interactant addresses an "ancillary matter" (p. 202), i.e. a matter that had remained marginal until that moment. In so doing, the conversation is restarted, but without the interactants having completely closed the ongoing sequence. Alignment and disalignment also play a role when a closing sequence approaches. Mondada & Traverso (2005) show that when alignment is observed, the closing of a conversational phase is accepted and aligned to by the participants, whereas when the interlocutors do not align with the proposed closure of the ongoing conversational phase, the closing movement is suspended and the ongoing conversational phase is reopened and extended. In this case, either there is a contrast on the topical or epistemic level, i.e. the interlocutor(s) change the topic or do not have the same epistemic access to the ongoing topic, or the first speaker aligns to the disaligning turn and the conversation takes a new direction. Finally, the leave-taking of workers' meeting in cafés (LeBaron & Jones, 2002) brings to light the accountability of endings (Laurier, 2008), which are achieved mostly through a collaborative construction of the closing environment: this happens not only through the conversation itself, i.e. through the subsequent turns at talk, but also in this specific context, finishing one's cup of coffee often coincides with topic closing and is followed by departure from the shop.[3]

These studies on L1 conversations focus mainly on the structural aspects of closing sequences and investigate the conversational moments in which a possible closure is initiated. They are based on a wide range of conversational data in different settings, from phone calls[4] to face-to-face interactions, each one showing specific aspects. For instance, a medical consultation is generally established on the basis of an agenda and authority, and epistemic asymmetries are present and oriented to during the conversation. On the contrary, a meeting in a café has most of the time no predetermined reason for taking place. Laurier (2008) comes to this observation in his conclusions:

> what might be distinctive about going for a coffee in the café is that it might be an occasion without "a' reason, thus, unlike the telephone call with its ever-present "reason for calling' (Sacks, 1995). The lack

of any particular intention over and above having some refreshment and conversation gives us the possibility for unmotivated talk.

(p. 178–179)

The main results of these lines of analysis identify specific structural, linguistic, and environmental resources for the initiation of closure when a conversation starts to fade. However, the link to the topical level of conversation is only partially addressed and is discussed in only a few papers. This is probably due to the difficulty of separating these two analytical levels (topical and sequential), and this is sometimes reflected in the chosen terminology. Namely, it is not always clear where the terminological and analytical boundaries among sequence, action, topic, and activity (especially storytelling) are set. This is an intrinsic limit of CA in closing sequences, because topic talk is such an underlying feature of conversations that it is not easy to completely separate it from other interactional features.

Topic closure in L2 talk-in-interaction has been investigated prominently in institutional contexts. For instance, Jeon (2003) has investigated the activity of closing an advising session at a university. His study aims at finding a relationship between ESL proficiency level and ways of closing the advising session. In a large database of video data from the University of Michigan, which included speakers of three ESL proficiency levels, the author first identifies three types of closure in relation to their structure. Some closings are abbreviated, i.e. some parts were missing (e.g. when the closure was abrupt); other closures are complete; and others again are extended, i.e. they contained a reopening sequence. Regarding the markedness of the closure, Jeon has found out that the higher the ESL proficiency level was, the more unmarked (i.e. smooth) the closure was. This suggests that the more proficient the speaker is, the better that speaker manages a session closure.

Mori (2004) studied a conversation between peers in an intermediate Japanese language class in North America. Her focus was on the sequence boundaries, which were occasionally made relevant by the speakers themselves. Particularly, the author highlighted the collaborative work of going in and out of subsequent sequences. This single case analysis concentrated on an interaction that happened after a teacher had assigned a task to the class. The students started the task but also engaged in repair sequences when lexical problems arose. In this case, code-switching (Japanese-English-Japanese) coincided with the sequence boundaries and was employed to mark the beginning and the end of the side sequence and of the topic at hand. The paper has shown what resources are employed by Japanese L2 speakers for collaborating in the closure of an ongoing sequence and of an ongoing topic and how L2 speakers show that they are orienting back to the task assigned by the teacher.

There is a striking point concerning the papers in the domain of SLA: none of them clearly addresses or includes the matter of topic in their analyses. It seems that the main concerns of these papers reside in finding the relationships between the accomplishment of a closing sequence and the L2 proficiency level of the investigated speakers. Consequently, great attention is paid to the lexical and prosodic resources used by the L2 speakers in the conversation. This is indeed an important and central aspect for researchers to investigate. However, fundamental papers like Sacks & Schegloff (1973) and Button (1987, 1990) have indicated that the closure is a conversational moment in which the matters at hand are oriented to by the conversationalists. Closure is, for example, an appropriate conversational place for either reopening a previously interrupted topic or for introducing a new one. However, it seems that research on L2 speakers has disregarded this aspect, i.e. that L2 speakers also have something that they want to talk about. Instead, they are often "treated" as users of a second language rather than as interactants participating in conversations with the linguistic resources at their disposal.

Keeping in mind these aspects of topic introduction and topic closure, I now turn to the analyses of examples from the TRIC L2 corpus described at the beginning of this volume. For topic introduction, I present the investigation of data from the data sets of two au pairs, Julie and Oksana, whereas for topic closure, I draw on the data from the data sets of three au pairs, Julie, Oksana, and Christine.

Notes

1. My English translation.
2. Schegloff (1990, 2007) also shows a detailed sequential analysis of sequence-closing sequences.
3. These studies are, of course, only examples of the three possible ways of addressing closure in conversation. Many other studies have been conducted on closing sequences in different contexts, such as phone calls (Antaki, 2002), television interviews (Clayman, 1989), health consultations (Heath, 1985, 1986; Robinson, 2001), and academic advisory sessions (Hartford & Bardovi-Harlig, 1992, Warga, 2005).
4. Raitaniemi (2014) proposes one of the most complete comparative analyses of phone calls endings in two languages, Finnish and German. Comparative studies within the domain of CA and interactional linguistics that are based on an actual comparison of two data sets in two different languages are rather rare (but see the papers collected in Sidnell, 2009).

References

Antaki, C. (2002). 'Lovely': Turn-initial high-grade assessments in telephone closings. *Discourse Studies*, 4(1), 5–23.
Ariel, M. (1988). Referring and accessibility. *Journal of Linguistics*, 24(1), 65–87.
Auer, P. (1984). Referential problems in conversation. *Journal of Pragmatics*, (8), 627–548.
Auer, P. (1988). On deixis and displacement. *Folia Linguistica*, 22(3–4), 263–292.

Berthoud, A.-C. (1991). Stratégies et marques d'introduction et de réintroduction d'un objet dans la conversation. *Bulletin CILA, 54*, 159–179.

Berthoud, A.-C. (1996). *Paroles à propos. Approche énonciative et interactive du topic.* Paris: Ophrys.

Berthoud, A.-C., & Mondada, L. (1992). Entrer en matière dans l'interaction: Acquisition et co-construction des topics en L2. *Acquisition et Interaction En Langue Etrangère (AILE)*, (1), 107–142.

Berthoud, A.-C., & Mondada, L. (1993). Traitement du topic: Aspects théoriques et acquisitionnels. *Bulletin CILA, 57*, 123–135.

Berthoud, A.-C., & Mondada, L. (1994). Gestion du topic et marquages énonciatifs dans des textes visant la construction de connaissances. *Les Carnets Di Cediscor*, (2), 139–152.

Berthoud, A.-C., & Mondada, L. (1995). Traitement du topic, processus énonciatifs et séquences conversationnelles. *Cahiers de Linguistique Francaise, 17*, 205–228.

Betz, E. (2011). Word choice, turn construction, and topic management in German conversation: Adverbs that are sensitive to interactional positioning. In M. T. Putnam (Ed.), *Studies on German-Language Islands*. Amsterdam and Philadelphia: John Benjamins Publishing Company.

Bolden, G. B. (2008). 'So what's up?': Using the discourse marker so to launch conversational business. *Research on Language & Social Interaction, 41*(3), 302–337.

Button, G. (1987). Moving out of closings. In G. Button (Ed.), *Talk and social organisation* (pp. 101–151). Clevedon: Multilingual Matters.

Button, G. (1990). On varieties of closings. In G. Psathas (Ed.), *Interaction competence* (pp. 93–148). Washington, DC: University Press of America.

Button, G., & Casey, N. (1984). Generating topic: The use of topic initial elicitors. In J. M. Atkinson & J. Heritage (Eds.), *Structures of social action* (pp. 167–190). Cambridge: Cambridge University Press.

Button, G., & Casey, N. (1985). Topic nomination and topic pursuit. *Human Studies, 8*, 3–55.

Clayman, S. E. (1989). The production of punctuality: Social interaction, temporal organization, and social structure. *American Journal of Sociology, 95*(3), 659–691.

Fox, B. (1987). Anaphora in popular written English. In R. Tomlin (Ed.), *Coherence and grounding in discourse* (pp. 157–174). Amsterdam: John Benjamins Publishing Company.

Gan, Z., Davison, C., & Hamp-Lyons, L. (2008). Topic negotiation in peer group oral assessment situations: A conversation analytic approach. *Applied Linguistics, 30*(3), 315–334.

Givón, T. (Ed.). (1983). *Topic continuity in discourse*. Amsterdam, Philadelphia: John Benjamins Publishing Company.

Grobet, A. (2002). *L'identification des topics dans les dialogues*. Bruxelles: Éditions Duculot.

Hartford, B. S., & Bardovi-Harlig, K. (1992). Closing the conversation: Evidence from the academic advising session. *Discourse Processes, 15*, 93–116.

Heath, C. (1985). The consultation's end: The coordination of speech and body movement. *International Journal of the Sociology of Language, 51*, 27–42.

Heath, C. (1986). *Body movement and speech in medical interaction*. Cambridge, UK, Cambridge University Press.

Heyman, R. D. (1986). Formulating topic in the classroom. *Discourse Processes*, (9), 37–55.
Holt, E. (2010). The last laugh: Shared laughter and topic termination. *Journal of Pragmatics*, 42, 1513–1525.
Jefferson, G. (1984). On stepwise transition from talk about a trouble to inappropriately next-positioned matters. In J. M. Atkinson & J. Heritage (Eds.), *Structures of social action* (pp. 191–222). Cambridge: Cambridge University Press.
Jeon, M. (2003). Closing the advising session. *Working Papers in Educational Linguistics* 18(2), 89–106.
Kim, Y. (2017). Topic initiation in conversation-for-learning: Developmental and pedagogical perspectives. *English Teaching*, 72(1), 73–103. DOI:10.15858/engtea.72.1.201703.73
König, C. (2013). Topic management in French L2: A longitudinal conversation analytic approach (pp. 226–250). *EUROSLA Yearbook 13*. Amsterdam/Philadelphia: John Benjamins Publishing Company..
König, C. (2014). Competenza interazionale in francese L2: l'esempio della 'parola ripresa' nella conversazione familiare. *Linguistica e Filologia*, 34, 135–165.
Laurier, E. (2008). How breakfast happens in the café. *Time & Society*, 17(1), 119–134.
LeBaron, D., & Jones, S. E. (2002). Closing up closings: Showing the relevance of the social and material surround to the completion of interaction. *Journal of Communication*, 52(3), 542–565.
Mondada, L. (1995). La construction interactionnelle du topic. *Cahiers de l'ILSL*, 7, 111–135.
Mondada, L. (2003). Parler topical et organisation séquentielle: l'apport de l'analyse conversationnelle. *Verbum*, 25(2), 193–219.
Mondada, L., & Traverso, V. (2005). (Dés)alignements en clôture. *Lidil*, 31, 35–59.
Mori, J. (2004). Negotiating sequential boundaries and learning opportunities: A case from a Japanese language classroom. *The Modern Language Journal*, 88(4), 536–550.
Morris-Adams, M. (2014). From Spanish paintings to murder: Topic transitions in casual conversations between native and non-native speakers of English. *Journal of Pragmatics*, 62, 151–165.
Morris-Adams, M. (2016). Negotiating topic changes: Native and non-native speakers of English in conversation. *International Journal of Applied Linguistics*, 26(3), 366–383.
Pekarek Doehler, S. (1999). Linguistic forms and social interaction: Why do we specify referents more than is necessary for their identification?. In J. Verschueren (Ed.), *Pragmatics in 1998*. (Vol. 2, pp. 427–447). Antwerp: International Pragmatics Association.
Pekarek, S. (1999). *Leçons de conversation: dynamiques de l'interaction et acquisition de compétences discursives en classe de langue seconde*. Fribourg: Presses Universitaires.
Pekarek Doehler, S. (2000a). Anaphora in conversation: Grammatical coding and preference organization. *Proceedings of the 24th Annual Penn Linguistics Colloquium*, 7(1), 183–196.
Pekarek Doehler, S. (2000b). Long distance pronominal anaphora: A grammar-in-interaction account. In P. Baker (Ed.), *Proceedings of the discourse, anaphora and reference resolution conference (DAARC)* (pp. 185–196). Lancaster: Center for Computer Corpus Research on Language.

Pekarek Doehler, S. (2001). Referential processes as situated cognition: Pronominal expressions and the social co-ordination of talk. In E. Németh (Ed.,) *Cognition in Language Use : Selected Papers from the 7th International Pragmatics Conference* (Vol. 1, pp. 302–316). Antwerp: International Pragmatics Association.

Pekarek Doehler, S. (2004). Une approche interactionniste de la grammaire: réflexions autour du codage grammatical de la référence et des topics chez l'apprenant avancé d'une L2. *Acquisition et Interaction En Langue Etrangère (AILE)*, 21(1), 123–166.

Pekarek Doehler, S. (2013). Conversation analysis and second language acquisition. In C. A. Chapelle (Ed.), *The encyclopedia of applied linguistics* (pp. 1–8). Blackwell Publishing. DOI:10.1002/9781405198431.wbeal0217

Perrault, C. R., & Cohen, P. R. (1981). It's for your own good: A note on inaccurate reference. In A. K. Joshi, B. Webber, & I. A. Sag (Eds.), *Elements of discourse understanding* (pp. 217–230). Cambridge: Cambridge University Press.

Quasthoff, U. A. (1984). On the ontogenesis of doing personal reference: Syntactic, semantic, and interactional aspects. *Folia Linguistica*, 28, 503–538.

Raitaniemi, M. (2014). *Die Beendigung von finnischen und deutschen Telefonaten. Eine interaktionslinguistische, kontrastierende Untersuchung*. Frankfurt am Main: Peter Lang.

Robinson, J. D. (2001). Closing medical encounters: Two physician practices and their implications for the expression of patients' unstated concerns. *Social Science and Medicine*, 53(5), 639–656.

Sacks, H. (1995). *Lectures on conversation* (Vol. 1 & 2). Oxford: Basil Blackwell.

Sacks, H., & Schegloff, A. E. (1973). Opening up closings. *Semiotica*, 8(4), 289–327.

Sacks, H., & Schegloff, E. A. (1979). Two preferences for the organization of reference to person in conversation and their interaction. In G. Psathas (Ed.), *Everyday language: Studies in ethnomethodology* (pp. 15–21). New York: Irvington Publishers.

Schegloff, E. A. (1986). The routine as achievement. *Human Studies*, 9, 111–151.

Schegloff, E. A. (1990). On the organization of sequences as a source of 'coherence' in talk-in-interaction. In B. Dorval (Ed.), *Conversational organization and its development* (pp. 51–77). Norwood, NJ: Ablex.

Schegloff, E. A. (2007). *Sequence organization in interaction* (Vol. 1). Cambridge: Cambridge University Press.

Seedhouse, P., & Harris, A. (2011). Topic development in the IELTS speaking test. *IELTS Research Report*, 12, 1–50.

Sidnell, J. (Ed.) (2009). *Conversation Analysis: Comparative Perspectives*. Cambridge: Cambridge University Press.

Stivers, T., & Heritage, J. (2001). Breaking the sequential mold: Answering more than the question during comprehensive history taking. *Text*, 21(1/2), 151–185.

van Compernolle, R. (2011). Developing second language sociopragmatic knowledge through concept-based instruction: A microgenetic case study. *Fuel and Energy Abstracts*, 43(13), 3267–3283. DOI:10.1016/j.pragma.2011.06.009

Warga, M. (2005). 'Je serais très merciable': Formulaic vs. creatively produced speech in learners' request closings. *Canadian Journal of Applied Linguistics*, 8(1), 67–93.

5 Topic Introduction

In this chapter, I present the analysis of two au pair girls, Julie and Oksana, for whom I have collected a total of 19 cases of topic introduction. In contrast to Julie and Oksana, I have no records of topic introductions in Christine's data. This can be explained by the results of the language test from her language school. In the test, Christine showed an A2 level of French L2, meaning she is the au pair from my database with the lowest French L2 level. This fact at least suggests that she might encounter more difficulties in taking the floor independently in order to introduce a new topic as compared to more advanced L2 speakers, such as Julie (B1 level). Moreover, the conversations in Christine's host family are characterized by a question–answer pattern during the whole duration of her stay. It is always a parent, generally the host father, that asks Christine questions about her daily activities, allowing her to describe what she did during the day. This pattern, however, influenced the possibilities for Christine to independently introduce a new conversational topic. But Christine never initiated a topic for herself.

In the first section, I show the analyses for Julie's data set (5.1), and I then continue with the investigations of Oksana's data (5.2). This is followed by a summary of findings (5.3) putting together the common points and the major differences found in the data and relating them to the research questions about L2 interactional competence and its development. The chapter ends with the presentation of three cases of topic shift (5.4), since this is considered a specific case of topic introduction. Although no longitudinal observations have been made for this action, it is still closely related to the accomplishment of topic introduction. For topic shift, too, I discuss the results in a summarizing section (5.5).

5.1 Advanced L2 Level: Julie[1]

The three examples from Julie's database next presented and analyzed highlight the resources that Julie exploits to open up a new topical sequence that allows her to introduce a new referent that can possibly become the conversational topic. The longitudinal data allows me to show changes in Julie's first turn for the achievement of topic introduction. Moreover, through a sequential analysis, I uncover the specific features of Julie's action of introducing a new topic and opening a new sequence with regard to what preceded. The results show, on the one hand, that Julie introduces a new referent in an appropriate sequential place for this type of action, thus showing from the beginning of her stay a high sensitivity to the sequential progression of conversation. On the other hand, her orientation toward the topical progressivity is an aspect that shows important changes over time.

I collected a total of 12 cases of topic introduction in Julie's data, and I will discuss representative examples from different points in time to show the accomplishment of the same action longitudinally.

5.1.1 Topic Introduction at the Beginning of the Stay

The first example for Julie, ex. 11, is from Julie's second audio-recording. At this time, she had been in Switzerland for almost two weeks. As with many other recordings, this one was made during dinnertime, while all the family (Marie, the host mother; Jordan, the older child; Vicente, the host father; and Manon, the younger child) were sitting at the table. I am interested in Julie's turn at lines 07 and 08, and I analyze it in two steps: first, I will describe the turn construction in terms of linguistic resources and information structure; second, I will make a sequential analysis of its placement in the interaction. This means looking at the precise moment in conversation in which the turn is uttered, identifying the action it accomplishes and placing it in context of the topical progression. All these aspects relate to Julie's interactional competence in French L2.

When Julie recorded this interaction, she was having dinner with her host family, and the children were playing loudly, jumping on the couch. Marie had addressed them beforehand, asking them to stop, but they had continued. In line 01, she addresses them again and tries to set an end to their games, which happens in line 06.

(11) Julie, 12.10.2009 *suivre la danse* "attend the dance class"

```
01  Mar: MAIS ÇA RECOMMENCE PAS  HEIN?=
         but  it  start again    NEG hunh
         but it doesn't start again does it?
02  Jor: =mais (xx)=
         but
03  Mar: =TU SORS DE CE DIVAN MANON S'IL TE PLAÎT.
         you exit from this couch Manon      please
         you get off the couch Manon would you?
04       (1.1)
05  Man: (non::::; m::::)
         (no:::, m:::)
06       +(6.3) ((soupirs des enfants en arrière-fond))+
                ((children are sighing in the background))
```

```
→ 07   Jul:  j'espère que je peux suivre
             I hope    that I  can  follow
→ 08         main- euh: de↑main (.) la: eh [la gy- euh: la
             d↑an[se=hein=hh.&
             morrow uh    tomorrow    the-F.sg. uh the-F.sg. gy uh the-F.sg
             dance course
             I hope that tomorrow I can keep up in the dance class
  09   Mar:                                [°(le)(x)-°
                                            the-M.sg.
                                                the
                        [danse.
                         dance course
                         dance lesson
  10   Jul:  &.h=parce que j'étais pas là une f↑ois +(↑ouh)
             ((en inspirant))+=f::
             because     I was  NEG there one time    uh
             ((in-breath))
             because I have missed one lesson
  11   Vic:  mhm.
  12   Mar:  ouais.
             yeah
  13   Jul:  ç:a va <telle>ment v↑ite
             it  goes   so      fast
             time passes so fast
  14   ((bruits des enfants))
       ((children make noises in the background))
  15   Jor:  mais Manon (xx)
             but   Manon (xx)
  16   (7.6) ((bruits des enfants))
             ((children make noises in the background))
  17   Mar:  mais des fois (.) c'est mieux d'arrêter une semaine
             but  some times      it's  better   to stop   a  week
             but sometimes it's better not to train for a week
  18         pis après tu reprends t'as l'impression que ça va
             mieux
             afterward then you start again  you have the impression that  it
             goes better
             and then when you start practice again you have the impression that it
             works better
  19   Jul:  o:ui?
             yes
  20   (.)
  21   Mar:  c'est comme courir
             it's like running
```

After Marie has asked the children to get off the couch, there is a long gap (line 06), after which Julie starts in line 07 with a sentence, *j'espère* "I hope," that projects a subordinate clause, which in this case is uttered with some difficulties in lines 07–08. We can gloss it with: *que je peux suivre demain la danse* "that I can attend the dance course tomorrow." She places herself as the subject of these clauses, and thus *je* "I" becomes the deictic center of both clauses. She also projects a predication about a future point in time, *demain* "tomorrow." The last element of the predication, *la danse* "the dance course," introduces a new referent in the sentence in the position of direct object. So Julie produces a sentence structure placing the sentence topic (*je*) in the canonical, pre-verbal position, and the focus (new information) in its classical direct object position. The object referent is a definite NP, which indicates that it is not presented as a "brand new referent" (Prince, 1981), but it is considered cognitively accessible to the interlocutors (Ariel, 1988). In fact, this referent was briefly mentioned earlier in the same conversation. Summing up, regarding the structuring of information on the sentence level, Julie deploys conventional L1-speaker-like linguistic means (cf. Berthoud, 1996; Berthoud & Mondada, 1995).

Sequentially, before this turn in lines 07–08, Marie and the children are concluding a discussion about the children's behavior and their being too noisy during the mealtime. The closing environment is observable in the following aspects. In line 01, Marie utters a turn that is formatted as an order and ends with a question tag (*hein*). The next relevant action should be for the children to perform what Marie asks (to be quiet). This is not the case, as we can see in line 02, where Jordan responds with a disaligning turn, beginning with a typical opposition marker, *mais* "but," but afterward his voice lowers, so that it is only possible to suggest what he utters. However, Marie in line 03 clearly orients toward the disaligning activity performed by her daughter Manon (who meanwhile continues to play and to be noisy), showing in this turn her orientation toward the local (contextual) sensitivity of this conversation (Bergmann, 1990). Subsequently, the pauses in lines 04 and 06 suggest that the ongoing course of action is coming to an end. In fact, no noises are audible in the recording except for Manon's unclear sound production in line 05. So the children have now performed the relevant actions projected by Marie's turns in lines 01 and 03, and this sequence can be heard by Marie and Julie as being closed.

Afterward, in line 07, it is Julie who self-selects and takes the floor and, by doing so, opens a possible new sequence in the ongoing conversation, thus orienting to what preceded as being closed. Julie expresses a hope, requiring some kind of recipient uptake. But she also shows some difficulties in producing her turn: see in line 08 the hesitation markers (*euh*), the vocal prolongations, and the repeated cutoffs, followed by self-repairs (*main- demain*; *la gy- la danse*). In response to these linguistic troubles, Marie twice provides the item that Julie is searching for (line 09). In the first case, Marie drops off the overlap, and in the second case, she proposes the item *danse* while Julie is already uttering this same item. Marie seems to display an orientation toward Julie's production difficulties and offers her assistance with a particular word-search problem.

Despite her troubles in the first turn in lines 07 and 08, Julie holds the floor and completes her utterances, accomplishing the opening of a new sequence. She does this by using herself as a deictic center for anchoring her discourse. But she also introduces a new referent (the dance course), which becomes the conversational topic of the interaction. All this indicates Julie's sensitivity to the sequential progression of conversation. But the same cannot be said for its topical progressivity. In fact, Julie starts a new sequence about a new matter that is not related to what preceded it: neither to the sequence about Marie and the children nor to what was done before that sequence. Julie does not use any misplacement markers to make the topic change explicit but starts her turn in line 07 in a rather abrupt way with a standard clause. This is interesting since it is not a typical way of opening a sequence about a new matter (Berthoud & Mondada, 1995; Button & Casey, 1984, 1985; Pekarek Doehler, 2004): there is a sort of mismatch in Julie's data between the sensitivity that she shows for sequentiality and her lack of sensitivity to topical talk. This is to say that she uses standard expressions, but the way she employs them seems to deviate from standard norms and may be typical for a speaker of French L2. Although she opens a new topical sequence, she does it without any markers related to its dependence or independence from the previous matter. We can therefore call this system of introducing a new topic an abrupt topic introduction.

5.1.2 Topic Introduction at the Middle of the Stay

The second example for Julie, ex. 12, is taken from a recording taped six months after Julie's arrival in Switzerland. During the recording, the whole family is preparing for dinner. At some point, Julie announces that during the winter, she wants to learn to ski powder snow. In this example, I am interested in Julie's turn in lines 05–06.

(12) Julie, 05.02.2010 *skier dans la poudre* "skiing powder snow"

```
    01  Mar: <c'est> bon j'ai rien dit=>j'ai cru qu'y avait plus
             de
             it's    good I have nothing said  I have thought that there was no
             more
    02       jambon=mais je l'ai trouvé<.
             ham     but   I it have found
             it's alright it's like I didn't speak I thought that there was no more ham
             but I found it
    03  +(5.0) ((bruits))+
             ((noises))
    04  (1.0)
→   05  Jul: m↑ais à la fin: (0.1) euh: (0.1) oui (0.1) à la fin
             de l'hiver
             but     at the end         uh         yes       at the end
             of  winter
→   06       je veux savoir (0.1) je veux (0.1) arri↑ver (0.5) à skier
             dans la poudre.
             I  want  to know     I want        to arrive        to ski
             in  the powder
             but by the end of the winter season I want to be able to ski powder snow
    07  (0.5)
```

84 Topic Introduction

```
08  Mar:  hein=hein
          unh hunh
09  Jul:  ↑et je veux faire-  eh-  eh-  arriver de  faire  (0.9)
          car↑ving
          and I    want to do  uh   uh   to arrive to  do carving²
          and I want to be able to do carving
```

Linguistically, line 05 starts with a discourse marker *mais* "but," which is very common in spoken French as an attention-getting device for claiming the floor and projecting more to come. Afterward, Julie introduces an adverbial construction, *à la fin* "in the end," which is interrupted by two short pauses, a hesitation marker (*euh*) and a self-regulation marker (*oui* "yes"), which seem to be directed at Julie herself rather than at her interlocutor. In fact, just after it, Julie repeats the first part of the adverbial construction *à la fin* "in the end" and completes it with a temporal specification, *de l'hiver* "of winter," identifying in this way a precise temporal context: at the end of winter. Subsequently, she introduces a predication about herself: as she did in the first excerpt, the *je* "I" becomes the deictic *origo* of the utterance, i.e. the utterance topic in a classic pre-verbal position. She expresses her wish to learn a new way of skiing, *skier dans la poudre* "ski on the powder," making relevant a subsequent uptake by her interlocutor.

For the sequential development, we also observe a similarity to the previous example. In ex. 11 and ex. 12, there is ongoing activity that is strongly related to the family context: Marie is searching for ham in the refrigerator, but she cannot find it. In line 01, we have Marie's pronouncement, which is produced with high volume and fast speed, so that she can resume the whole activity that was going on until that moment. Because no one reacts to Marie's resumption, one can consider the problem solved. After some seconds of noise in line 03 (the participants are preparing the meal) and a silent pause of 1.0 seconds in line 04, Julie self-selects in line 05, opening a possible new sequence and clearly indicating the preceding activity as being closed. As in ex. 11, Julie shows some difficulties (a repetition in line 05 and a change of communicative project in line 06), but she manages to introduce new information and a new referent (a particular type of skiing) in the focal position of her utterance (ski on the powder), which subsequently becomes the conversational topic. In fact, even though not immediately after Julie's turn, Marie acknowledges it with a minimal response (*hein-hein*, line 08), thus inviting her to continue her telling. Julie progresses after Marie's minimal reaction, adding a new turn in line 09.

If we compare this second excerpt with the first one, we observe some common features:

1. A preceding sequence and topic are collaboratively closed.
2. A pause that is in this second case partially filled with noises coming from the kitchen.

3. Julie self-selects proposing a new conversational topic that is anchored to the "I" as sentence topic.

There is a difference, however, in Julie's turn architecture: in ex. 11, she introduces the new matter in an abrupt way, whereas in ex. 12, she accomplishes a more complex contextualization and interactional work, allowing her interlocutor to anchor the new topic in a particular time constellation. Therefore, even though she uses a new pronouncement for nominating a possible new topic (Button & Casey, 1985), she accomplishes more interactional work for projecting the upcoming topical disjunction.

5.1.3 Topic Introduction at the End of the Stay

The third example is part of the last recording done by Julie during her stay; this means ten months after her arrival in Switzerland. In this recording, Julie and Marie are discussing the preparation of Julie's departure. I will concentrate especially on Julie's turn from lines 06 to 12.

(13) Julie, 16.06.2010 *qu'est-ce que je voulais* "what I wanted"

```
   01    Man:  j'ai dit [(peut-être)] un cauchemar?
               I have said   maybe      a   nightmare
   02    Jul:           [ouais.      ]
                         yeah
   03    Mar:  ↑mh↑m.=
               mhm
   04    Jul:  =°ehm.°
               uhm
   05    (1.1)
→  06    Jul:  °<qu'est-ce> >que je voulais,<° (0.1) .hh >AH OUI=.
               h< j'ai
               what        that I  wanted                  oh  yes
               I have
→  07          télépho↑né ehm:: (0.4) avec ma=Mama::n et j'ai
               démandé euh
               called      uhm           with my mom    and I have
               asked       uh
→  08          (0.4) qua::nd (0.4) eh ben en f↑ait si tu ↑veux le
               ↑jeu:di tu
                     when        uh well in fact  if you want on
               Thursday you
→  09          peux encore aller >travailler<=c'est ↑bête si tu
               va:s-
               can still   go    to work       it's stupid if you
               go-
→  10          restes ici.
               stay here
               what did I want, oh yes, I have called my mom and have
               asked her when (she will arrive) well in fact if you want,
               on Thursday you can still go to work, there is no need for
               you to stay at home
```

```
11   Mar:   [°(x)(oui).°
                yes
12   Jul:   [parce que on- on part le- à midi?
             because   we  we leave the-M.sg. at noon?
             because we will not leave until noon
13   (0.2)
14   Mar:   ↑si mais bon >faut quand même que tu prépares tes
            choses
            yes but well  need     anyway    that you prepare  your
            things
15          tranquille↑ment<,
            calmly
            yes but still, you need to prepare all your stuff with no rush
```

Linguistically, in line 06, Julie's first utterance, though it has the syntactic form of a question, functions as a misplacement marker, which strongly projects more to come. This utterance lacks the final rising intonation typical of questions but is constructed syntactically as an interrogative, the most important feature being the question marker *qu'est-ce que* ("what"). This utterance functions as a misplacement marker rather than as an actual question, showing the discontinuity of the upcoming topic and action with regard to the preceding ones. This is visible, first, in the lower voice volume, which suggests that this question is formulated as self-directed rather than directed at an interlocutor (Steinbach-Koehler & Thorne, 2011), and, second, in the fact that Marie does not orient to it as projecting an answer. In fact, after a micro-pause, Julie produces *ah oui* "oh yes" with higher voice volume and accelerated voice speed. This item is also preceded and followed by in-breath and marks the beginning of the actual utterance, which has—as seen before—*je* "I" in topical, pre-verbal position and a new referent in its second, focal part (Julie's mother). This time, again, the utterance is interrupted by two micro-pauses and two hesitation markers (*ehm:* and *euh*, in line 07). This accounts for some difficulties that Julie is encountering, and after a third micro-pause in line 08, Julie changes her communicative project. She marks this using the marker *eh ben* "uh well" and the adverb *en fait* "in fact/actually." In lines 08 and 09, Julie formulates a proposition to Marie, which makes an acceptance or a refusal from her relevant. After a short pause in line 10, it seems that Marie is accepting (line 11), but there is an unclear segment, and her turn is overlapped by Julie's increment in line 11: she delivers an account for her preceding proposition, possibly because Marie's reaction is a little bit delayed. The conversation proceeds afterward about the organization of Julie's departure.

Focusing now on the sequential organization of this excerpt, we observe a similar structure to the preceding examples. First, a sequence is getting closed: in ex. 11 and ex. 12, the closed sequences were strongly bound to an extra-linguistic activity (in ex. 11, children making noises; in ex. 11, preparing dinner), whereas in ex. 13, the ongoing activity is storytelling and is pursued by Marie, reporting the nightmare that her daughter had the night before. Lines 03 and 04 show minimal recipient reactions, both from Marie and from Julie: these features are typical of a sequence being closed, and they prepare the field for a smooth passage to a new topic and to a new sequence. In fact, Julie's *eh'* in line 04 can be considered a "pivotal element," in the sense that it belongs both to the closing sequence and to the opening sequence. Retrospectively, line 04 aligns to Mom's minimal response in line 03, showing the slow exhaustion of the topic and of the activity—the climax of the story being reached before that moment. Prospectively, line 04 indicates Julie's claim for the floor, and although it is followed by a rather long pause, it pre-announces a possible upcoming self-selection by Julie. In fact, in line 06, Julie self-selects and produces a complex turn introducing a new conversational topic that is independent of the previous one.

Compared with the preceding excerpts, ex. 13 shows Julie's different way of structuring the turn that introduces a new conversational topic. In this excerpt, her preparatory work starts possibly already in line 04, when she shows her willingness to take the floor. However, the main prefacing and linking work is accomplished in line 06. With the question, "what did I want?" functioning as a misplacement marker, Julie projects a change in the topic progressivity of conversation, indicating that what comes next is not related to the previous ongoing activity and topic. The "oh yes" in line 06, contributes both to prepare the interlocutor for the new upcoming topic and to help Julie resume her thoughts in order to better structure the continuation of her turn.

5.2 Intermediate L2 Level: Oksana

I collected a total of seven cases of topic introduction for Oksana during the period September 2010 to May 2011. In addition to these tapes, there are 14 recordings with only the children.

For my analysis, I first focus on the sequential placement of topic introduction, which reveals that a new topic is introduced when the previous sequence and topic are collaboratively closed. I then describe the linguistic and prosodic resources employed by Oksana for introducing a new topic. This description refers to the turn architecture and the introduction of referents in an ongoing conversation. The most important aspects, showing a similarity to Julie's data, concern the sequential placement of the topic introduction and the employed resources for the turn construction. However, I also document an important difference between the two au pairs, and this is related to the type of topic, i.e. to their possible newsworthiness or interest for the interlocutor. This relates to the interactional aspects of recipient design that Oksana brings more to the foreground than Julie does. This aspect will be addressed after the analyses.

5.2.1 Topic Introduction at the Beginning of the Stay

In the first example from Oksana's data set, she is discussing with Pierre, the host father, whether it is necessary to buy a new mixer for the kitchen. Afterward Oksana starts talking about her daily activity with the child, Nadège. I focus especially on Oksana's turn in line 07.

(14) Oksana, 28.09.2010 *aujourd'hui* "today"

```
01   Oks: mh PAS POUR ÇA: mais pour gâteau:
              mh not for  this but for  cake
02        normalement avec les yeux:=et avec les
          usually     with  the *eyes and with the-pl.
03        far↑ine peut-être ↑mais pour ça?
          flour-sg. maybe    but  for  this
          no not for doing this, but usually when you bake a cake with eggs and flour
          maybe it helps but not for this
04   (..)
05   Pie: je le regarde (lui) qu'est-ce qu'il y a demain.
          I look at it-M.sg. (it-M.sg.) what is there         tomorrow
          I will see tomorrow what I find
06   (1.3)
→ 07 Oks: ehm OK ↑eh:m (..) eh quoi nou::s avons faire aujourd'hui?
          uhm OK uhm       uh what  we    have-3ps.pl.pres do-inf. today
          uhm OK uhm uh what have we done today?
08   (.)
09   Pie: voilà oui.
          there you go yes
10   Oks: eh: Nadège?
          uh  Nadège
11   Nad: èh?
          (reaction similar to "what?")
12   Oks: qu'est-ce que nous avons faire aujourd'hui?
          what      that we  have-3ps.pl.pres. do-inf. today
          what have we done today?
13   (...)
14   Oks: nous allons (aller;allés) à côté de lac=oui?
          we  go-3ps.pl.pres. (go-inf.;gone-3ps.pl.) to the lakeside yes
          we have gone to the lake, haven't we?
15   (...)
16   Oks: [oui ?]
              yes?
17   Pie: [tu] as été faire une promenade?
              you have been do  a   walk
          have you gone for a walk?
18   (...)
19   Nad: non.
          no
20   (.)
21   Oks: non=non nous allo::ns eh:: jouer avec le ballon-
          no   no  we  go-3ps.pl.pres. uh play-inf. with the ball-
22        eh dans le sable=parce que il y a u- une liè,
          uh in   the sand    because  there is a- a-F.sg. *place-M.sg.
          no no we went playing with the ball uh in the sand because there is a place
```

```
23   (..)
24   Oks: une liè pou:r euh=
          a-F.sg. *place-M.sg. for  huh
          [there is] a place for
25   Pie: =+un lieu. ((Pie corrige la prononciation de Oks))+
          a-sg.M. place ((corrects Oks's pronunciation of "place"))
          a place
26   Oks: une lieu [pour] jouer^avec ballon ↑mhm?
          a-sg.F. place for play-inf. with ball mhm
          [there is] a place for playing with the ball, isn't there?
27   Pie:          [mhm]
                    mhm
```

This example comes from Oksana's first recording, made a few days after her arriving at her host family's home. She and the host father, Pierre, are having dinner at home, and Oksana is describing what she did during the day with Nadège. I am interested in line 07, when Oksana self-selects after a previous sequence and topic are collaboratively closed down and a long pause occurs.

From lines 01 through 05, Oksana and Pierre are making decisions and arrangements for buying a new mixer, since the one that they have does not work anymore. Pierre's final statement in line 05 marks the closure of this sequence and topic. This is also observable in the long pause that occurs after this turn. Longer pauses are namely found in closing implicative contexts (cf. Button, 1990) and in relation to the introduction of or a change in conversational topic (cf. Maynard, 1980).

After a 1.3-second pause, Oksana utters a turn that simultaneously aligns with Pierre's closing turn in line 05 while claiming the floor for herself. Her *ehm OK ehm* "uhm OK uhm" functions as alignment to Pierre closing, though delayed, because it does not topicalize any other element of Pierre's statement. The double hesitation marker *ehm*, the second of which is also prolonged, allows Oksana to claim the floor for herself, also blocking a possible further talk by Pierre. In so doing, she keeps talking after a micro-pause, introducing the next conversational topic, i.e. what she and Nadège did that day. Pierre align with Oksana's turn and topicalizes it straightforwardly in the next turn (line 09). In lines 10 and 12, Oksana also tries to involve Nadège in the retelling of their day, but the child does not react to this invitation. In line 14, then, Oksana offers a description of their daily activity, fishing for Nadège's confirmation with a questioning turn ending, *oui?* ("yes?"). Given that no reaction follows, Oksana fishes again for the child's answer, in line 16, but again with no success. At this point, Pierre formulates another question, which he addresses to Nadège, namely if she had gone for a walk. Nadège finally answers with a minimal negative response. Oksana then self-selects and explains to Pierre that they were at the lakeside playing with the ball, since there is a sandy play area.

A look at the sequential placement of Oksana's turn in line 7 uncovers similar features to Julie's examples. Two aspects can be observed. First,

Oksana self-selects after a long pause has occurred and no one else is taking the floor. Second, Oksana's turn contains a news announcement in the form of a question, the news being here what she has done with Nadège in the afternoon. As a question, her turn necessarily projects as a next action an answer from her interlocutor. This shows that Oksana orients to what precedes as being closed.

5.2.2 Topic Introduction in the Middle of the Stay

The next example, taken from a recording after one month of her stay, shows some differences in Oksana's topic introduction methods. In this recording, Oksana and Pierre are talking about some free-time activities that are suitable for children. The focus of this excerpts is on Oksana's turn in lines 13–14.

(15) Oksana, 31.10.2010 *piscine* "swimming pool"

```
01   Pie: on peut lever les barrières,
          one can take away the   barriers
02   (.)
03   Pie: comme ça >la-< la boule elle va [pas&
          in so doing the-sg.F. the-sg.F. bowl it-sg.F. doesn't go
04   Oks:                                 [oui:,
                                           yes
05   Pie: &à droi[te ou à gauche.
          to the right  or  to the left
```
[lines 1–3–5] you can take away the barriers so that the bowl doesn't roll out to the right or to the left
```
06   Oks:         [ehm.
                   uhm
07   (.)
08   Oks: .hhm
09   Pie: ouais: par>ce qu'autrement< c'est pas inté°ressant°°.
          yeah   because otherwise     it's  not  interesting
          yes because otherwise it wouldn't be so interesting for little children
10   (5.0) ((eating-related noises))
11   Pie: mais elle aime BIEN.
          but  she   loves well
          but she really loves it
12   (4.0) ((eating-related noises))
→ 13 Oks: peut être je: (2.6) je vais:: à:: pi↑scine avec
          na°dège°(0.4)
              maybe  I           I  go    to swimming pool with
              Nadège
→ 14      cette +°°(sean)°° ((semaine)).
          this  (wrong pronunciation for "week") week
          maybe this week I will got to the swimming pool with Nadège
15   (2.5)
16   Pie: alors mar↑di, (.) c'est là où l'eau elle est-
          elle est chaude.
          well  Tuesday     it's  then where the water it-sg.F. is
          it-sg.F. is warm
          well on Tuesday the water is always particularly warm
```

```
17   (1.3)
18   Oks: mh?
19   (1.0)
20   Pie: les mar↑dis  (0.4)  l'eau elle est chaude.
          the tuesdays         the water it-sg.F.  is warm
          on Tuesday the water is always warm
21   (.)
22   Pie: elle fait trente:  >je sais plus<  environ trente degrés.
          it-sg.F. makes 30   I don't know anymore  about   30   degrees
          the water has 30 degrees, or about 30 degrees, I'm not so sure anymore
```

Oksana and Pierre are having dinner at home. From line 01 to line 09, Pierre is explaining to Oksana how it is possible to let little children play bowling, namely via the use of barriers on both sides of the track, so that the bowling balls do not drop off. Pierre concludes his explanation with the comment that otherwise the game is not interesting to the children (line 09). During the long pause in line 10, both interactants are heard eating. In line 11, Pierre self-selects and adds another comment, a more specific one concerning the bowling experiences of his daughter Nadège: *mais elle aime bien* "but she really loves it." As an assessment, this turn functions as closing implicative. In a similar way as in his preceding turn in line 09, no reaction comes from Oksana. At this point, there is another long pause (line 12), and again some eating-related noises are heard. After this pause, Oksana self-selects and introduces a possible new conversational topic. Through a news announcement (Button & Casey, 1985), she informs Pierre that she might go to the swimming pool with Nadège that week. She constructs her turn as follows: she begins with the adverb *peut-être* "maybe," which functions as a modal particle. Then she positions herself as the deictic *origo* of this sentence. A vocal prolongation on the subject and a long intra-turn pause immediately after it suggest some difficulties in turn construction. After the pause, Oksana repeats the subject and continues with a predication (lines 12–13): *je vais à piscine avec Nadège cette semaine* "I go to the swimming pool with Nadège this week." This predication contains a spatial and a temporal indication and an indirect object (with Nadège). In conclusion, placing herself in the canonical subject position, Oksana constructs a long and complex predication, which delivers to her interlocutor all the contextual clues needed to establish a conversational topic.

Regarding the sequential position of Oksana's turn, Pierre was explaining to the au pair girl how to let children play bowling in a way that allows them to have fun too, i.e. with some sort of barriers so that the ball surely arrives at the end of the path without escaping to the right or to the left. His two last turns (lines 09 and 11) get no reaction from Oksana, at least nothing verbal. Line 11 can then be seen as an attempt by Pierre to fish for a response from Oksana: the turn is uttered after a long pause (in which the interlocutors are eating), but it is topically bound to turns before the long pause. Moreover, it contains a final, summarizing statement to what Pierre has explained before; thus, it gives Pierre's explanation sequence a clear closing trait. After summarizing statements, some sort of alignment (or even affiliation) from one's interlocutor is expected (Selting, 1994), but this does not happen here. The two long pauses in lines 10 and 12 recall a typical closing environment (Holt, 2010; Schegloff, 2007), when the topics fade and no interactant adds anything to keep them going. It is therefore at a precise conversational moment that Oksana self-selects in line 12, namely when no one else is requiring the floor and when the preceding topic and sequence have faded out.

Oksana constructs her turn in a fashion that shows her orientation toward the preceding sequence and topic as being closed: she does not start with a linking device; instead, she starts with a modal particle that shows no bond (either topical or sequential) with the preceding turns and sequences, and she positions herself as the sentence topic (Reinhart, 1981), whereas before it, the sentence topic was the child. Nadège is thus shifted from the place of sentence topic to the indirect object place in Oksana's predication.

If we look at the sequential moment of Oksana's self-selection and at the resources she employs, she is accomplishing the introduction of a new topic via a news announcement. This is not my opinion, but what the speaker is audibly and accountably doing with the resources that she has at her disposal. Interestingly, however, Pierre acknowledges Oksana's topic introduction in a delayed way. It might well be that he does something nonverbal, maybe with his eyes or his head. But we do not have access to this information. Pierre goes ahead with the conversation and explains something about the water temperature in the swimming pool on Tuesday (line 15). This explanation adds a piece of information for Oksana, but it also functions as an alignment to Oksana's previous turn: since she announced that she would probably go to the swimming pool with the child, the father informs her about which day it is better to go on, to better enjoy the water.

To sum up, in this example, Oksana accomplishes a more complex topic introduction than he had in the previous one. She uses a modal adverb to weaken both her viewpoint and the content of her news announcement, since it is essential for her to receive Pierre's authorization for the activities she plans to do with the child. Therefore, a modal particle successfully plays the role of indirectly requesting permission without directly requesting permission. This is an important activity concerning the protection of one's face and the management of intersubjectivity in conversation: it allows for the construction of a common ground regarding both the planned activities and the relationship between the interactants. Managing intersubjectivity in this case means to establish an interpersonal and a professional relationship that can be preserved for future occasions and that Pierre and Oksana can build on during the conversations that are still to come. Oksana's predication in her topic introduction turn is also more complex than the one in the preceding example, though some speech troubles are still to be seen (pauses and vocal prolongations). Finally, the sequential placement of this topic introduction shows a great similarity to Julie's data, since it takes place after a previous sequence has been closed.

5.2.3 Topic Introduction at the End of the Stay

I now turn to the last example from Oksana's collection from her last recording, after eight months of stay. She is talking with Pierre about his sports activities for the next evenings. I am particularly interested in Oksana's turns in lines 10 and 12.

(16) Oksana, 31.05.2011 *volley* "volleyball"

```
01  Oks:    +°c'est pas gra[ve°  ((loin de l'enregistreur))+
             it's    not  bad     ((away from recorder))
02  Pie:                  [non: je pense pas?
                           no    I don't think so
03  Agn:    (OUI ELLE) A DIT PAS GRAVE.
            (yes she)  has said not  bad
            yes she said it's not bad
04  (4.1)
05  Agn:    ei- elle a dit pas grave hein.
                 she has said not bad   eh-INTERJ
            she said not bad did she?
06  (1.6)
07  Nad:    ↑A:::h hihihihi
08  Oks:    °>mh OK tiens<.°
              mh OK hold
              mh OK here you go
09  (.)
→10 Oks:    [aujourd'hui::&
             today
11  Nad:    [gna:m gna:m.
→12 Oks:    &tu j/u/::: volley- +volleyball, ((prononciation anglaise))+
            you *play   volley   volleyball   ((English pronunciation))
13  (.)
14  Oks:    comment on dit ça °en français°?
            how     one says this  in French
            do you play volleyball (English pronunciation) today? how do you say it
            in French?
15  Pie:    aujourd'hui je- je vais jouer du + volley. ((prononciation
            today         I   I  go   play DET volley   ((French
16          française))+
            pronunciation))
            today I'm going to play volley ((French pronunciation, lexeme "ball" is
            skipped in French))
17  Oks:    +volley. ((prononciation française))+
             volley   ((French pronunciation))
18  Pap:    >ouais c'est-< c'est [(xx)
             yeah   it's    it's
```

94 Topic Introduction

```
19  Oks:                    [c'e:st eu:h +volleyball,
                             it's    uh    volleyball
20        ((prononciation anglaise))+
          ((English pronunciation))
          it's volleyball ((English pronunciation))
21  Pie: volley+ball ((prononciation anglaise))+ >oui oui<. on dit
          volleyball    ((English pronunciation))       yes yes  we say
22        aussi du volley+ball ((prononciation française))+ hein?=
          also  DET volleyball    ((French pronunciation))    INTERJ
          volleyball ("ball" with English pronunciation)) yes yes. we also say vol-
          leyball (("ball" with French pronunciation))
23  Oks: =aha.
24  Pie: en français. (.) [on a]
          in French          we have
25  Agn:                    [ON PEUT] DIRE FOOTBALL
                             one can say football
26  (. .)
27  Oks: n:on c'est pas la même=
          no   it's  NEG the same
          no it's not the same
28  Pie: =c'est pas la même chose on dit
           it's  NEG the same thing   we say
29        foot+ball ((prononciation anglaise))+
          football       ((English pronunciation))
30        on dit baseket+ball ((prononciation anglaise))+ (.)
          we say basketball        ((English pronunciation))
31        basket+ball ((prononciation française))+
          basketball        ((French pronunciation))
32        disons en français c'est basketball football (.)
          let's say in French   it's   basketball  football
33        [mh.]
          it's not the same thing. we say football (("ball" with English pronuncia-
          tion)) we say basketball (("ball" with English pronunciation)) (pause)
          basketball (("ball" with French pronunciation)). we can say in French
          it's basketball football mh.
34  Agn: [+football ((en riant))+]
           football       ((laughing))
35  Pie: +ball ((prononciation anglaise))+ c'est eu:h (..) en anglais?
           ball  ((English pronunciation))   it's   uh      in English?
          ball ((English pronunciation)) it's in English
36  Agn: a
37  Pie: oui c'est le:: >c'est avec le travail?<
          yes it's   the-sg.M. it's   with  the  work?
          yes it's with my work colleagues that I play volleyball
38  (.)
39  Oks: mhm=
40  Pap: =on s'en↑traîne parce que le dix-huit juin on a:: (..)
           we  train ourselves because the eighteenth of june we have
41        on a un tournoi.
          we have a tournament
          we are training because on June eighteenth we have a tournament
42  Oks: °aha d'accord°.
          aha alright
```

The whole family is having lunch together, and Oksana is discussing Pierre's plans for the evening while preparing something to eat for the children. Oksana starts her turn in line 10 with a temporal locator, *aujourd'hui* "today," and is immediately overlapped by Nadège's noises related to her eating activity (line 11). Oksana continues her turn immediately after and places Pierre (in the second-person singular) in the canonical place of sentence topic (Reinhart, 1981), i.e. the subject *tu* "you" is now the deictic center of her turn. The predication concerns his activity: the VP (verbal phrase) j/u/ *volley- volleyball* "play volleyball," though the verb is pronounced in a non-standard way, completes Oksana's question; i.e. she asks Pierre if he is going to play volleyball that evening. By means of a new inquiry (Button & Casey, 1984), Oksana takes the floor, thus proposing a possible conversational topic, and she also projects a next relevant action, namely an answer from Pierre. However, after a short pause (line 13), she self-selects again and asks Pierre for help, since she shows some uncertainty about the pronunciation of the lexeme "volleyball" in French. In line 15, Pierre offers his lexical help, though in an embedded correction (Jefferson, 1987), i.e. answering Oksana's question, *aujourd'hui je- je vais jouer du volley* "today I- I'm going to play volleyball." Right after this answer, Oksana repeats the lexeme with the standard French pronunciation and so confirms that she has understood Pierre's repair. In line 18, Pierre self-selects and initiates a turn that seems to be designed as an explanation (*c'est- c'est-* "it's- it's-"). However, Oksana overlaps this turn in line 19 and utters another clarification request concerning the right pronunciation of the word "volleyball." Pierre repeats the item in line 20 and acknowledges Oksana's pronunciation at turn ending with a fast and repeated "yes yes." After the side sequence concerning the pronunciation issues has been closed (line 35), Pierre picks up Oksana's conversational topic and develops it further, explaining that he plays volleyball with his colleagues since they have a tournament coming up.

Looking at the sequential placement of Oksana's self-selection in line 12, it is again done in a sequentially relevant place, namely after a previous sequence has been closed. The closing environment is observable in the following aspects: in lines 03 and 05, Agnes (the older daughter) is commenting on an expression that Oksana used in line 1. In line 03, Agnes highlights it with louder voice, whereas the repetition in line 05 is characterized more by a normal voice volume. However, no one reacts to her assessments, such as those in the long pauses in lines 04 and 06. As Maynard (1980) noticed, a topic change generally occurs when one topic line slowly fades, i.e. when no interactant contributes to the maintenance of the ongoing topic. This is particularly clear when longer pauses are seen between turns, because this means that they are prospecting a response from their interlocutors, but nothing comes. After this, a topic change generally occurs. In fact, in this example, no one reacts to Agnes's turns; Nadège produces some laughter-like noises in line 7; and Oksana, who was preparing toast for her, refers to it in line 8 by saying °*mh OK tiens*° "mh OK here you go." The lower voice volume also suggest that this turn is not conceived for furthering the conversation. Only then does Oksana self-select and change the topic: she introduces a new one. She herewith orients toward the preceding sequence and topic as being closed, and with a new temporal reference, she makes it clear to her interlocutor that she is introducing something new to the conversation. However, Oksana self-selects, again initiating a repair with a metalinguistic question on the pronunciation of the word "volley." The silence before in line 13 is short, but the absence of an answer is noticeable. By asking the metalinguistic question in line 14, Oksana treats her English pronunciation as a possible reason for Pierre's lack of an answer. Although it contains an embedded correction, line 15 ignores line 14 and responds to the question in line 12. By doing this, Pierre treats Oksana's English pronunciation as understandable and not a source of difficulty. In line 17, Oksana refuses to let the pronunciation issue go away, and the pronunciation differences between French and English become the conversational topic until line 36. In line 37, Pierre once more answers Oksana's original question from line 12, though differently from how he answered in line 15.

In his answer, Pierre does not just offer the item with the correct pronunciation but also embeds the words in a complete (standard) sentence, accomplishing thus a double action. On the one hand, he answers Oksana's question from lines 10–12; i.e. he aligns to her topic introduction. On the other hand, his turn construction contains elements that account for a subtle management of intersubjectivity. The standard pronunciation is syntactically embedded in the sentence and is therefore not directly addressed; i.e. the linguistic problem is corrected in passing. This allows for a face-saving action: Oksana is not being addressed as incompetent by the more expert French speaker. Managing intersubjectivity means here to accomplish a coordinated work of language clarification in a way to preserve the good-working interpersonal and professional relationship between the interlocutors. In the last two examples, then, I have shown how the actions of topic introduction and repair can be closely intertwined and happen in a timely way that helps maintain intersubjectivity during the conversation.

5.3 Summary of Findings

I have collected all the cases in which Julie and Oksana accomplish topic introduction in an ongoing conversation. This action is recurrent and stable so several examples could be compared. I have concentrated particularly on the sequential environment of topic introduction and on the resources mobilized by the L2 speakers to accomplish it.

5.3.1 The Sequential Environment: Sequence Opening After a Closed Sequence

In my data, the au pairs are shown to introduce new conversational topics after a previous sequence has been closed. This means that the previous turns are closing implicative (Holt, 2010), projecting no more talk to come on the same matter and followed by a pause. It is after this pause that Julie and Oksana self-selected and produced a turn that introduces a new conversational topic, which needs to be ratified by their interlocutor in order to become the actual conversational topic at hand. This feature of topic introduction, namely its placement after a closed sequence, did not show any changes over time, so I considered it a crucial aspect of my object of analysis.

In relation to my question about the development of L2 interactional competence, these findings show that Julie and Oksana already possess a high level of L2 interactional competence. With their topic introductions, they showed a strong orientation toward the topical and the sequential organization of the ongoing conversation. This ability might come from their L1, but they also manage to apply it in a locally relevant, accountable, and observable way in their L2 conversations.

5.3.2 The Turn Architecture: Linguistic and Prosodic Resources

Julie showed interesting changes over time in her way of participating in the conversation. At the beginning of her stay, she made no use of discourse markers of any kind to show to her interlocutor that she was introducing a new conversational topic. The introduction happened in a rather abrupt way, with no preparatory work for her interlocutor. This way of introducing a topic is rather unusual, because such an action of disjunction generally requires extra conversational work by a speaker to prepare the interlocutor for the new upcoming topic and to signal its newsworthiness.

In the second excerpt, Julie exploited some linguistic items that "prepared the field" for her interlocutor. The discourse marker *mais* "but" and the temporal locator *à la fin de l'hiver* "at the end of winter" made observable for Marie that the upcoming talk was not related to the preceding one. Although the discourse marker alone created a rather weak disjuncture from the preceding talk, it nonetheless showed that Julie was orienting slightly more toward the preceding turns. On the other hand, the contextualization clues in her first turn showed a stronger orientation toward the upcoming turns, thus highlighting Julie's prospective perspective.

Finally, the third excerpt showed a complex conversational work accomplished by Julie. She started her turn possibly even before her actual self-selection; i.e. Julie was seen collaborating in a closing implicative environment. Simultaneously, with the same turn, Julie projected a possible continuation and self-selected after a pause. By doing this, she oriented again backward by uttering a self-directed question that functioned as a misplacement marker: she oriented to what preceded as completed and closed. At the same time, she oriented again forward, projecting something new to come. In fact, the *ah oui* "oh yes" and the previous misplacement marker stood as preliminaries for the central utterance in the turn, the information that Julie delivered afterward concerning her future departure. This was reformulated in the moment by Julie through a change in her communicative project, but eventually, the information was delivered to Marie and gave her the occasion for an alignment. The consequence was that Julie's first turn in the last excerpt was much longer than her first turns in the other two excerpts and accomplished fine interactional work, making Julie's orientation toward the topical progress of conversation evident and something she was accountable for.

Oksana's data showed a more stable picture of her methods for introducing a new conversational topic. The main difference is in her bringing up news announcements at the beginning in order to introduce a new conversational topic, whereas toward the end, she employed more news inquiries.

Between Julie and Oksana, there is an interesting difference concerning the management of recipient design in relation to topic introduction, which I discuss next.

5.3.3 Difference Between Julie and Oksana: Management of Recipient Design

My investigations have shown that Julie tended to introduce topics that are self-attentive, whereas Oksana seemed to introduce topics that are more other directed (cf. Bolden, 2006). More specifically, Julie introduced topics that are of personal concern: in the examples presented, she started talking about her dance class, then about her skiing experiences and wishes, and finally about her mother's arrival. Clearly, in the last example, this is also important for Marie's day's agenda. Julie proposed she also normally go to work, whereas Marie rejected this offer, explaining that the preparation of Julie's departure may take some time. A look at the other examples from Julie's collection, however, attested to this tendency: within the 12 cases I collected, there are only four instances in which Julie introduced an other-attentive topic.

In contrast to Julie, Oksana tended to introduce other-attentive topics. Of the three discussed examples, in two cases, she introduced a topic of great relevance to her interlocutor (Nadège's school day and Pierre's volleyball training), but only once did she introduce a self-directed topic, namely when she said that she wanted to go to the swimming pool with Nadège. However, even in this case, it is noticeable that it is not only a matter of personal interest but also a request of permission, asked of Pierre; i.e. it is about his daughter and the activities that Oksana is allowed to do with her. For Oksana, I collected a total of seven cases, and in not one of them did she introduce a topic related to herself (her interests, wishes, past experiences, etc.). This difference between the two au pairs was quite intriguing. It can be related to the difference in their ages (Oksana is 22, whereas Julie is 18), which might influence the way they work for their host families. Moreover, in Oksana's host family, only the host father is present, so discussing his interests and those of the children's might be more relevant. The conversational dynamics that take place in these two host families are different in other ways as well, and this too can influence how the au pairs treat conversational topics. I will return to this point in my concluding chapters.

After showing how topic introduction is managed by the au pairs during their stay, I now turn to the management of topic shift, which I consider as a specific type of topic introduction. For this action, I present a total of three examples, one for each au pair (5.4). A summary of findings concludes this analytical chapter (5.5). I propose a synchronic and not a longitudinal analysis of topic shift and topical backlinking to pinpoint several aspects of topic progression that are central to the description and the conceptualization of the nature of L2 interactional competence.

5.4 Topic Shift

Topic shift is an omnipresent activity that contributes to topic management throughout the body of conversations. Speakers use a variety of resources and practices to manage topic progression in real time. For these reasons, it is rather difficult to build a collection of cases that can be used to show changes over time, and I therefore do not show longitudinal data for this case. Topic shifts happen with every turn at talk, in the sense that interlocutors bring the conversation further and therefore necessarily transform the conversational topic (cf. Morris-Adams, 2014). Maynard (1980) proposed a first general description of this mechanism:

> Topic shifting procedures . . . are regular features of ongoing topical talk, and are ways in which transformations can be done on a prior utterance in order to occasion a set of mentionables in a present utterance. It is in this sense, that *structural* matters are crucial to the description and understanding of topical talk.
>
> (p. 272, emphasis in the original)

There are two main points in Maynard's description. First, one can look at what happens in an ongoing conversation: conversational topics can be analyzed by taking their unstable nature into consideration. Second, this changing nature relies on structural properties of interaction: it is not only a matter of content or of content interpretation, but at stake are also the features of interactional structure and sequences. These underlying features are more general than content, since content varies from conversation to conversation, but the structural properties of conversation and turns at talk are generalizable. It is, then, through these structural matters that topic shifts are accountable for the interlocutors and analyzable for the analyst.

The question to ask, then, is, how can topic shifts in conversation be analyzed? In other words, how is it, then, that one can continually shift topics yet maintain relevance (Garcia & Joanette, 1997: 94)? The researchers indicate the main principle that makes it possible to continuously shift topics in conversation while letting the same conversation look coherent: relevance. This is best shown in the next example (ex. 17).

5.4.1 Topic Shift Through Reference Shift

Interactional topics have been observed to flow almost seamlessly into one another, and our common sense suggests that it happens exactly that way. Grice (1975) illustrated that participating in conversation generally means to "[m]ake [a] conversational contribution such as is required, at the stage at which it occurs, by the accepted purpose or direction of the talk exchange in which you are engaged" (p. 45). He terms this the "principle of cooperation," and much literature has shown how cooperation functions in conversation, for instance by demonstrating how interactants incessantly orient toward the preceding turn with regard to its design and its content: "[interlocutors] work towards a common purpose thereby explaining the fact that conversations are not a series of disjointed remarks" (Garcia & Joanette, 1997: 95). This cooperation is illustrated in the following example, which comes from Oksana's database. Oksana and Pierre are talking about ice rinks in their respective home countries, Poland and Switzerland. I am particularly interested in line 13.

(17) Oksana 25.10.2010 *stadion glace* "ice stadium (ice rinks)"

```
03   Oks: ma (.) par exemple ici en suisse vous avons (..) euh stadion?
          but     for  example here in Switzerland you-2.pl. have-1.pl  uh  stadium
04   (.)
05   Pie: ou[i.
          yes
06   Oks:    [avec glace dans chaque grand (.) [hm: vi?
             with  ice   in   every   big            *city
          but, for instance, in Switzerland do you have an ice rink in every big city?
07   Pie:                                      [hm::
08   (2.4)
09   Pie: .h hm::: chaque grande ville ↑ouais disons >on peut presque
                   every   big    city   yeah   say   one can  almost
```

```
10          dire< maintenant oui.
            say       now       yes
         in every big city, yes, we can say that nowadays
11  (...)
12  Pie: oui [.hh
         yes
→13 Oks: [mais en pologne je sais pas où est:: °stadion glace°.
         but   in  Poland  I don't know where is    stadium   ice
         well, in Poland, I wouldn't know where there is an ice rink
14  (.)
15  Pie: ouais il n'y a peut-être pas beaucoup.
         yeah    there aren't   maybe      a lot
         yeah, maybe there aren't so many there
16  (2.2)
17  Pie: ouais.
         yeah
18  (..)
19  Pie: bon celui où on a été à ((ville)) c'est un vieux stade
         good that one where we have been in ((city)) it's    an  old  stadium
20       hein=c'est- je crois que c'est le- c'est le: le:: le plus
         INTERJ it's-  I  believe that it's   the- it's   the  the  the oldest
21       vieux stade::du groupe A de- du: la première ligue
         stadium of    group    A of- of the-M.sg. the-F.sg. first league
22       si tu veux suisse=hein.
         if you want  swiss  INTERJ
         well, that one where we have been in ((city)) is an old rink, I think this is
         probably the oldest one of the first Swiss league
23  (..)
24  Oks: °mhm°
25  Pie: ligue nationale A.
         national league A
         first national league
```

In ex. 17, Oksana asks her host father, Pierre, if every big city in Switzerland has an ice rink (a couple of days before they went to see a hockey game at an ice rink). Oksana's question is split between line 03 and line 06. In line 03, she starts her inquiry by geographically indexing the referent *stadion* "stadium," which she introduces as a turn-final item. In line 05, Pierre is positively answering this question when Oksana overlaps his answer (line 06) and increments her question with a series of specifications concerning the stadium: she is asking about ice stadiums in big cities. After a long pause, Pierre initiates a repair (line 09) and then repeats his positive response *ouais* "yeah." However, this time he adds some remarks that moderate his answer: *disons* "let's say," *on peut presque dire* "one can almost say." Nevertheless, his turn ends with a positive response (line 10), which he repeats after a pause (line 12). In line 13, overlapping Pierre's intake of breath, Oksana self-selects and produces a turn that initiates a topic shift: she affirms that she does not know where there are ice rinks in Poland (her home country). As Maynard (1980) recalls, there are many strategies for accomplishing a topic shift: in example 17, Oksana shifts the geographical reference frame for the same referent (ice rinks). By virtue of a disjunctive marker at turn beginning (*mais* "but," line 13), she prepares the field for a possible contrastive proposition to come. In fact, her statement compares two countries (Switzerland and Poland) regarding the presence of ice rinks (the referent she introduced with her first inquiry, lines 03 and 06), and she positions herself as an unknowing party. In conclusion, while the main referent is maintained, the contextual frame is changed, and in this way, the au pair girl is able to manage a topic shift that takes the conversation in a new direction.

Another possibility for shifting the topic is through a pivot-shifting, i.e. by using an already-introduced referent to address new aspects that concern it. This practice is discussed in the next subsection.

5.4.2 *Topic Shift Through Pivot-Shifting*

The next example is from Julie's database. Here, Marie is telling a story about a kitchen tool she has just bought, which is the same used by Didier Cuche (a famous professional athlete). The naming of the athlete coincides with the story climax, and after Julie and Victor have reacted to this announcement, Julie shifts the conversational topic by addressing another aspect concerning Didier Cuche's health condition (line 78).

(18) Julie 16.02.2010 Didier Cuche

```
57   Mar:  =mais °°je pense pas.°° .h et pi:s euh >il me dit< +C'EST
            but      I don't think so       and then uh    he tells me   it's
58         LA MÊME (.) QUE DI- QUE DIDIER CUCHE.((voix souriante))+
            the same    as di-  as Didier  Cuche  ((laughing voice))
           but I don't think so, but then he told me, it's the same as Didier Cuche
59   (1.2)
60   Mar:  mais lui il en a un plus grande mais il utilise le même truc.
            but him-DIR he DIR has a bigger    but  he  uses   the same thing
           he (Didier Cuche) has a bigger one, but still of the same thing
61   (0.8)
62   Mar:  ts.=
63   Jul:  =ah ouais.=
            oh yeah
64   Mar:  =j'ai dit +ah bon be:n on sera aux prochains ((voix
           souriante))+
            I have said  oh good well   we will be   at the next    ((laughing
            voice))
65         +jeux olympiques. ((en riant))+
            Olympic Games ((laughing))
           then I've said, well then, we will attend the next Olympic Games.
66   Vic:  ((rit))
            ((laughs))
67   Mar:  ((rit))
            ((laughs))
```

```
68  Jul:  ((rit))
          ((laughs))
69  Jul:  ouais c'est ça. ((rit))
          yeah   that's it  ((laughs))
70  (1.7)
71  Jul:  ↑ah ouais (0.2) alors c'est bien ce tr↑uc je=pen[se.
          oh yeah         then   it's good  this thing  I  think
          oh yeah, so this thing must be very good, I guess
72  Mar:                                                   [+ouais ((en
                                                            yeah
73        riant))
          ((laughing))
74  (0.7)
75  Mar:  .h >parce qu'après j'ai dit< mais:=c'est encore- y a encore
          because afterward  I've said but   it's   still-  is there also
76        une ↑boule dessus >il dit< ouais=ouais c'est tout un:
          one bowl over it he says  yeah yeah   it's all one
          because then I've asked, if there is another bowl on top of it, and he said
          yes, it's all in one
77  (1.2)
→78 Jul:  mais Didier Cuche il a: (0.5) ts. aussi des problèmes
          avec son
          but  Didier Cuche  he has         also some problems
          with his
79        ge↑nou?
          knee
          but (by the way) Didier Cuche also has some problems with his knee,
          hasn't he?
80  (0.2)
81  Jul:  tu sais?
          you know
          do you know that?
82  Mar:  boh.
          buh
83  (0.7)
84  Mar:  je pense (.) ↑ouais ...
          I   think    yeah ...
```

Marie reaches her story climax in lines 57–58, when she announces that she has found out that Didier Cuche uses the same kitchen tool she has just bought for herself. The climax is characterized by a higher voice volume and a laughing voice (Selting, 1994). It is noteworthy that 1.2 seconds of pause follow, in which her coparticipants do not react to her story. Marie then self-selects after the pause and expands her story with a downgrading assessment of the previous one: she says that Didier Cuche has a bigger kitchen tool, but in the end, they both use the same thing (line 60). Again, a 0.8-second pause follows, after which Marie produces a tongue slam. Julie reacts at this point with a weak alignment (Pomerantz, 1984) in line 63, onto which Marie latches her next turn, thus soliciting an affiliative response to her story. She makes a joke (lines 64–65) about the fact that they, too, will be at the next Olympic Games (implying that they will be there with Didier Cuche), and at this moment, Victor and Julie laugh, affiliating with Marie's joke (lines 66–68). Afterward, Julie self-selects and proffers a concluding remark: *ouais c'est ça* "yeah that's it" (line 69). After a long pause, she self-selects again and proffers another concluding remark, assessing that she thinks that the tool must be good (line 71). Marie overlaps Julie's last TCU and aligns to her assessment (line 72). After a pause, she then self-selects and continues her telling about the kitchen tool: she has asked for more information about the components of this tool. In line 77, a longer pause occurs (1.2 seconds), and in line 78, Julie self-selects and shifts the conversational topic with a pivotal movement; i.e. she employs a left dislocation ("*Didier Cuche il a*" Didier Cuche he has), which marks a topical restart while remaining related to the ongoing topic through the adverb "*aussi*" (also). In fact, she asks if Didier Cuche also has problems with his knee and solicits a response after a micro-pause (line 80): *tu sais?* "you know?" (line 81). From line 82 onward, the conversation continues about Didier Cuche's knee condition and the health conditions of competitive athletes.

There are several noteworthy aspects about Julie's turn in lines 78–79. First, she self-selects at an appropriate interactional moment, i.e. after a story has ended and a long pause has taken place. Second, she uses an opposition marker at turn beginning (*mais* "but"), which prepares the field for upcoming talk that might be disjointed from the preceding talk. In fact, this is partially the case: Julie takes the conversation in a new direction while anchoring it to an already-introduced referent. Third, she accomplishes the shift through a left dislocation: this allows her to reintroduce an already-named referent and to promote it to the status of sentence topic and thereby to propose it as conversational topic for the upcoming talk. The turn in lines 78–79, then, pinpoints Julie's competence in shifting the topic using referential expressions and turn design; moreover, this turn also shows Julie's orientation toward the conversation progression and its structure, particularly through the precision timing of her self-selection.

5.4.3 Topic Shift Through Multiple Reference

The next example comes from Christine's database. In it, Christine accomplishes a topic shift by indirectly introducing two possible people who can correspond to the referent introduced in line 492 (*ta soeur* "your sister"). During the recording, the whole family is sitting at the table and is having dinner. It is one of the children, Cédric, that initiates an inquiry addressing Christine.

(19) Christine 21.09.2010 *ma soeur* "my sister"

```
492 Ced:  ta soeur elle habite où?
          your sister-DIR she-SUBJ lives where
          but where does your sister live?
```

```
493 (..)
494 Chr: MOI?
         me?
495 (..)
496 Ced: [TA SOEU:R.
          your sister
497 Rac: [ta soeur.
          your sister
498 (.)
499 Chr: AH MA SOEUR avec moi à la maison.
         oh my sister  with me   at home
         oh! my sister! she lives with me at home.
500 (..)
501 Chr: au weekend (.) +au moment à ((LOCALITE)) ((voix
         souriante))+
         at the weekend    at the moment in   ((place))        ((laughing
         voice))
         during the weekend, at the moment, she stays at ((place)) [her boy-
         friend's place]
502 (..)
((pendant 7.4sec les enfants crient—incompréhensible))
((for 7.4 seconds the children are screaming very loudly—incomprehensible))
503 Chr: tu as VU (0.1) déjà ma sœur.
         you have seen       already my sister
         you have already seen my sister.
504 (.)
505 Chr: Manon.
         Manon
506 (..)
507 Pas: oui::,
         yes
508 Chr: mais Leïla pas encore.
         but  Leïla  not yet
         but Leïla not yet
```

Cédric inquires about Christine's sister in line 492 asking where she lives. After a short pause, Christine initiates a repair on the reference (line 494), which is responded to in overlap by Cédric and his mother, Rachel (lines 496–497). In line 499, Christine initiates the third turn of this repair sequence with a change-of-state token (*ah* "oh") and repeats the repaired referent (*ma soeur* "my sister") continuing the turn with the response to Cédric's inquiry: *avec moi à la maison* "with me at home." After a short pause, Christine self-selects and expands her turn with a specification: she explains that, at the moment, her sister spends her weekends in another place—so to say that she lives in two places. For a long moment, then, the children are very loud, and the parents are busy keeping them calm. Once the children have calmed down, Christine self-selects and addresses Cédric again with a turn that states that he has already seen her sister (line 503). She then increments this turn by adding her sister's name (line 505). After a short pause, it is Pascal, the host father, who responds to this statement with a confirmation (line 507), which is, however, prolonged and which terminates with a continuing intonation, accomplishing a request for more information. Indeed, in line 508, Christine produces a turn stating that he has not yet seen her other sister, Leïla. Christine's topic shift is a double one and is accomplished over three turns at talk. Starting from the fact that Cédric has introduced the referent "your sister," Christine first changes the conversational direction in line 503 by establishing a new relationship between the introduced referent and her interlocutor. In fact, Cédric's question was merely about the place where Christine's sister lives. However, such news inquiries (Button & Casey, 1985) offer the possibility for expanding one's response, and this is exactly what Christine does in line 503. After her responses in lines 499 and 501, accomplishing the next relevant action after an inquiry, she expands her responses, shifting the topic in line 503 and she does so by addressing a new aspect of an already-introduced referent. Moreover, she is able to accomplish another topic shift with her turn in line 508, since she further disambiguates the referent that she talked about: in fact, she herewith states that she has not only one sister but two and that Cédric has seen only one of them, namely Manon.

5.5 Summary of Findings

These three examples illustrate how the au pairs manage conversational topic shifts and thus present a window onto this aspect of their L2 interactional competence.

The conception of topic shift I have worked with is intuitive and relies on common-sense interpretation, as reported in Sacks (1995: 566):

> A general feature for topical organisation in conversation is movement from topic to topic, not by a topic-close followed by a topic beginning, but by a stepwise move, which involves linking up whatever is being introduced to what has just been talked about, such that, as far as anybody knows, a new topic has not been started, though we're far from wherever we began.

The shifts I have analyzed happen stepwise in Sacks's sense: they link up what is being talked about, and they are located in adjacently placed turns. As I have shown, all three L2 speakers manage stepwise conversational topic shifts, independently of their L2 proficiency level. This is a central point for my analysis, since this allows me to pinpoint several features of L2 interactional competence.

First, the au pairs show that they are able to build a new relationship between the conversational topic so far and marginal or new aspects of the same topic. They accomplish this though some available contextual clues that they can manipulate and change. These linkages recall the features of displaced language, as defined by Auer (1984):

In displaced passages of interaction, the *origo* may be left on any of its dimension, or on all simultaneously. Whereas an element of a language system is either deictic or non-deictic, an utterance can be more or less *umfeld*-dependent.

> (p. 269, emphasis in the original)

Specifically, Oksana links the Swiss situation to the Polish one as far as the presence of ice rinks is concerned; Julie addresses the health condition of a known Swiss athlete after knowing what kitchen tools he uses; and Christine shifts the focus of attention from one of her sisters to the other. This means that when the au pairs address a new aspect of an ongoing conversational topic, they not only create the possibility for a new class of mentionables (see Maynard, 1980) but also displace the focus of attention on another point/place/referent in space and time (Auer, 1984). In so doing, however, they continuously show their interpretation of the just-happened talk while adding new material for the upcoming talk. This action requires not only L2 linguistic skills but also an incessant attention to the conversational flow, especially to its sequential structure. The au pairs are, then, able to start and accomplish a topic shift at the content level because they are already able to orient to the conversational structure of adjacency pairs and larger sequences.

Second, topic shifts are another means for L2 speakers to participate in a conversation and to collaboratively work on the conversational topic. With my data analyses, at the beginning of this chapter, I have demonstrated that au pairs are able almost from the beginning of their stay to introduce new conversational topics. In this section, I have shown that they are also able to shift ongoing topics by using different resources, including semantic relationships at the reference level as well as pivot-shifting. This, however, only happens in collaboration with their interlocutors, as the next part from Julie's ex. 18a illustrates.

(18a) Julie, 16.02.2010 *genou* "knee"

```
77  (1.2)
78  Jul: mais Didier Cuche il a: (0.5) ts. aussi des problèmes
         avec son
         but  Didier  Cuche he has           also    some problems
         with  his
79       ge↑nou?
         knee
         but (by the way) Didier Cuche also has some problems with his knee,
         hasn't he?
80  (0.2)
81  Jul: tu sais?
         you know
         do you know that?
82  Mar: boh.
         buh
```

108 Topic Introduction

```
83   (0.7)
84 Mar: je pense (.) ↑ouais . . .
     I   think       yeah . . .
```

The topic-shifting movement begins in line 78, but Julie shows her orientation toward the new conversational topic by explicitly soliciting a response from her interlocutor in line 81. With this example, I highlight the centrality of the collaborative nature of topic shift, especially the fact that L2 speakers can observably orient toward this collaboration, as Julie's participation has just shown.

Notes

1. The analysis of these three examples was already the object of König (2013). In the present study, the analyses have been refined and partly modified.
2. Carving is a particular way of skiing by cutting the snow with the ski edge to avoid losing speed.

References

Ariel, M. (1988). Referring and accessibility. *Journal of Linguistics*, 24(1), 65–87.
Auer, P. (1984). Referential problems in conversation. *Journal of Pragmatics*, (8), 627–548.
Bergmann, J. R. (1990). On the local sensitivity of conversation. In I. Marková & K. Foppa (Eds.), *The dynamics of dialogue* (pp. 201–226). New York: Harvester Wheatsheaf.
Berthoud, A.-C. (1996). *Paroles à propos. Approche énonciative et interactive du topic*. Paris: Ophrys.
Berthoud, A.-C., & Mondada, L. (1995). Traitement du topic, processus énonciatifs et séquences conversationnelles. *Cahiers de Linguistique Francaise*, 17, 205–228.
Bolden, G. B. (2006). Little words that matter: Discourse markers 'So' and 'Oh' and the doing of other-attentiveness in social interaction. *Journal of Communication*, 56(4), 661–688. http://doi.org/10.1111/j.1460-2466.2006.00314.x
Button, G. (1990). On varieties of closings. In G. Psathas (Ed.), *Interaction competence* (pp. 93–148). Washington, DC: University Press of America.
Button, G., & Casey, N. (1984). Generating topic: The use of topic initial elicitors. In J. M. Atkinson & J. Heritage (Eds.), *Structures of social action* (pp. 167–190). Cambridge: Cambridge University Press.
Button, G., & Casey, N. (1985). Topic nomination and topic pursuit. *Human Studies*, 8, 3–55.
Garcia, L. J., & Joanette, Y. (1997). Analysis of conversational topic shifts: A multiple case study. *Brain and Language*, 58, 92–114.
Grice, H. P. (1975). Logic and conversation. *Syntax and Semantics*, (3), 41–58.
Holt, E. (2010). The last laugh: Shared laughter and topic termination. *Journal of Pragmatics*, 42, 1513–1525.
Jefferson, G. (1987). On exposed and embedded correction in conversation. In G. Button & J. R. E. Lee (Eds.), *Talk and social organization* (pp. 86–100).

Clevedon, UK: Multilingual Matters. [Originally in *Studium Linquistik* (1983), vol. 14, 58–68.]

König, C. (2013). Topic management in French L2: A longitudinal conversation analytic approach (pp. 226–250). *EUROSLA Yearbook 13*. Amsterdam/Philadelphia: John Benjamins Publishing Company.

Maynard, D. W. (1980). Placement of topic changes in conversation. *Semiotica*, 263–290.

Morris-Adams, M. (2014). From Spanish paintings to murder: Topic transitions in casual conversations between native and non-native speakers of English. *Journal of Pragmatics, 62*, 151–165.

Pekarek Doehler, S. (2004). Une approche interactionniste de la grammaire: réflexions autour du codage grammatical de la référence et des topics chez l?apprenant avancé d?une L2. *AILE Acquisition et Interaction en Langue Etrangère, 21*, 123–166.

Pomerantz, A. (1984). Agreeing and disagreeing with assessments: Some features of preferred and dispreferred turn shapes. In J. M. Atkinson & J. Heritage (Eds.), *Structures of social action* (pp. 57–101). Cambridge: Cambridge University Press.

Prince, E. F. (1981). Toward a taxonomy of given-new information. In P. Cole (Ed.) *Radical pragmatics* (pp. 223–255). New York: Academic Press.

Reinhart, T. (1981). Pragmatics and linguistics: An analysis of sentence topic. *Philisophica, 27*(1), 53–94.

Sacks, H. (1995). *Lectures on conversation* (Vol. 1 & 2). Oxford: Basil Blackwell.

Schegloff, E. A. (2007). *Sequence organization in interaction* (Vol. 1). Cambridge: Cambridge University Press.

Selting, M. (1994). Emphatic speech style: With special focus on the prosodic signalling of heightened emotive involvement in conversation. *Journal of Pragmatics, 22*(Special Issue: Involvement in Language), 375–408.

Steinbach-Koehler, F., & Thorne, S. L. (2011). The social life of self-directed talk: A sequential phenomenon? In J. K. Hall, J. Hellermann, & S. Pekarek Doehler (Eds.), *L2 interactional competence and development* (pp. 66–92). Bristol, UK: Multilingual Matters.

6 Topic Closure

The preceding chapter has shown what L2 speakers do in conversation when they introduce a new conversational topic: how they coordinate this work with their interlocutor(s), what resources they employ, and where they choose to introduce a topic in an ongoing conversation. Similarly, this chapter presents the conversational work done by the au pairs Julie, Oksana, and Christine when they participate in the closure of a conversational topic. I will show how the L2 speakers participate in this collaboratively achieved endeavor. Having presented the literature review in Chapter 4, I proceed here directly to the data investigations and show three examples for each au pair. In total, I have collected 85 cases of topic closure. In this chapter, I follow the same pattern as in Chapter 5 and start with Julie's data (6.1). I then present Oksana's data (6.2) and finally Christine's data (6.3). The chapter closes with a summary of findings (6.4) that leads to the concluding chapters of this book.

6.1 Advanced L2 Level: Julie

In Julie's recordings from September 2009 to June 2010, I found 42 instances of topic closure. The following three examples are taken from Julie's corpus at two points in time. I present the linguistic and sequential analysis for each, which sets the ground for discussing what happens at the topical level.

6.1.1 Topic Closure at the Beginning of the Stay

The first example comes from Julie's second recording in October 2009. She had been in Switzerland for about five weeks at that time. At the moment of recording, the host family is having dinner and Julie is telling them something about her day with the children. Specifically, she is reporting on going to the bakery with the children and buying two cups of hot chocolate. The saleswoman then asked her if she should make the cocoa tepid. Julie did not know this word yet, so she first looked a bit surprised before understanding what the word meant.

Topic Closure 111

(19) Julie, 10.12.2009 *lauwarm* (German word)[1] "tepid"

```
01   Jul:  à: la b:oulangerie elle m'a- (0.3) euh: j'ai demandé deux
            at the    bakery     she  me-IND      uh   I've I asked   two
02         (0.4) euh cacaos?
             uh     cocoas
           at the bakery I've asked for two cups of cocoa
03   (0.6)
04   Jul:  et  puis ehm  (0.3) elle m'a  [demandé&
           and then uhm         she  me-IND asked
05   Jor:                                [DEUX cac[aos.
                                          two   cocoas
06   Jul:                                         &[ah je l- je les
                                                    fait
                                                   oh I  l-  I  them
                                                    make
07         <ti↑èdes>.
            tepid
           and then she (the saleswoman) has asked me if I wanted tepid cups of cocoa
08   (0.3)
09   Jul:  et moi j'ai- (0.3) <tièdes>? ((rit))=
           and me  I have      tepid    ((laughs))
           and I've (looked/said) tepid? ((laughs))
10   Mar:  =((rit))=
            ((laughs))
11   Jul:  je >ne savais< pas qu'est-ce que ça °veut dire°°.=
           I   didn't know NEG  what           this   means
           I didn't know what this means
12   Mar:  =ah ouais.=
            oh  yeah
13   Jul:  =↑oui lauwarm.
            yes  tepid (in German)
14   (0.3)
15   Jul:  c'est- ouais.=
           it's    yeah
16   Vic:  =↑mh=
            mh
17   Jul:  =c'est pas ↑chaud pas f[roid.=
           it's   NEG  warm   NEG  cold
           it's neither warm nor cold
18   Mar:                         [>ouais ouais<.
                                   yeah   yeah
19   Jul:  ((respiration forte))
           ((loud respiration))
20   +(6.1) ((Man saute et rit))+
            ((Man jumps and laughs))
21   Jor:  mais ma↑non c'est pas <drô:le> hein.
           but   Manon  it's  NEG  funny  INTERJ
           come on Manon this is not funny, is it?
22   (8.1) ((Man rit))+
            ((Man laughs))
23   Mar:  ou↑ais c'est bien pis  comme ça ↑nous l'après-midi
           on peu:t
           yeah   that's fine then like this   we   the afternoon
           we can
```

```
24            se donner rendez-vous en v↑ille.
              give us an appointment    in the city
              yeah it's alright like this, so in the afternoon we can meet in the city
25  (0.3)
26  Jul:  oui.
          yes
27  (0.3)
28  Mam:  toi    tu peux aller direct-
          you-DIR you-SUBJ can go directly
29        mais toi t'as beaucoup de ch↑oses à pr↑endre?
          but you-DIR you-SUBJ have a lot of things to take
30        pour aller à la gym ou-  ça va.
          for   go    to the gym or  it's fine
          but do you have many things to carry on yourself for going to the gym
          or is it fine like this?
31  (0.2)
32  Jul:  non: ça va.
          no   it's fine
```

The sequence develops as follows: from line 01 to line 10, Julie reports of her visit to the bakery with the children. There she bought two hot chocolates, and the saleswoman asked her if she wanted them tepid. This word was new to Julie, who asked the saleswoman what that meant. This is reported in line 09, where Julie repeats the question she has asked to the saleswoman, i.e. the item itself with a rising intonation (tepid?). She closes this turn with a laugh, which Marie aligns with and affiliates in line 10 with more laughter. Lines 09 and 10 constitute a closing implicative environment insofar as the interactants show aligning and affiliating turns at the end of a storytelling sequence.

Subsequently, in line 11, Julie self-selects and utters a summarizing conclusion to her preceding story, thus stating that she did not know what the word meant. Marie aligns with it in line 12, but with a minimal continuative response (*ah ouais* "oh yeah"). Julie aligns herself with Marie's turn in line 13 in that she confirms the comprehension by the host mother (*oui* "yes") and repeats the problematic item in her L1 (German: *lauwarm* "tepid"). After a short pause, Julie self-selects in line 15 and reopens the conversation, starting to deliver another possible explanation for the same lexical item (see the cutoff in *c'est-* "it's-"), but then she stops and realigns with Marie's previous display of understanding, producing the confirmation item *ouais* "yeah." Vic also aligns at this point in line 16 with Julie with a minimal alignment token, which also functions as a topicalizer and thus invites Julie to continue her story. In fact, in line 17, she ties back to her previous turn in line 15 by reproducing the same beginning: *c'est* "it's." And this time, she also continues with a full word explanation, which rephrases the term "tepid." Toward the end of Julie's turn, Marie in line 18 produces a double alignment token, characterized by a faster speech pace, which overlaps Julie's end of the turn. In line 19, Julie produces only a long inhale, and then the conversation is subsequently relaunched by the children, who are apparently playing nearby. From line 23, Marie continues the conversation; i.e. she recalls the organization plans they were discussing early on in the same conversation and reopens the topic of the activities that are planned for the next day (see Pochon-Berger & Pekarek Doehler, 2015 for the complete analysis of the story closings concerning this example).

6.1.2 Topic Closure in the Middle of the Stay

The next example also comes from Julie's second recording. This span of conversation temporally follows ex. 19. The family is still having dinner together, and Julie has just addressed the issue of the dance class that she did not attend the previous week (see ex. 11, Chapter 5). In relation to this, she has expressed the wish of still being able to dance after this pause. Marie, the host mother, explains to her that sometimes it is better to stop for a while in order to be able to completely follow the lessons again. The example shows the closure of this sequence.

(20) Julie, 10.12.2009 *c'est comme courir* "it's like running"

```
01 Mar:   mais des fois (.) c'est mieux d'arrêter une semaine pis après
          but  some times      it's better to stop  one   week   then afterward
02        tu reprends t'as  l'impression que  ça va  mieux.
          you restart you have the impression that it goes better
          you know, sometimes it's better to make a pause for a week and then
          when you restart you have the impression that everything runs smoother
03 Jul:   o:ui?
          yes
          really?
04        (.)
05 Mar:   c'est comme courir.
          it's  like   running
          it's like jogging
06        ((Jul et Mar rient))
          ((Jul and Mar laugh))
07 Jul:   je ne sais pas.
          I don't know.
08        (.)
09 Jul:   peut-↑être?
          maybe
10        (3.7)
11 Jul:   °je vais voir:°
          I'll see
12        (1.8)
13 Mar:   non (.) parce que (xx) °je n'ai rien à faire hein°
          no          because     I don't have anything to do INTERJ
          no, please, go ahead, I don't have anything to do, do I?
```

In this case, Julie is telling Marie that she has missed one dance lesson, so she is worried about not being able to follow the instructions in the next one. Marie answers that it will indeed be better, because a pause can sometimes be helpful (lines 01–02). In line 03, Julie produces a request for specification or confirmation of Marie's turn (see the final rising intonation). In line 05, Marie responds with a generalizing explication, *c'est comme courir* "it's like running," which projects the end of the sequence; i.e. it marks the beginning of a closing implicative environment (cf. Drew & Holt (1995) on idiomatic expressions and topic termination). In fact, this turn is followed by joint laughter of both (Julie and Marie), line 06. As shown in the literature review, laughter, and especially joint laughter, is seen to be relevant in closing implicative environments (Holt, 2010). However, after a short pause, Julie self-selects and produces a disaligning turn in line 7, *je ne sais pas* "I don't know," which Marie does not respond to. I treat Julie's turn as disaligning because in line 03 she has already shown her skepticism about Marie's interpretation of the whole situation as advantageous for her (i.e. for Julie). After a micropause, Julie downgrades her disalignment, uttering *peut-être* "maybe" in line 09 with a final rising intonation and attenuates therein her previous disaligning turn. In this case too, Marie does not react, and a remarkably long pause follows Julie's turn (line 10). In line 11, Julie self-selects again and proposes a future-oriented statement, which she utters with a lower voice volume, *je vais voir* "I'll see." In so doing, she overtly projects the end of the sequence and of the topic at hand. In fact, after another, longer pause, Marie's turn in line 13 is directed to the attention of her children.

This example shows a more complex closing sequence than the previous one does. Here Julie manages her disalignment starting immediately in line 02 with her inquiring turn, *oui?* "yes?" And that possibly questions Marie's knowledge or epistemic stance about the dance lessons. Julie extends the closing sequence after a first possible closure in line 05 and in line 06, when she and Marie laugh together. Julie proposes several summarizing and generalizing statements (lines 07, 09, and 11) that are typical of closing sequences. Moreover, Julie also manages the absence of recipient reaction by her interlocutor by downgrading her disaligning statements, and the conversation flows toward a topic change (Maynard, 1980). The downgrading takes place, in my opinion, because Julie softens her first utterance, "I don't know," after having shown some skepticism about Marie's perception of the whole situation as advantageous for Julie. However, by adding "I'll see" in line 11, she opens up to the possibility that Marie is right, and in so doing, Julie changes the trajectory of her stance in a more positive way.

6.1.3 Topic Closure at the End of the Stay

I now turn to the last example for Julie. At the moment of recording, Julie had been staying in Switzerland for seven months. During the recording, she is eating with Marie and is telling Marie something about a girl she knew from Belgium who also spent some time in Switzerland.

(21) Julie, 23.03.2010 *elle est très sympa* "she is very nice"

```
01  Jul: pis on a parlé   toujours de suisse j'ai dit .h ah bientôt
         then we have talked always    about Switzerland I've said oh  soon
02       je veux aller en suisse >et pis elle me dit<  ouais
         I  want to go   to Switzerland and then she  me told    yeah
03       c'est bien:: c'est che:r c'est ((rit))
         it's  good   it's expansive it's  ((laughs))
         and we have also always talked about Switzerland. I've said that I
         want to go there as soon as possible (alternatively: that I will soon go
         there) and then she told me that (Switzerland) is good, expansive and
         ((laughter))
04  Mar: mh:
05       (. . .)
06  Jul: °elle >avait< parlé°.
         she    had     spoken
         she had told me
07       (4.8)
08  Jul: °elle est très sympa.°
         she  is  very nice
09       (1.0)
10  Mar: ah
11       (4.4)
12  Jul: hh. alors (.) >je sais< pas.
             well        I don't know
         in the end, I don't know
13  Mar: mh=(nous) à pâques >je sais< pas ce qu'on va faire,
         mh  we    for Easter  I know   NEG what  we'll do
         we neither, I don't know what we are going to do for Easter
```

Marie and Julie are planning the period of Easter, and Julie has started saying that she may go to visit a friend of hers. Subsequently, she tells Marie something about this friend of hers, and toward the end of her telling, Julie explains what this girl once told her about Switzerland. Parallel to the preceding example, Julie comes to the climax of her story, signaled by her prosody from lines 1 to 3, and especially by her laughter in line 03, inviting laughter from her interlocutor. Instead, in line 04, Marie produces only a minimal response token, which is in itself aligning but disaffiliating (see Selting, 1994 on emphatic speech style). Julie responds to this after a pause of almost one second by an increment of her telling: in line 06 Julie produces a new turn, which works by summarizing her previous words, *elle avait parlé* "she had spoken" (meaning maybe "she had told me"). Julie's voice volume is lower in this turn, a feature of closing implicative environments. Moreover, Julie herein orients toward the minimal and disaffiliating response from Marie in line 04.

116   *Topic Closure*

This turn offers Marie another possibility for reacting, but it does not happen for a remarkably long time (line 07). In line 08, Julie produces another final statement, also implicating a closure, *elle est très sympa* "she is very nice." A closer look at Julie's prosody reveals that her voice is lower and somehow softened. After a 1.0-second pause, Marie reacts to this turn again with a minimal response, line 10. After a longer pause, Julie produces a resuming turn in line 12, marked by the resuming connector *alors* "so" and the final statement *je sais pas* "I don't know." It is impossible to clearly state which previous conversational topic Julie is addressing with this final statement: this could be related to her plans for the Easter period, or it could be a generalizing final statement about her friend. Only after this turn does Marie react to Julie with a topical reorientation of the talk, projecting an explanation about her state of affairs for the Easter period.

So far, I have shown what Julie does in closing implicative environments:

- She produces generalizing and summarizing statements.
  (cf. Button, 1990; Holt, 2010)
- Her generalizing and summarizing statements are sometimes produced in an incremental way, thus soliciting recipient reaction. In so doing, she shows her orientation toward a preference for alignment and affiliation at this point in conversation.
  (cf. Pochon-Berger & Pekarek Doehler, 2015; Selting, 1994)
- Linguistically seen, she uses standard French expressions such as "I don't know" and "I'll see."
  (cf. Jeon, 2003; Warga, 2005)
- Her prosody is adapted to the closing implicative environments: softened voice, lower speech speed, final falling intonations.
  (cf. Holt, 2010)

These summarizing observations raise an earlier central question: what about changes over time? As compared to the examples of topic introduction in Chapter 5, no real changes are seen to have taken place. I have considered two main points for finding an answer to this question. First, Julie's advanced L2 level could make it difficult to find any relevant differences in her way of collaborating in closing sequences (this point is in line with what Jeon [2003] finds out in academic advising sessions). Closing sequences are places in which generalizing or summarizing statements and formulaic expressions are typically found (Drew & Holt, 1995; Holt & Drew, 2005). Since Julie's L2 level is already so advanced, I could not find any differences in her closing contributions at the beginning or at the end of her stay.

A second question that arose: is such a sojourn too short a span of time to consider for tracing change? Or, to rephrase, should I not consider the longitudinal aspect for this microcosm but rather strive for a cross-sectional comparison? Finally, a third, methodological question can be addressed: what is the difference between tracing "actions" and their accomplishment in contrast to tracing linguistic elements and their diversification in interactional uses over time? I discuss these questions in Chapter 7.

For now, it suffices to clarify that my doubts about the differences I have documented in the ways the au pairs introduce and close a conversational topic were change driven. I started my analyses with the impression that changes happen longitudinally for topic introduction, and I then assumed that the same thing would happen with topic closure. Instead, topic closure was characterized by stability over time. But before discussing this point any further, I continue with the presentation of the longitudinal data I have collected from Oksana.

6.2 Intermediate L2 Level: Oksana

I have collected a total of 19 cases of topic closure for Oksana's recordings, which took place between September 2010 and May 2011. As with Julie's data, I present a sequential analysis that also includes the linguistic and prosodic features of the closing turns-at-talk. In general, Oksana's data show her active participation in the construction of topic closures. However, there are two main differences in her data compared to Julie's data:

1. Oksana seems only to align with her interlocutor's closing initiations, whereas Julie initiates closing herself.
2. Oksana's resources differ from those at Julie's disposal probably because of their different French L2 level.

The following analyses show these two points more in detail and are also summarized at the end of this subsection.

6.2.1 Topic Closure at the Beginning of the Stay

The first example is taken from Oksana's first recording. She is having dinner with the host father, Pierre, and the younger child, Nadège. Oksana and Pierre have just discussed buying a new mixer for the kitchen, and the example begins with Pierre stating that he will search for it the next day.

(22) Oksana, 28.09.2010 *quoi nous avons faire* "what we did"

```
01 Oks: c'est:- parce que c'est (.) c'est mixer le nom de cette chose?
        it's-   because   it's        it's  mixer the name of this   thing
     because is it mixer the name of this thing?
```

Topic Closure

```
02   (..)
03   Pie:  oui s- c'est- s::: c'est un mixer normal, ↑toi ce que tu
           yes  i-   it's-  i      it's  a normal mixer    you-DIR what you-SUBJ
04         penses c'est le robot.
           think about it's the food processor
           yes a normal mixer. what you are thinking about is the food processor.
05   Oks:  o- oui parce que s- c'est bon pour gâteau?
           y- yes because   i- it's  good for  cake
           yes, because it's good for baking a cake
06   (..)
07   Oks:  [(x)-
08   Pie:  [mh=oui.=
            mh yes
09   Oks:  =↑ah ↑OK.
            oh  OK
10   (..)
11   Pie:  tu penses c'est nécessaire u:n plus grand?
           you think  it's   necessary    a  bigger one
           do you think that a bigger one is necessary?
12   (...)
13   Oks:  mh PAS POUR ÇA: mais pour gâteau: normalement avec les
           mh not for   this but   for  cake   usually       with the-pl.
14         yeux:=et avec les far↑ine peut-être ↑mais pour ça?
           *eyes  and with the-pl. flour-sg.  maybe   but for this
           no not for doing this, but usually when you bake a cake with eggs and
           flour maybe it helps but
           not for this
15   (..)
16   Pie:  je le regarde (lui) qu'est-ce qu'il y a demain.
           I look at it-M.sg. (it-M.sg.)  what is there        tomorrow
           I will see tomorrow what I find
17   (1.3)
18   Oks:  ehm OK ↑eh:m,
           uhm OK uhm
19   (..)
20   Oks:  e:h quoi nou::s avons faire aujourd'hui?
           uh  what    we  have-3ps.pl.PRES. do-INF. today
           what have we done today?
21   (.)
22   Pie:  voilà oui.
           go ahead yes
23   (...)
24   Oks:  nous allons aller à côté de lac=oui?
           we   go-3p.pl.PRES. go-INF to the lakeside yes
           we went to the lakeside, didn't we?
25   (...)
26   Oks:  [oui?]
            yes?
27   Pie:  [tu] as été faire une promenade?
            you have been do       a    walk
            did you go for a walk?
28   (...)
29   Nad:  non.
            no
```

```
30   (.)
31   Oks: non=non nous allo::ns eh::  jouer avec le  ballon-
          no  no   we go-3ps.pl.PRES uh   play-INF with the ball-
32        eh dans le sable=parce que il y a u- une liè,
          uh in   the sand  because      there is  a-  a-sg.F. *place
          no, we went playing with the ball in the sand because there is a place
          (non-standard pronunciation)
```

From lines 01 to 04, Pierre and Oksana are cooperatively solving a language-related issue; i.e. they are identifying the same object that they should buy soon, and Pierre clarifies in lines 03–04 that what Oksana is thinking about is a big food processor, when they might only need a normal mixer. Oksana then asks if the processor would be good for preparing cakes, and Pierre confirms it in line 08. Oksana's turn in line 09 acknowledges Pierre's answer and is also closing implicative by means of the final falling intonation and the absence of topicalizers. Pierre self-selects afterward, readdressing the topic at hand and asking Oksana if she thinks that they need a bigger machine (line 11). Oksana answers in lines 12–13, explaining that it is not necessary for their everyday use, so Pierre states that he will look for a mixer the next day (line 16). A long pause follows, after which Oksana self-selects in line 18. She produces a first hesitation marker, then an acknowledgment token (OK), and then another, prolonged hesitation marker. This last item ends with a continuative intonation; i.e. Oksana prepares the field for more to come and requests the floor for herself. There is subsequently a short pause, in which, however, no one else takes the floor, and Oksana continues in line 05. After another hesitation marker (*e:h*), she introduces a new conversational topic, namely her daily activities with the child: what did we do today? (line 20). It is also possible that Oksana addresses this turn to Nadège, the child. However, it is Pierre who acknowledges Oksana's turn in line 22, saying "yes, there you go," showing also his orientation toward the newsworthiness of Oksana's upcoming talk.

This introduction is characterized by a final rising intonation, which makes it resemble a question. However, Oksana does not inquire about Pierre's day; instead, she is the one who describes something about her day. The final rising intonation functions rather as a request for permission: do you want to hear what we did today? After a micro-pause, Pierre responds positively to the question and aligns to this new topic line with the topicalizing turn *voilà oui* "go ahead yes." The conversation continues with Oksana telling him what she did during the day with Nadège, namely that they went to play at the lakeside.

This example shows that Oksana's participation in the closing sequence is minimal: in line 09, she produces an acknowledging turn after an explanation that she received from Pierre. The final falling intonation in her turn initiates a closing implicative environment.

However, as often happens in closing sequences (cf. Sacks & Schegloff, 1973), Pierre reopens the sequence and the topic at hand (Button & Casey, 1988/1989; Bolden, 2008), delaying the topic closure. In line 18 too, Oksana minimally acknowledges Pierre's final statement, which initiates the closing, and through her repeated hesitation markers, she at the same time claims the floor for herself. In so doing, she shows her orientation toward the preceding sequence and topic as being closed.

6.2.2 Topic Closure in the Middle of the Stay

The next example is from Oksana's fifth recording. At that moment, she had spent almost four months in Switzerland. In this example, she is planning to travel home for the Christmas holidays. She and Pierre are discussing the possibility of taking Oksana to the train station.

(23) Oksana, 13.12.2010 *ce sera lundi* "it will be on Monday"

```
01  Oks: mais ce sera:: (.)  [euh lundi.
         but   it willbe      uh Monday
         but it will be on Monday.
02  Pie:                     [(pa) (x) .
                              (pa) (x)
03  (...)
04  Pie: <lundi>,
         Monday
05  (1.2)
06  Pie: anna elle a l'école le lundi   à::: sept heures et demi,
         anna she  has the school the Monday at   half past seven
         anna goes to school on Monday at half past seven
07  (1.6)
08  Pie: °ouais:: j'arrive à huit heures à:: fribourg,°
         yeah I arrive at eight o'clock in Fribourg
         yeah I arrive at eight o'clock in fribourg
09  (2.5)
10  Pie: ↑non: je crois que c'est >>bon<<.
         no   I  think that it's      good
         no, I think it works
11  (..)
12  Oks: ↑non c'est bon.
         no   it's  good
         no, it works
13  (.)
14  Oks: c'est bon.
         it's  good
         it works
15  (..)
16  Pie: on regardera encore si jamais les horaires.
         we will look again    if never  the timetables
         if necessary, we can take another look at the timetables
17  (.)
```

```
18   Pie:  si jamais on peut-  °°peut voir°°.
            if    never   we can     can  see
            if necessary, we can see (i.e. we can organize ourselves otherwise)
19   (1.8)
20   Pie:  <et autrement autrement> oui comme >je t'ai dit< la clé
            and otherwise otherwise   yes  as    I you-DIR have told the key
21         tu l'as vue aujourd'hui?
            you-SUBJ it have seen today
            and otherwise, as I told you, have you seen the key?
```

In line 01, Oksana concludes her explanation stating that her journey will be on a Monday. Her last TCU is overlapped by Pierre's turn in line 02, but his words are not clearly audible. Oksana's turn suggests (at least) that this information can possibly be problematic for some reasons. She starts her turn with a contrastive conjunction (*mais* "but"); the VP is prolonged on the final vocal (*ce sera::* "it will be::"); and this is followed by a micro-pause and a hesitation marker. This turn architecture sustains Oksana's stance about a possible problem in relation to her leaving on a Monday morning, since she has knowledge of the activities that normally take place on that day. After a long pause (line 03), Pierre reacts to Oksana's statement. He first repeats the day at slower speed and with a continuative intonation, thus claiming the floor again for himself. A longer pause follows, and then Pierre continues with the first information about the beginning of school of the older daughter. In this case too, he concludes the turn with a continuative intonation, thus self-selecting for the next possible slot. In line 07, another long pause takes place, after which Pierre again claims the floor for himself. In line 08, he delivers a turn with a lower volume. This is also observable in the beginning affirmative token *ouais::* "yeah." For the third time in a row, he concludes his turn with a continuative intonation, thus again projecting more to come. Another long pause takes place (this time even longer than the preceding two), and Pierre self-selects again in line 10, delivering his final statement. He starts with a higher voice pitch, thus marking a prosodic contrast with the previous turn. The first item is a negative particle (*non* "no"), which marks the end of Pierre's previous contributions. In fact, he had structured his previous turn in a chronological order and a list of three following elements: "on Monday + Anna goes to school at half past seven + I arrive at eight o'clock." Structuring his contributions like a list, he has claimed and obtained the floor for himself for a longer time, thus putting on hold the normal machinery of turn-taking. Oksana has aligned to this, since she has not verbally taken the floor until Pierre had finished with the list. It is only afterward that she self-selects in line 12 and aligns to Pierre's final statement by recycling his prosodic and syntactical pattern *non c'est bon* "no it's good." This alignment is already closing implicative in itself, since it displays an agreement between the interlocutors. After a micro-pause, however, Oksana self-selects again in line 14 and repeats her agreement in a shorter form: *c'est bon* "it's good." This turn is also closing implicative, since it again ratifies Oksana's agreement with her interlocutor's standpoint.

122 *Topic Closure*

However, after a short pause, Pierre self-selects and therein postpones the closure. With his turns in lines 16 and 18, he tries to reopen the previous topic of the time of Oksana's journey and suggests that they can have another look at the timetable if necessary. His turn in line 18 ends not only with a lower voice volume but also with a final falling intonation. The following pause is long, and there are no audible reactions to Pierre's last turn from Oksana. He then self-selects and clearly orients toward the preceding sequence and topic as being closed: he begins his turn in line 19 with an additive particle, *et* "and," followed by a repetition of the word *autrement* "otherwise." Moreover, he utters this turn beginning with a slower speech speed, in order to secure Oksana's attention. By means of a news inquiry (Button & Casey, 1985), he introduces a new matter concerning the house key. Thus, he overtly shows his orientation toward the upcoming talk as being disconnected from what preceded.

This example shows a rather prolonged closing sequence: there are four closing implicative turns, the first two by Oksana and the other two by Pierre. In a similar way, Pierre does not verbally react to Oksana's turns in lines 12 and 14, and Oksana does not verbally react to Pierre's turns in lines 16 and 18. Through these actions, the closing sequence is prolonged after Oksana shows her agreement in lines 12 and 14 toward Pierre's considerations (lines 4 to 10). The closure is marked rather by Pierre's turn in line 20 with his introduction of a new topic through a marked and disconnecting turn. To sum up, Oksana's participation in the closing sequence is longer in this example than it was in the previous one, although no great differences can be seen in the linguistic and prosodic means that she employs in her turns.

6.2.3 Topic Closure at the End of the Stay

The last example for Oksana comes from her last recording, thus almost nine months after her arrival in Switzerland. She is talking with Pierre about fruits coming from other nations, and they address the aspect of health safety when eating some exotic fruits.

(24) Oksana, 31.05.2016 *je pense c'est pas mi-* "I think it's not mi-"

```
01   Pie:  <ou:ai:s> (...) >je sais< que- au brésil ça fait euh- ils
           yeah              I know    that in brasil this makes uh they
02         disent toujours c'est pas très bon mais (.) mais ça:
           (.) +ah
           say    always    that's NEG very  good but      but this
           oh
03         >ça ça< vient des états-unis? ((high pitched voice))+
           this this comes  from the USA
           I know in brasil it is said to be not so good, but this one comes from the US
04   (...)
05   Oks:  °mhm.°
06   (1.6)
```

```
07   Pie:   [(bon)-
             well
08   Oks:   [↑et je pense c'est pas mi- c'est pa::s=
             and I   think  it's  NEG mi-  it's  NEG
             and I think that it's not better (mi- is the beginning part of "mieux"=better)
             it's not
09   Pie:   =non: [c'est rien marqué.
             no     it's  nothing marked
             no, it's not even labeled
10   Oks:          [le- plus- plus pire que: (°collaboratif°)
                    the   more   more  bad   that   (collaborative)
                    the worst that (in collaboration?)
11   Pie:   ou:ais (.) n↑on >y a< <aucune eu:h (..) notice euh->
             yeah        no    there's not any   uh       note   uh
             there's no note at all
12   Nad:   ((chante en arrière-plan))
             ((sings in the background))
13   (2.1)
14   Pie:   >non non< c'est bon.
             no   no    it's  good
15   (1.5)
16   Oks:   °d'accord.°
             alright
17   (..)
18   Pie:   ouais (.) super.
             yeah       great
19   Oks:   .h alors à jeudi on va: à:: aquaparc?
             well at thursday we go  to  water park
             so, do we go to the water park on Thursday?
```

From lines 01 to 03, Pierre delivers an explanation about exotic fruits and what is generally labeled as good or dangerous. He concludes his turn with a high-pitched TCU. Oksana minimally responds to this turn after a long pause with a lowered voice acknowledgment token (*mhm*). Another, longer pause takes place, and then Pierre self-selects, but this is overlapped by Oksana's turn in line 08. She starts with a high pitch on the first turn item, takes the floor, and delivers an assessment about the fruit. Her turn is characterized by a cutoff (*c'est pas mi-* "it's not mi-"), followed by an incomplete sentence (*c'est pas* "it's not"). The last item (*pas*) is also prolonged. The cutoff and the vocal prolongation suggest some troubles in the turn delivery. Pierre self-selects, and in a latched turn, he takes up Oksana's stance without providing any lexical help. On the contrary, he seems to align with Oksana's stance by stating that there are no marks of any kind on the fruit. Meanwhile, Oksana self-selects again and overlaps Pierre's turn: she seems to further her previous turn, but also in this case (line 10), she shows some lexical troubles (see the several cutoffs, the repetition of *plus* "more," and the final word produced with a lower voice volume (°*collaboratif*° "in collaboration"). In line 11, Pierre first aligns to Oksana's stance with a weak affirmative token (*ouais* "yeah") and then continues with a reformulation of his previous turn *non y a aucune notice* "no there is no note." Oksana does not react immediately to this turn: in line 12, Nadège sings something in the background, and then a longer pause follows in line 13. In line 14, Pierre self-selects and produces the first closing implicative turn: *non non c'est bon* "no no it's good." Oksana's reaction is nevertheless delayed, after a 1.5 second pause: she aligns to Pierre's turn in line 16 with a low volume *d'accord* "alright." After a short pause, Pierre self-selects and again utters two aligning and closing implicative items: *ouais super* "yeah great." Thus, the closing sequence is accomplished. This is observable in Oksana's next turn, with which she introduces a new conversational topic and thus orients toward the preceding one as being closed.

To conclude, Oksana's participation in topic closure is active from the beginning. She shows an appropriate use of agreeing tokens, such as "*OK*" and "*d'accord*," which she employs in closing implicative environments. Sometimes, longer pauses are seen in the transcripts; however, the interactants are having dinner, and this can be a possible cause for some delays in the response-giving turns. The second example shows a longer closing sequence, characterized not only by long inter-turn pauses but also by a different turn-taking mechanism. Oksana seems to appropriately contribute to the closure and continuously shows her orientation toward the topical and the structural levels of the ongoing conversation. The main differences when compared to Julie's participation in topic closure reside in the fact that Oksana does not initiate closing herself but rather collaborates in the closing sequence once it has been initiated by her interlocutor. Moreover, the linguistic resources that she employs are fewer and not as diversified as those used by Julie.

In the next section, three examples for the au pair Christine are discussed. This au pair has the lowest French L2 level in my database. The data contain rather short closing sequences, but on the other hand, these excerpts show a constant change in Christine's way of participating into closing and thus allow for tracing her learning trajectory in this specific practice.

6.3 Beginner L2 Level: Christine

In Christine's data, 24 cases of topic closure were identified. The examples come from recordings at different moments in time, between September 2010 and February 2011. The first is from Christine's first recording when she had been in Switzerland for one week. A particular aspect regarding Christine's recordings is that the whole family is always present during the recordings. However, not all the members are at the table all the time, and they are also not always engaging in a conversation with Christine. It is nevertheless a remarkable feature of Christine's family situation. Christine was consistent with the recordings, and they were always done during the evening meal time.

6.3.1 Topic Closure at the Beginning of the Stay

The participants in the following example are Christine, Pascal (the host father), Rachel (the host mother), Cédric (the older son), and Daniel (the younger son). The host parents are inquiring about Christine's language teacher at school, and the au pair explains to them that her language teacher is pregnant.

(25) Christine 21.09.2010 *sept huit* "seven eight"

```
01  Pas: pis Christine elle est gentille ta maîtresse?
         then  Christine  she  is  nice       your teacher
         well Christine is your teacher nice?
02  (...)
03  Pas: à- (h)au cours [(x) ((rit))
         a-     at the class  (x) ((laughs))
         in your language class? ((laughter))
04  Chr:                 [à l'école?
                          at school?
05  Dan: [((bruits))
          ((noises))
06  Chr: [((rit)) oui:
          ((laughter)) yes
07  (.)
08  Dan: ((bruits pendant 2.3sec))
         ((noises for 2.3seconds))
09  Pas: [hein?
          INTERJ
          is she?
10  Chr: [elle a u:n- comment on dit.
          she  has a-sg.M.  how does one say
          she has a, how do you say it?
11  Dan: [((bruits))
          ((noises))
12  (.)
13  Chr: avec une bébé dans la ven[tre.
         with a-sg.F. baby in the-F-SG tummy
         she has a baby in her tummy
14  Pas:                          [↑enceinte.
                                   pregnant
15  (.)
16  Chr: oui elle est enceinte.
         yes  she  is  pregnant
17  Pas: ah::: d'accord.
         oh    alright
18  (..)
19  Pas: [(ah super.)
          oh great
20  Rac: [combien de mois?
          how many months
          in which month is she pregnant?
21  (...?)
```

```
22  Ce?: ((bruits))
         ((noises))
23  Chr: quoi?
         what?
24  Rac: en combientième mois?
         in   what       month
         in which month is she pregnant?
25  (..)
26  Chr: je ne sais pas.
         I don't know
27  (.)
28  Ce?: (xxx) [PARCE QUE
                because
29  Chr: mais je crois peut-être (...) sept? huit? ((rit))
         but  I believe maybe           seven eight ((laughs))
         but well maybe she is in the seventh or eighth month ((laughter))
30  (.)
31  Ced: elle (ha[bite où    ta  sœur?
         she       lives where your sister
         where does your sister live?
32  Pas:          [ah.
                   oh
33  Chr: mhm.
34  ((tous rient pendant 1.3sec))
    ((everyone laughs for 1.3sec))
35  Ced: ta sœur elle habite où?
         your sister she lives where
         where does your sister live?
```

In line 01, Pascal asks Christine whether the teacher is nice, and Christine answers positively. In line 10, then, Christine expands the topic at hand, saying that her teacher is pregnant. This information is delivered with some problems; see Christine's turns in lines 10 and 13, in which she utters the metalinguistic question "how do we say it?" and then explains what she is trying to say—"she has a baby in her tummy." When the repair is accomplished, in line 16, Pascal produces two generalizing statements, in lines 17 and 19, with which a possible closure is projected (cf. Drew & Holt, 1995 on the use of proverbs). However, Rachel reopens the topic at hand by asking Christine how far along the pregnancy is. Here too, Christine shows some difficulty in delivering the answer; see her repair initiation in line 23. Once she has answered Rachel's question in line 29, Pascal reacts to this in a delayed and minimal way; see line 32. Christine herself also responds in a minimal way to Pascal's turn, in line 33. With these two turns, the ongoing topic is closed.

Between Christine's turn in line 33 and Pascal's minimal response in line 32, Cédric asks Christine a question about where her sister lives. However, neither Christine nor the other family members orient toward his question. Pascal's reaction overlaps Cédric's question, and afterward, Christine aligns to Pascal's final and minimal reaction with a minimal reaction token in line 33. This leads to general laughter from the whole family in line 34. Afterward, Cédric again asks Christine the same question about her sister, and the conversation continues about that matter, so that the previous sequence and topic have been closed.

6.3.2 Topic Closure in the Middle of the Stay

The next example is from Christine's fourth recording, at which point she had been staying in Switzerland for three months. As usual, she is having dinner with her host family. Ex. 26 was recorded after Christine has explained to her host parents that on one of the following days, a friend of hers will come to visit to spend some time with her. The example contains the end of Christine's explanation, particularly the moment in which she reveals her friend's name.

(26) Christine, 02.12.2010 *sans—e* "without—e"

```
01  Chr: elle s'appelle aussi sandrine come ma ↑sœur.
          she  is named    also   sandrine  like my sister
          her name is sandrine, like my sister
02  (..)
03  Pas: ah: d'accord ou↑ais.
          oh  alright   yeah
04  (..)
05  Chr: mais sans +e ((lettre))+ en fin.
          but without e  ((letter))  in the end
          but without the final -e ((letter))
06  (6.9) ((bruit de service))
          ((noise of plates))
07  Rac: ↑bon (...) qui c'est qui veut encore une ↑crêpe?
          well         who is it who  wants again  a   crêpe
          well, who wants another crêpe?
08  (.)
09  Pas: oui: oui:
          yes  yes
10  Chr: oui volontiers.
          yes, gladly
11  (...)
12  Mam: tu les préfères à quoi les crêpes °Christine.°
          you the-pl.F.DIR. prefer what kind the crêpes Christine
          what kind of crêpes do you prefer, Christine?
```

In line 01, Christine is telling her host parents that her friend has the same name as her sister, Sandrine. After a short pause (line 02), Pascal reacts to Christine's turn in line 03 with a change-of-stake token (Heritage, 1984), an acknowledgment token (*d'accord* "alright"), and a final affirmative token (*ouais* "yeah"). After another short pause (line 04), Christine self-selects in line 05 and increments her previous turn, delivering an explanation specifically on the name of her friend: *mais sans -e en fin* "but without an -e at the end." Verbally, no one responds to Christine's turn, and a long pause follows, during which only some noises from the table are heard. In line 07, Rachel self-selects and initiates a turn with *bon* "well," which functions as a resuming and restarting device (Local, 2004). A closer look at the prosody of this item suggests that she uses a higher pitch at the beginning of the word, clearly marking a new onset and projecting more to come. After a longer intra-turn pause, she asks her interlocutors if they want some more crêpes. In the subsequent turns, Pascal and Christine respond to Rachel's question, and Rachel asks Christine another question (line 12). The final turns of this example clearly show the interactants' orientation toward the sequence and the topic at hand until line 05. Christine's turn in line 01 delivers an explanation, which is aligned to by Pascal. His turn in line 03 is already closing implicative, since he does not topicalize any elements in Christine's previous turn. However, she self-selects afterward and therefore postpones the actual sequence and topic closure. In this example, the closure is observable in lines 01 through 04, where the closure of an explanation is collaboratively achieved by Pascal and Christine. Then, in line 05, Christine reopens the topic at hand with a post-next-turn increment, which, however, does not receive any audible reactions from her interlocutors. It is, however, possible that the interactants reacted in some nonverbal ways to Christine's final statement in line 05, but none of the video data support this speculation. The closure is observable in the turn uttered by Rachel in line 07: therein she begins with a disjunction marker (*bon* "well"), which indicates a cut from the preceding sequence and topic. The next relevant activity is then overtly addressed by Rachel, who asks who wants another crêpe.

6.3.3 Topic Closure at the End of the Stay

The last example from Christine's data set comes from her last recording, i.e. almost six months after her arrival in Switzerland. The family is having dinner together. In the example, Christine is telling Rachel, the host mother, what she did during the last weekend, because she was in a place near a hotel where the host family also spent a couple of days on holiday.

(27) Christine, 22.02.2011 *c'était rigolo* "it was funny"

```
01   Pas:  elle était sympa la piscine là-bas.=
           she²  was   nice  the swimming pool down there
           the swimming pool there was nice
02   Rac:  ouais mais on avait déjà été aussi: seulement à la piscine
           yeah  but   we had already been also  only        at the swimming
           yeah, but we had already been there only at the swimming pool.
03   Pas:  ouais.
           yeah
04   Rac:  en dormant pas:
           without sleeping
           without staying overnight
```

```
05  Ced:   (XXXXX)
06  (. . .)
07  Ced:   m:::=
08  Pas:   m↑hm.
09  Chr:   ↑mais en soir on a fait    euhm toujours quelque chose
           but  in  evening we have done uhm  always   some    thing
10         avec les autres familles?
           with  the  other  families
           but we usually always did something with other families in the evening
11  (.)
12  Chr:   c'est presque euhm (..) (xx) presque
           it's  almost   uhm              almost
13         là-bas [((rit))
           down there ((laughs))
           it's almost there ((laughter))
14  Rac:          [ah ouais.
                   oh yeah
15  Chr:   ou(h)ais(h).
           ye(h)ah(h)
           yeah ((laughing))
16  Rac:   c'est vrai.
           it's  true
17  Chr:   oui: c'était rigolo(h).
           yes  it was  funny(h)
           yes, it was funny ((laughing))
18  +(3.0)((enfant chantonne en arrière-fond))+
           ((a child is singing in the background))
19  Pas:   ah pis les vacances scolaires c'était: la semaine passée.
           oh then the  school   holidays   it was   last   week
           and then the school holidays were last week.
20  Chr:   oui de berne.
           yes of bern
           yes, those of bern[3]
```

From lines 01 to 08, Pascal and Rachel are collaboratively revealing that they had also been where Christine was the weekend before. In lines 09–10, Christine talks about the evenings there, where they all did something with the other families. In lines 12–13, Christine has spatially identified the place of her holiday, where she spent some time with her family, and starts laughing. Overlapping her laughter, Rachel aligns to this with an acknowledgment token in line 14: *ah ouais* "oh yeah," which is repeated by Christine in line 15 with a laughing voice. Rachel then utters a final statement: *c'est vrai* "it's true," in line 16, to which Christine ties up her aligned turn in line 17. After an initial confirmative item (*oui* "yes"), she recycles the syntactic pattern used by Rachel and produces *c'était rigolo* "it was funny." The recycled pattern differs from the one of Rachel in the temporal feature of the VP: whereas Rachel's statement is in the present tense, Christine's statement is in the past tense.

After a long break in the conversation, due to some loud noises produced by one child, Pascal in line 19 asks Christine about the school holidays of the week before. Although the general topic might be seen to be somehow related to the previous one (Christine's retelling of her activities during the holiday period), Pascal presents his news inquiry as introducing something new and disconnected from the preceding talk (see especially the initial change-of-state token, which is retrospectively oriented, and the following adding particle *pis* "and," which is prospectively oriented).

To conclude, although Christine's linguistic resources seems to be more reduced as compared to those of Julie and Oksana, she shows over time an increased participation in joint topic closure. In fact, by the end of her stay, Christine is engaging more actively in topic closings through recycled syntactic patterns and tying techniques, which allow her to align in a more visible way to her interlocutor's turn.

6.4 Summary of Findings

In this chapter, I have discussed the accomplishment of topic closure by three French L2 speakers, namely the au pairs Julie, Oksana, and Christine. At the beginning of their sojourns, they were acknowledged to have, respectively, a B2, B1, and A2 proficiency level in French L2. These reference levels have structured my investigations. To discuss the similarities and differences in the accomplishment of topic closure, I recall the questions I asked after the first analyses of Julie's data: are longitudinal changes of topic closure observable, or should, in this case, cross-sectional comparisons be preferred?

6.4.1 Main Findings Regarding the Participation in Topic Closure

As uncovered in the analyses of Julie's interactions, this au pair seems to have a rather stable pool of methods for participating in topic closure. Probably corresponding to her advanced French L2 level, she can appropriately use typical closing implicative expressions (OK, fine), also with final falling intonation. When her interlocutor does not immediately react to her closing initiating turns, she is able to propose new closing implicative turns that solicit her recipient's response, and she generally finds one. She can therefore manage a possible disalignment in a closing sequence and shows herewith her orientation toward both the topical and the structural levels of the ongoing conversation.

Oksana's data have shown that she seems at the beginning to only minimally participate in closing sequences. She is soon seen to manage a prolonged topic closure composed of longer, complex, and reformulated turns from her interlocutor. She exhibits an orientation toward the particular rules of turn-taking when her interlocutors claim the floor, and she aligns to their stance-taking turns by letting them finish and by self-selecting only afterward. The main finding for Oksana concerns her participation in the closure; i.e. she aligns to her interlocutor's closing initiation, whereas she does not initiate closure herself. Although her French L2 level is intermediate, she also employs typical French closing implicative expressions (alright, it's good) at the right conversational places, from the beginning of her stay.

Christine's data have shown the most remarkable changes over time. In the first example, she participates only minimally in the topic closure: the closure is instead led by her interlocutors, and she limits herself to align to their topic lines (Covelli & Murray, 1980). As time passes, she changes her way of participating in topic closures: she uses more formulaic expressions (it was funny), and she does not limit her contribution to only one turn but instead produces two or three closing implicative turns and therefore participates more actively in the joint construction of topic closure.

6.4.2 Topic Closure: Longitudinal Observations and Stability Over Time

Topic introduction (Chapter 5) has been analyzed through the lens of longitudinal observations. In this case, investigations from different points in time have shown to what extent the accomplishment of one and the same action has changed over time. These observations have shed more light on our understanding of L2 interactional competence and its development over time.

In principle, I expected that my investigations on topic closure would lead to similar conclusions. However, this was not the case, as this chapter has shown. The actional microcosm of topic closure shows stability rather than changes in its accomplishment. That is to say, longitudinal observations of topic closure lead to a picture of this action that is more characterized by stability than by changes—at least as far as my database is concerned. Resources for participating in closing sequences seem to appear already at the beginning of the L2 learning process, at least in the corpus I have investigated.

Several features of topic closure may help explain this. First, topic closures are accomplished while different courses of action are carried out (Heritage & Sorjonen, 1994). A conversational topic can be developed, such as within the framework of storytelling or of an explanation, so the large background activity influences the interactants' participation in it.

Second, topic closures can be investigated either by looking at their initiation or by looking at how speakers participate in them. My data have highlighted that the au pair Julie initiates topic closures, whereas Oksana and Christine instead participate in the closures initiated by their interlocutors. If we put it in relation to the existing literature on topic closure (or sequence closure, more broadly), it is possible to assume that a relationship between the proficiency level of the L2 speakers and their ability to participate in a more active way in topic closures may exist. After the investigations of Julie's data, the outcomes show that she has a broader linguistic repertoire for managing closing implicative environments at her disposal than do Oksana and Christine. Oksana's and Christine's participations in topic closure are limited to minimal or generalizing expressions that they do not change or elaborate on; i.e. the expressions used do not show any variation over time. In this sense, my results seem to align with as Jeon's (2003) and Warga's (2005) outcomes.

Third, also the time span in which data are collected influences the results: following an au pair for six months is different from collecting the au pair's data for nine or ten months. At this point should only be said that maybe a cross-section comparison can uncover other similarities or differences among the ways au pairs participate in topic closure. From my investigations, the impression arises that the main differences are seen between Julie and Oksana on the one hand and Christine on the other hand. However, a cross-sectional comparison makes sense only if more subjects are included, so that for every French L2 proficiency level enough speakers are considered.

The next chapters put the results of the analyses in contrast by presenting a description of L2 interactional competence (Chapter 7). Specifically, the nature and the development of L2 interactional competence are addressed. Finally, Chapter 8 contains some concluding remarks about the present study and about other possibilities for future research in the domain of CA-SLA and its eventual application in the world outside the classroom.

Notes

1. As mentioned earlier, Julie's L1 is German. Occasionally, she uses it in the conversations with the host family, especially with the host mother, who knows a bit of German herself.
2. "She" refers to the "swimming pool." In French "la piscine," i.e. "the swimming pool," is feminine. In this turn, Pascal produces a left-dislocated construction, starting with the direct object *elle* at turn beginning, which is then rephrased in the matrix sentence "*la piscine*," this lexeme having the subject status in the matrix sentence.
3. In Switzerland, the Cantons have school holidays during different periods.

References

Bolden, G. B. (2008). 'So what's up?': Using the discourse marker so to launch conversational business. *Research on Language & Social Interaction*, 41(3), 302–337.

Button, G. (1990). On varieties of closings. In G. Psathas (Ed.), *Interaction competence* (pp. 93–147). Washington, DC: University Press of America.

Button, G., & Casey, N. (1985). Topic nomination and topic pursuit. *Human Studies*, *8*, 3–55.

Button, G., & Casey, N. (1988). Topic initiation: Business-at-hand. *Research on Language & Social Interaction*, *22*, 61–92.

Covelli, L. H., & Murray, S. O. (1980). Accomplishing topic change. *Anthropological Linguistics*, *22*(9), 382–389.

Drew, P., & Holt, E. (1995). Idiomatic expressions and their role in the organization of topic transition in conversation. In M. Everaert, E.-J. van der Linden, A. Schenk, & R. Schreuder (Eds.), *Idioms: Structural and psychological perspectives* (pp. 117–132). Hillsdale, NJ and Hove, UK: Lawrence Erlbaum Associates Publishers.

Heritage, J. (1984). A change-of-stake token and aspects of its sequential placement. In J. M. Atkinson & J. Heritage (Eds.), *Structures of social action: Studies in conversation analysis* (pp. 299–345). Cambridge: Cambridge University Press.

Heritage, J., & Sorjonen, M.-L. (1994). Constituting and maintaining activities across sequences and prefacing as a feature of question design. *Language in Society*, *23*(1), 1–29.

Holt, E. (2010). The last laugh: Shared laughter and topic termination. *Journal of Pragmatics*, *42*, 1513–1525.

Holt, E., & Drew, P. (2005). Figurative pivots: The use of figurative expressions in pivotal topic transitions. *Research on Language & Social Interaction*, *38*(1), 35–61.

Jeon, M. (2003). Closing the advising session. *Working Papers in Educational Linguistics*, *18*(2), 89–106.

Local, J. (2004). Getting back to prior talk: And-uh(m) as a back-connecting device. In E. Couper-Kuhlen & C. Ford (Eds.), *Sound patterns in interaction: Cross-linguistic studies of phonetics and prosody of conversation* (pp. 376–400). Amsterdam and Philadelphia: John Benjamins Publishing Company.

Pochon-Berger, E., & Pekarek Doehler, S. (2015). Direct reported speech in storytellings: Enacting membership categories and negotiating experiential and epistemic entitlements. *Text and Talk*, *35*(6), 789–813.

Sacks, H., & Schegloff, A. E. (1973). Opening up closings. *Semiotica*, *8*(4), 289–327.

Selting, M. (1994). Emphatic speech style; With special focus on the prosodic signalling of heightened emotive involvement in conversation. *Journal of Pragmatics*, *22*(Special Issue: Involvement in Language), 375–408.

Warga, M. (2005). 'Je serais très merciable': Formulaic vs. creatively produced speech in learners' request closings. *Canadian Journal of Applied Linguistics*, *8*(1), 67–93.

7 Nature and Development of L2 Interactional Competence

This study has dealt with the observation of how au pairs learn or improve their French L2 over time while staying with host families in the French-speaking part of Switzerland. The analytical object of topic management has been segmented into two actions, namely topic introduction (Chapter 5) and topic closure (Chapter 6). In both cases, longitudinal investigations have been carried out, in which the following aspects have been considered: the linguistic resources employed by the au pairs, the structural features of their topic introduction and closures, and finally the comparison of their strategies at different points in time.

In this chapter, I summarize the main findings from both analytical chapters, and I address two main aspects related to the concept of L2 interactional competence. First, I depict the nature of L2 interactional competence as it emerges from my investigations (7.1). Second, I discuss the aspects related to the development of L2 interactional competence in relation to analyses of topic introduction and of topic closure (7.2). Finally, I conclude the chapter with a more general discussion about the study of L2 interactional competence (7.3).

7.1 On the Nature of L2 Interactional Competence

When the research project TRIC-L2 was started at the University of Neuchâtel in 2010, the central point addressed was its longitudinal design. At that time, only a few studies were known that had dealt with data collection over time within the domain of CA-SLA (Brouwer & Wagner, 2004; Cekaite, 2007; Hellermann, 2005, 2006, 2007, 2008; Jeon, 2003; Young & Miller, 2004). However, even while tracking changes over time in the ways that the au pairs accomplished specific actions in conversation, such as introducing or closing topics, discussions over the nature of L2 interactional competence were ineluctable.

In this section, I present the main aspects of the nature of L2 interactional competence that have emerged after my analyses: interactional competence is more than mere linguistic competence (7.1.1), this competence is locally constructed in conversation and is therefore also shared in its nature (7.1.2), and finally, in the meaning of "interactional competence," a full array of abilities is comprised that goes beyond language per se (7.1.3).

7.1.1 L2 Interactional Competence: Not Only Linguistic

The investigations presented in this study are based on the documentation of how topic introduction and topic closure are accomplished by three au pairs at different points in time. My observations are based on a cross-sectional comparison that has shown some general tendencies about the accomplishment of topic shift and topical backlinking in French L2 talk. The first important tendency is that all three au pairs accomplish topic introduction and topic closure. This means that none of these actions is strictly dependent on the L2 proficiency level of the speakers. This is important in better understanding L2 interactional competence because this shows that speakers already know how to manage conversational topics from their L1 experiences and that they can also achieve this endeavor in their L2.

However, there is a striking point: the data do not document a simple transfer from the L1 to the L2; the au pairs do not straightforwardly transport L1 linguistic resources into the investigated environments in the L2 talk. Instead, my data have shown, first, that the au pairs employ typical linguistic resources of the French language to accomplish topic introduction and topic closure. As far as topic introduction is concerned, a development of resources for preparing the field for the upcoming talk was observed, which indicates that the au pairs develop a sort of context sensitivity throughout their sojourn. Similar findings are presented in the recent work by Pekarek Doehler & Berger (2018) on the interactional work accomplished by the same au pair, Julie, for framing a new story during ongoing conversations. A closer look at topic closure highlights that the possible resources (like summarizing statements or generalizing expressions) seem to be at the disposal of the au pairs from the beginning. What changes is that the L2 speakers become, over time, more active in their participation in the topic closures and also increasingly manage possible absences of reaction from their interlocutors.

More principally speaking, looking at developmental or longitudinal data through the lens of CA and with a focus on L2 speakers' L2 interactional competence implies more than looking at linguistic and prosodic features of talk. For instance, conversational topics were seen to be introduced at specific interactional places, such as after a previous topic and sequence were closed. This suggests that the action of topic introduction is characterized by essential structural features that are language-independent. This means, on the one hand, that the L2 speakers use the linguistic resources that they have at a certain time in order to collaboratively accomplish an action with their interlocutors. On the other hand, this also means that the au pairs overtly (observably) orient toward the general progression of the conversational flow. In other words, the L2 speakers are able to recognize the interactional loci that are suitable for clearly showing their orientation toward topic boundaries.

If it is so, that the au pairs can orient toward the conversation progression—and I argue that my investigations have shown this—then my results align with the point made by Hall et al. (2011), Nguyen (2011), and Taguchi (2015): L2 interactional competence is not merely linguistic in nature; it also relates to other resources that are locally made available and collaboratively managed in the conversation by the participants themselves.

7.1.2 L2 Interactional Competence: Local and Shared

The word "collaborative" brings me to the next point. The au pairs collaborate with their interlocutors to manage topics during an ongoing conversation. The actions of introducing and closing a topic can be achieved only if the interactants work together. To do so, they have to constantly monitor each other's reactions; i.e. they have to continuously check on the other's (dis)alignment with themselves.

In the case of topic management and in equal measure for both topic introduction and topic closure, a double-check is needed. On the one hand, the L2 speakers have to monitor whether their interlocutors are following the new or the old topic line (Covelli & Murray, 1980); on the other hand, the au pairs also have to monitor the structural development of the ongoing conversation, i.e. to determine whether the turns at talk, the pauses or silences, the marked sequence boundaries, and so on allow for the start of a new topic line or if they instead implicate closing (Holt, 2010).

After the investigations of data from three different au pairs, the results show that all three are able to introduce and close a conversational topic. They make their orientation toward the topic boundaries locally relevant in that they show their interlocutors how they are positioning themselves regarding what preceded. They therefore skillfully use linguistic and prosodic cues (like contextualization cues for topic introduction). Moreover, they are able to search (and wait) for their interlocutors' affirmative reactions; i.e. they wait until it is actually possible to bring the introduced topic further, or in the case of topic closure, they wait until no more comments and reactions follow.

The analysis of topic management in a second language helps depict the local and shared nature of L2 interactional competence. As many other studies (Hall et al., 2011; Kasper & Wagner, 2011; Mondada & Pekarek Doehler, 2004; Mori & Hasegawa, 2009; Pekarek Doehler, 2006; Taguchi, 2015) have demonstrated, L2 interactional competence cannot be studied only by means of a speaker's production in the L2, because L2 interactional competence is composed of many different abilities that are made observable during the interactions and that are employed in close coordination with one's interlocutors. As Mondada & Pekarek Doehler formulate,

> Even when it does not appear to be so, learning is interactional because it is always rooted in activities, in language games, in forms of experience. There are, in fact, activity types that our common sense (and much of the technical literature on acquisition) does not immediately or generally associate with social interaction. Instead, these tasks are viewed as being typically individual or as being concerned with noninteractional objects and objectives.
> (Mondada & Pekarek Doehler, 2004: 505)

Learning, i.e. the acquisition and mobilization of a panoply of abilities in relation to topic management, can be summarized as follows: the ability to recognize and choose the interactional place for introducing a new conversational topic; the ability to use the most appropriate linguistic and prosodic resources for marking the topic introduction; the ability to recognize a closing implicative environment; and, finally, the ability to align (or disalign) to one's interlocutor during topic closure. Possessing these abilities and improving them over the time of their sojourns render the au pairs increasingly competent French L2 speakers.

7.1.3 L2 Interactional Competence: Many Abilities, One Term

In my study, I have demonstrated how topic management relates to L2 interactional competence: it is a part of it, because this competence is not merely linguistic or structural. It is a socially related competence; it is shared in its nature; it is locally oriented to in everyday conversations; and its nature can be grasped only if the concept of competence is linked to its intrinsic social origin.

Interacting in a second language implies not only speaking that language but also socially acting in that language. This peculiarity of L2 interactional competence has already been discussed in several papers (Eskildsen, 2018; Kasper & Wagner, 2011; Pekarek Doehler, 2006; Sahlström, 2011; Hall, 2018). Eskildsen (2018: 69) offers a clear summary:

> the actual building of interactional competence is socially accomplished and a matter of biographical experience and discovery. Whatever language they are learning and whenever they are doing it, people must learn the new language-specific ways of accomplishing social action by participating in interaction with local co-participants.

They learn these in a very bottom-up, trial-and-error fashion as they observe, eavesdrop, appropriate, control and calibrate semiotic resources, picked up from the environment, for accomplishing locally occasioned social actions.

Interactional competence embraces several abilities and is not restricted to only the linguistic knowledge of the L2 speaker. In my study, I have concentrated on topic management and have shown that for managing topics in conversation—i.e. for introducing, shifting, and closing them—a multitude of abilities is required and deployed by the L2 speakers. They orient toward the structural features of conversation, such as sequence and activity boundaries; they manage intersubjectivity and recipient design; they are able to open and close a conversational topic; and they do all this while managing several other interactional activities, such as repairing communication problems or agreeing or disagreeing with one's interlocutor.

For now, the only actual label usable for identifying the L2 speakers' knowledge and abilities is the term "interactional competence." In a recent paper, Hall (2018) has settled the question of distinguishing between interactional competence and interactional repertoires. For her, this distinction should be made since the latter indicates objects of L2 learning, i.e. new methods that are language-specific (in my case, they are French L2–specific), whereas the former refers to a more general and abstract concept of a generic competence of interacting specific to human beings. There may be a difference in the perspectives between scholars from the field of CA-SLA and scholars from other research fields (such as education), and this terminological distinction (competence/repertoire) could be useful for avoiding misunderstandings. However, since most of the studies on the features of L2 interactional competence seem to refer to the objects of learning, I choose to continue to use this term to characterize the findings from my study but follow the development of the terminological discussion just started.

In the next section, I propose a discussion about the developmental nature of L2 interactional competence as I observed through the analyses of topic management in French L2 talk-in-interaction.

7.2 On the Development of L2 Interactional Competence

In the preceding chapters, I have investigated how speakers of French L2 manage topics in everyday conversations. My analyses have been based on the investigation of two distinct actional microcosms: topic introduction and topic closure. These investigations have brought to light the methods that L2 speakers recurrently employ to introduce and close topics in ongoing interactions, pointing out the collaborative nature of topic management.

7.2.1 Topic Introduction: Summary of Findings

The study of topic introduction and how it changes over time has dealt with the data of two au pairs: Julie and Oksana, both having rather advanced L2 proficiency levels (B2 and B1, respectively). The specific case of topic shift, instead, has been illustrated with the data also of the third au pair, Christine. For Christine, no case of topic introduction was found. For Julie and Oksana, I have collected a total of 19 cases of topic introduction.

7.2.1.1 Topic Introduction

My analyses have shown that topic introduction was always initiated by the au pairs when the previous topic and sequence were closed. The closing-implicative environment manifested itself in the data through

1. Closing implicative turns (summarizing and generalizing statements, final falling intonation, no new topicalizers).
2. The presence of a final agreement.
3. A longer pause.

After the pause, the L2 speaker self-selected and introduced the new conversational topic. The interactional locus in which the L2 speakers introduced a new conversational topic has shown the most stable features, in my collection of cases.

Regarding the linguistic and prosodic features of topic introduction, both Julie and Oksana have shown some changes in the methods that they employed to introduce the new conversational topic. Generally speaking, the au pairs have become more proficient and more efficient in accomplishing this action, especially as regards the interactional work done for preparing their interlocutors for the upcoming talk. This interactional work is observable, at turn beginning, in the use of misplacement markers or attention-getting devices, in the deployment of more contextual clues for anchoring the new topic, and in the growing length of their turns-at-talk.

In so doing, the L2 speakers increase the visibility of their orientation toward the conversation progression; i.e. they show an augmented context sensitivity (cf. Pekarek Doehler & Berger, 2018) in relationship to topic-bound activities (cf. Sacks, 1995). Accomplishing a more accurate and finer preparation of the fieldwork before introducing a new conversational topic, Julie and Oksana demonstrate more clearly to their interlocutors that they are orienting toward what preceded as being closed, so that one of the possible next relevant actions might be a new topic introduction. With a clearly observable display of orientation toward these structural and topical features of conversation, the L2 speakers also choose to introduce a new topic in an interactional place that is appropriate for this action. Moreover, the finer interactional work achieved for introducing a new conversational topic also shows another type of orientation by the au pairs, namely their orientation toward the conversational aspect of recipient design (Nguyen, 2011). By better preparing their interlocutors for the upcoming talk, the au pairs show their ability to actively integrate their interlocutors in the ongoing conversation; i.e. they are shown to be not only "passive spectators" of the conversations but rather engaged partners in the same conversational activity.

7.2.1.2 Topic Shift

I have presented cases of topic shift as well (section 5.4). I consider topic shift to be a particular case of topic introduction because the au pairs change the topical line (Covelli & Murray, 1980) with some strategies so that the conversation goes in another direction, although they have not actually introduced a completely new conversational topic. The au pairs from my database exploited three different strategies to accomplish a topic shift: they shifted the actual reference; they have used a pivot-shifting; or they exploited a case of multiple reference. It is clear that there are other possibilities for shifting a topic at hand that I have not addressed. But already with the three cases that I have sketched, it is possible to identify some common features of this action.

In general, the L2 speakers have shifted the current topic by addressing some marginal aspects of it (this recalls to some extent the stepwise transition described by Jefferson, 1984). What this action shows is that all three au pairs were able to do so, which means that all of them were able to identify the current topic and identify other, heretofore-neglected but still-related aspects of it. For doing this, in turn, they have to be able to recognize when it is possible to address these other aspects and, moreover, how to do so in a way that is clear also to their interlocutors. What the au pairs show, then, is their ability to manage the L2 interactional repertoires (Hall, 2018), i.e. the objects of their L2 learning process. They have learned in and through the daily interactions with(in) their host families.

7.2.1.3 Observability of the Development of L2 Interactional Competence

A longitudinal comparison was made for the data of the au pairs Julie and Oksana. In both cases, it revealed that the methods for introducing a topic in conversation changed from what can be called a more abrupt toward a smoother topic introduction. This change is observable especially in the finer, more-context-sensitive interactional work that is accomplished by the au pairs at turn beginning. I have termed the initial way of introducing a new conversational topic an "abrupt topic introduction" because the new topic was introduced "out of the blue." This means that although the previous sequence and action had been closed, no preparatory work for the interlocutor was done (e.g. see Julie's first example). The preparatory interactional work comes out over time particularly through the use of misplacement markers, attention-getting devices, contextualization information, and some hesitations or spur-of-the-moment changes in syntactical patterns. The result is a longer, more complex first turn for introducing a new conversational topic.

In these observations, I see the strength of my longitudinal investigations. They have shown how the same L2 speaker accomplishes the same action over time, and because of this stable starting point (speaker + action), it is possible to draw the changes in the L2 speaker's methods for introducing a conversational topic. The development of L2 interactional competence, then, goes at the same pace as these changes are observable. It is possible to talk about the development of the au pairs' L2 interactional competence in the sense that they show more clearly what they orient toward (e.g. the preceding sequence and topic, the interests of their interlocutors, the family agenda). This is so because they orient in a more sensitive way toward the structural and topical features of conversation (cf. Kim, 2017).

Within the longitudinal design, I have also drawn some comparisons between the two au pairs, Julie and Oksana, that mainly concern their L2 proficiency level and the nature of the introduced topic. In fact, Oksana's topic introductions seemed to me to be generally more addressee oriented than Julie's topic introductions. Oksana is shown to introduce more often some topical lines that are related to Pierre's interests (like cooking, playing volleyball, or sports more generally—such as when they talk about the ice rinks). I have not carried out an actual cross-sectional comparison, so this is merely a discussion of some tendencies that I see in my data.

Perhaps these personal differences in the type of conversational topics introduced can be related to the relationship between the au pairs and their host families, i.e. to the degree to which the L2 speakers are (getting) integrated in the family life. A main difference concerning this aspect is that in Oksana's host family, only the host father is present, since he and his wife are separated. The situation being like this, it is more likely that Oksana and Pierre get to know each other better and faster than Julie and her host parents, who live together, so they are present differently and talk differently with Julie. The time for getting acquainted may then vary because of the family constellation.

Another aspect that may affect the repertoire of introduced conversational topics is the age difference between the au pairs. Oksana is four years older than Julie, so it is possible that she has taken up the role of caregiver in a different way than Julie has. Finally (but related to this last point), a reflection can also be made about the previous experiences of the au pairs, because these can also influence how Oksana and Julie treat conversational topics in relation to their interlocutors. However, I know little about their previous life, so it has not been possible to investigate this aspect.

7.2.2 Topic Closure: Summary of Findings

The study of topic closure and its changes over time has dealt with the data of all three au pairs: Julie, Oksana, and Christine. In conclusion, I have collected a total of 85 cases of topic closure and have shown three representative examples for each au pair. Every example was taken from a different point in time, so that, in the end, it was possible to retrace an eventual trajectory of the changes in the way the au pairs close a conversational topic.

7.2.2.1 Sequential and Linguistic Aspects of Topic Closure

The data have shown that many features are found regularly in topic closure sequences: first of all, the presence of long inter-turn pauses. This is a typical clue for some troubles in the change of speakership, i.e. an appropriate interactional moment for closing the topic at hand and moving on with the conversation (see Maynard, 1980). The second feature is the use of shorter turns containing formulaic language ("that's it," "there you go"), as well as summarizing and generalizing statements (cf. Drew & Holt, 1995, 1998; Holt & Drew, 2005). When no new topicalizers are found and no one adds new topical material, then the interactional context can be identified as closing implicative (cf. Holt, 2010). Finally, these sequences feature a final, longer pause, after which a speaker self-selected and introduced a new conversational topic. These features were present in the data of all three au pairs from the beginning of their stays and can therefore be considered stable and reliable aspects for the constitution of a collection of cases and for the analysis of topic closure.

A consideration of the linguistic and prosodic features of the topic-closing turns has demonstrated that changes are more observable in Christine's data, which means that, over time, she participated more actively in the action of topic closure. This is observable in the following aspects:

1. The quantity of her turns, i.e. Christine produces more turns when a topic closure is occasioned (at the beginning of her stay, she participated with one turn, whereas at the end of her stay, she produces two or three turns).
2. The type of language she employs, i.e. she uses more formulaic language (it's funny, it's right, that's it).

The investigations of the data from Julie's and Oksana's data sets have shown fewer changes in the accomplishment of the action of topic closure. It holds true for both au pairs that they use, from the beginning of their sojourns, typical resources for closing implicative environments, such as formulaic language, final summarizing statements, and final falling intonations in their closing implicative turns. In addition to this, the lexical repertoire of expressions retrieved through the corpus shows a certain stability too, a typical feature of topic closures.

7.2.2.2 Observability of the Development of L2 Interactional Competence

A longitudinal comparison was carried out for all three au pairs. In the cases of Julie and Oksana, this comparison has shown no particular changes over time; i.e. the action of topic closure seems to be characterized rather by stability than by change (Hauser, 2013). Christine's data, instead, depicted some changes in the way she participates into topic closure, and I have described this change as a more appropriate, or more skillful, participation in topic closure. It was observable in the increasing quantity of Christine's turns-at-talk and in the closing-implicative expressions that have appeared more often toward the middle and the end of her sojourn. A comparison among the three au pairs has shown that the differences were mainly in personal skills and depended on the interactional constellations in the host families. On the one hand, then, there are Julie and Oksana, who have a more advanced French L2 proficiency level, and on the other hand, Christine, who has a less advanced French L2 proficiency level. This result suggests that the action of topic closure shows more longitudinal changes when the L2 speaker's proficiency level is rather low. In other words, topic closure appears to be an actional microcosm that tends to stabilize over time and with an increased L2 proficiency level, or it is something that is learned early.

7.3 L2 Interactional Competence and Its Development Over Time

In a recent volume, Taguchi (2015) rephrases Hall et al.'s (2011) definition of L2 interactional competence as follows:

> iinteractional competence views language ability as a dialogic construct, locally situated and jointly constructed by participants in discourse. . . . Interactional competence considers participants' skilful use of a variety of linguistic and interactional resources at the task of joint meaning creation.
>
> (p. 1)

I take this rephrasing as a starting point for my remarks on L2 interactional competence and its development over time. The first aspect to be considered is that L2 interactional competence is distributed among participants. As introduced in Chapter 3, L2 interactional competence cannot be analyzed as the product of one mind, specifically of the L2 speaker's mind, because this competence is situated and collaboratively activated in and through interaction, i.e. when at least two interactants come together and one of them is an L2 speaker.

7.3.1 L2 Interactional Competence and Topic Introduction

My investigations of topic introduction have explicitly addressed the distributed nature of L2 interactional competence in two ways. First, I have analyzed the turns produced by the L2 speakers for them to introduce a new conversational topic, and my analyses have included linguistic, prosodic, and sequential features. Second, larger sequences have been investigated too, in which the interlocutors' reactions were found; i.e. only by taking into consideration the larger ongoing activities was it possible to say something about how the L2 speakers were able to manage new conversational topics in the ongoing interactions. This is so because the action of introducing a new conversational topic is jointly accomplished by all interactants on a turn-by-turn basis; i.e. I could only see turn after turn how the participants positioned themselves in the preceding turn-at-talk (cf. Firth & Wagner, 1997). Hence, only then was it possible to recognize if the proposed topic also stabilized as the topic at hand or if it was rejected by the other interactants.

Another point I find interesting in Taguchi's words is her use of the adjective "skillful": "participants' skilful use of . . . resources." "Skillful" in this context refers to the use of resources and practices to accomplish locally relevant social actions. The observation of the data refers uniquely to how the L2 speakers employ the resources they have available at the moment of the ongoing conversation. In my case, with the analyses of topic introduction, I have pinpointed that the L2 speakers change their introductory methods, rendering them smoother. In other words, the au pairs contextualize their topic introductions more (see also Hellermann, 2007 on task opening) by delivering a range of special and temporal information as well as information on other people or events. Moreover, the "smoothness" of their introduction relies on the use of an array of resources that signal different things to their interlocutors:

1. They are claiming the floor for themselves (self-section).
2. They are orienting to what preceded as concluded.
3. They are about to introduce something new (and to some extent disjointed from what the current topic had been so far).

In so doing, the au pairs deploy over time a more elaborated topic introduction and thereby show a stronger orientation toward their addressees (König, 2013; Taguchi, 2015; Kim, 2017). This result is in line with the study by Nguyen (2011) on recipient design in the domain of pharmacy consultation and on how it changes over time. Indeed, Sacks et al. (1974) had already pointed out that recipient design is a feature of conversations that also influences the choice and the management of conversational topics (p. 727). As this study has shown, topic introduction can be analyzed also in relation to recipient design: rendering the introduction more elaborated and smoother, i.e. making the effort of a finer interactional work for preparing the field for the upcoming talk, allows the interlocutor to be prepared for the next conversational topic. This in turn makes it easier for the interactants to collaboratively construct a topical sequence (cf. the studies by Covelli & Murray, 1980; Maynard & Zimmerman, 1984).

Moreover, when new conversational topics are introduced in a smoother way, the conversation can flow without interruptions. In fact, with an appropriate introduction, misunderstandings can be avoided; i.e. repair sequences can be prevented from happening (although, of course, there is no guarantee of this, since everything can be repaired in conversation).

The changes in the L2 speakers' methods for introducing a new conversational topic suggest that a long-lasting and continuous learning process is taking place during their sojourns. This learning process, however, does not concern merely the second language. There is more going on in this learning context: the au pairs are becoming members of the host families (cf. Farina et al., 2012; Pochon-Berger et al., 2015). This means that they get more acquainted with the interactional dynamics of these families, they get more involved in the children's lives, and they share increasing information and knowledge with the host parents. These aspects in turn affect how the L2 speakers manage the introduction of new conversational topics. Especially the growing body of shared knowledge between them and the host family members seems to help the au pairs in their process of topic management. This result is in line with what is presented in a recent study by Kim (2017) on two Japanese brothers learning English. In fact, when the common ground is stabilized and the interactants know each other better, it seems easier for them to introduce new topics in conversation without having to explain why they want to talk about this or that matter—because they know the interests of their interlocutors better.

To conclude, then, the analysis of the au pairs' methods for introducing a new conversational topic has uncovered an ongoing, underlying L2 learning process that has been shown in the changes in the methods that they used to introduce a new topic. This L2 learning process has been shown to be sociocultural-linguistic in nature, but surely not only linguistic (Sahlström, 2011). In my data, I have demonstrated L2 learning in a noninstitutional setting, like the family. Changes were observable in the methods that the au pairs have used to introduce a new conversational topic, the introduction becoming smoother and more contextualized during their sojourn with the host families. In a nutshell, the longitudinal changes in the au pairs' methods for introducing topics display their orientation toward the family and the interactional contexts they are acting in.

7.3.2 L2 Interactional Competence and Topic Closure

The situation with topic closure is a bit different, since the relation between this actional microcosm and the development of L2 interactional competence seems to be less clear than the relation between this development and topic introduction. Despite fewer striking changes being documented longitudinally, more interesting observations were made between the participants. On the one hand, other important aspects emerge that relate L2 interactional competence to changes in the methods for closing a topic. In this case, the development of L2 interactional competence seems to be more observable at the linguistic level of the closing turns. On the other hand, then, it is possible to discuss the stability of topic closure over a longer period of time. I now address both aspects of this actional microcosm.

Topic closure seems to be related to the existence of a possible agenda that underlies the whole conversation. Closing a topic projects either a new topic or the restart/resumption of a previous one. I have stated in my introduction that everyday conversations, especially in families and during mealtimes, are not based on an agenda; i.e. there is no previous schemata to follow about the topics to be discussed. However, at the same time, I have noticed in every conversation of my database the presence of something like a "virtual agenda." I have put it in relation mainly to the family activities, and these are of two types: the ones that are still to be organized and the others that were carried out during the day by the au pair with the children. These two activity types are always discussed in the conversations of my data sets. Other topics are sometimes present (like the telling of some personal experiences by the interactants), but the conversations, even though they are informal and familiar in nature, always have the aim of checking on the au pair's work and of organizing the upcoming days.

Considering this underpinned and non-declared agenda as an underlying feature of everyday family interactions sheds more light on the cases of topic closure, because finding agreement and the smooth passage to a next matter gain great social importance. In this sense, a thoroughly positive result is the fact that in Julie's and Oksana's data the topic closure sequences ran smoothly from the beginning of their stays.

On the one hand, Julie's and Oksana's data have shown that these two au pairs were able from the beginning to manage prolonged closing sequences and, in different occasions, the absence of recipient reactions too. If these results do not show some sort of development of their L2 interactional competence over time, they show that Julie and Oksana have a stable L2 interactional competence in the management of topic closure. Christine's data, on the other hand, have depicted more similarities to the data on topic introduction. First, the investigations have brought to the surface some changes in Christine's methods for closing a topic, such as more active participation in topic closures and the use of final, generalizing expressions. Second, the analyses have pointed out a change in the way she more clearly agrees with her interlocutors and ties her closing turns to theirs.

These changes over time in Christine's data, again, show the social nature of L2 interactional competence, since changes in her ways of participating in topic closure are to be related to her participation with the host family (Hellermann, 2011). In fact, Christine does not widen her vocabulary, nor does she proffer fewer error-free turns. Instead, she positions herself more clearly in her interlocutors' stances and, hence, becomes more active in the action of topic closing itself (Farina et al., 2012).

References

Brouwer, C., & Wagner, J. (2004). Developmental issues in second language conversation. *Journal of Applied Linguistics*, 1, 29–47.

Cekaite, A. (2007). A child's development of interactional competence in a Swedish L2 classroom. *The Modern Language Journal*, 91, 45–62.

Covelli, L. H., & Murray, S. O. (1980). Accomplishing topic change. *Anthropological Linguistics*, 22(9), 382–389.

Drew, P., & Holt, E. (1995). Idiomatic expressions and their role in the organization of topic transition in conversation. In M. Everaert, E.-J. van der Linden, A. Schenk, & R. Schreuder (Eds.), *Idioms: Structural and psychological perspectives* (pp. 117–132). Hillsdale, NJ and Hove, UK: Lawrence Erlbaum Associates Publishers.

Drew, P., & Holt, E. (1998). Figures of speech: Figurative expressions and the management of topic transition in conversation. *Language in Society*, 27(4), 495–522.

Eskildsen, S. W. (2018). Building a semiotic repertoire for social action: Interactional competence as biographical discovery. *Classroom Discourse*, 9(1), 68–76. DOI: 10.1080/19463014.2018.1437052

Farina, C., Pochon-Berger, E., & Pekarek Dohler, S. (2012). Le développement de la compétence d'interaction: une étude sur le travail lexical. *Tranel*, 57, 101–119.

Firth, A., & Wagner, J. (1997). On discourse, communication and some fundamental concepts in SLA research. *The Modern Language Journal*, 81(3), 285–300.

Hall, J. K. (2018). From L2 interactional competence to L2 interactional repertoires: Reconceptualizing the objects of L2 learning. *Classroom Discourse*, 8(1), 25–39.

Hall, J. K., Hellermann, J., & Pekarek Doehler, S. (Eds.) (2011). *L2 interactional competence and development*. Clevedon: Multilingual Matters.

Hauser, E. (2013). Stability and change in one adult's second language English negation. *Language Learning*, 63(3), 463–498.

Hellermann, J. (2005). Syntactic and prosodic practices for cohesion in series of three-part sequences in classroom talk. *Research on Language & Social Interaction*, 36(1), 105–130.
Hellermann, J. (2006). Classroom interactive practices for literacy: A microethnographic study of two beginning adult learners of English. *Applied Linguistics*, 27(3), 377–404.
Hellermann, J. (2007). The development of practices for action in classroom dyadic interaction: Focus on task openings. *The Modern Language Journal*, 91(1), 83–96.
Hellermann, J. (2008). *Social Actions for Classroom Language Learning*. Clevedon: Multilingual Matters.
Hellermann, J. (2011). Members' methods, members' competencies: Looking for evidence of language learning in longitudinal investigations. In J. K. Hall, J. Hellermann, & S. Pekarek Doehler (Eds.), *L2 interactional competence and development* (pp. 147–172). Clevedon: Multilingual Matters.
Holt, E. (2010). The last laugh: Shared laughter and topic termination. *Journal of Pragmatics*, 42, 1513–1525.
Holt, E., & Drew, P. (2005). Figurative pivots: The use of figurative expressions in pivotal topic transitions. *Research on Language & Social Interaction*, 38(1), 35–61.
Jefferson, G. (1984). On stepwise transition from talk about a trouble to inappropriately next-positioned matters. In J. M. Atkinson & J. Heritage (Eds.), *Structures of social action* (pp. 191–222). Cambridge: Cambridge University Press.
Jeon, M. (2003). Closing the advising session. *Working Papers in Educational Linguistics*, 18(2), 89–106.
Kasper, G., & Wagner, J. (2011). A conversation-analytic approach to second language acquisition. In D. Atkinson (Ed.), *Alternative approaches to second language acquisition* (pp. 117–142). London, New York: Routledge.
Kim, Y. (2017). Topic initiation in conversation-for-learning: Developmental and pedagogical perspectives. *English Teaching*, 72(1), 73–103. DOI:10.15858/engtea.72.1.201703.73
König, C. (2013). Topic management in French L2: A longitudinal conversation analytic approach (pp. 226–250). *EUROSLA Yearbook 13*. Amsterdam/Philadelphia: John Benjamins Publishing Company.
Maynard, D. W. (1980). Placement of topic changes in conversation. *Semiotica*, 263–290.
Maynard, D. W., & Zimmerman, D. H. (1984). Topical talk, ritual and the social organization of relationships. *Social Psychology Quarterly*, 47(4), 301–316.
Mondada, L., & Pekarek Doehler, S. (2004). Second language acquisition as situated practice. *The Modern Language Journal*, 88(4), 501–518.
Mori, J., & Hasegawa, A. (2009). Doing being a foreign language learner in a classroom: Embodiment of cognitive states as social events. *IRAL: International Review of Applied Linguistics in Language Teaching*, 47(1), 65–94. DOI:10.1515/iral.2009.004
Nguyen, H. T. (2011). Achieving recipient design longitudinally: Evidence from a pharmacy intern in patient consultations. In J. K. Hall, J. Hellermann, & S. Pekarek Doehler (Eds.), *L2 interactional competence and development* (pp. 173–205). Clevedon: Multilingual Matters.
Pekarek Doehler, S. (2006). Compétence et langage en action. *Bulletin Suisse de Linguistique Appliquée*, 84, 9–45.

Pekarek Doehler, S., & Berger, E. (2018). L2 interactional competence as increased ability for context-sensitive conduct: A longitudinal study of story-openings. *Applied Linguistics*, 39(4), 555–578.

Pochon-Berger, E., Pekarek Doehler, S., & König, C. (2015). Family conversational storytelling at the margins of the workplace: The case of au pair girls. In L. Grujicic-Alatriste (Ed.), *Discourse studies in diverse settings: Dissemination and application* (pp. 86–108). Bristol: Multilingual Matters.

Sacks, H. (1995). *Lectures on conversation* (Vol. 1 & 2). Oxford: Basil Blackwell.

Sacks, H., Schegloff, E. A., & Jefferson, G. (1974). A simplest systematic for the organization of turn-taking in conversation. *Language*, 50(4), 696–735.

Sahlström, F. (2011). Learning as social action. In J. K. Hall, J. Hellermann, & S. Pekarek Doehler (Eds.), *L2 interactional competence and development* (pp. 45–65). Clevedon: Multilingual Matters.

Taguchi, N. (2015). *Developing interactional competence in a Japanese study abroad context*. Bristol: Multilingual Matters.

Young, R. F., & Miller, E. R. (2004). Learning as changing participation: Discourse roles in ESL writing conferences. *The Modern Language Journal*, 88(4), 519–535.

8 Conclusion(s)

This last chapter of the study is dedicated to a more general discussion on different aspects that concern the investigation of L2 interactional competence and especially some didactical and pedagogical implications of this type of research. In its first section (8.1), I present a summarized version of the answers to my research questions in order to close the circle and to show to what extent my investigations have been helpful in finding answers. Then, in a second and final section (8.2), I address some implementation issues that are recently being discussed more often within the domain of CA-SLA, namely what practical contributions can arise from CA-SLA research outputs for the domains of education and of professional practices.

8.1 Answering the Research Questions

In the introduction to this book, I have sketched the research questions that have guided my investigations and can now formulate answers for them. One of the first questions that came up concerned how L2 speakers manage conversational topics in everyday interactions. With my investigations, I have individuated different methods exploited by the au pairs in managing conversational topics. On the one hand, I have concentrated on topic introduction and have uncovered some common sequential features for accomplishing this action, namely that the au pairs introduce a new conversational topic after a previous sequence and topic have been closed. This means that the L2 speakers show their orientation toward what preceded as being closed. On the other hand, the analysis of the linguistic and prosodic means employed by the au pairs has revealed the use of a wide array of resources for marking the initial topic boundary, ranging from hesitation and misplacement markers to a variety of contextualization cues.

Given the longitudinal design of the research project, a second question arose about how the practices for managing topic change over time. After some previous analyses, a further question was needed, namely if all practices are subjected to change over time or only some of them. My analyses have demonstrated that change is more clearly observable for topic introduction than for topic closure. The au pairs Julie and Oksana seem to develop a repertoire of strategies to accomplish a smoother topic introduction; i.e. they learn over time how to prepare the field for their interlocutors and how to achieve a more sensitive recipient design by producing longer and more complex turns. Topic closure instead seems to be more stable; i.e. the investigations have shown almost no changes, at least for Julie and Oksana. The analysis of Christine's data has nevertheless highlighted that she does adapt her methods for closing a current topic over time, especially through a more active participation in topic closing environments.

After reaching these first results, new considerations could be made. On the one hand, there was the investigation into what such investigations of topic management can tell about the nature of L2 interactional competence. As was shown throughout this volume, L2 interactional competence is not easy to grasp, because it is a multilayered competence and presents itself under a variety of facets. It is possible to deal with it through the lens of specific actions, such as topic introduction or topic closure, whose investigations have revealed the array of resources mobilized by the au pairs during their sojourns for interacting appropriately with their host families. The description of these resources and the documentation of the related abilities deployed by the L2 speakers has contributed to a description of the nature of L2 interactional competence.

On the other hand, this study was concerned with the usability of longitudinal investigations into topic management to gain a better understanding of the development of L2 interactional competence. The longitudinal analyses in this volume have uncovered exactly to what extent change happens in the methods that the au pairs deploy to manage topics in conversation. It has been shown that they learn how to make their orientation toward the structural and the topical progression more observable and accountable for their interlocutors. This is to say, the L2 speakers have learned how to show in a more context-sensitive way what they orient toward and what they deal with during an ongoing interaction.

With this study, I have explained what CA is, how its methodology works, and how it is possible (and why it is useful) to apply it to the study of L2 talk in interaction, i.e. how one comes from CA to CA for SLA (Markee, 2005; Pekarek Doehler, 2013). This research has developed over several steps that have been presented in this book: data collection and transcription, data analysis, and research outputs. The decision to concentrate on conversational topics was tricky given that "CA is a rigorously empirical approach to social interactions" (Sidnell, 2010: 35): it is necessary to analyze the data from the emic perspective of the interactants, without being driven by a priori hypotheses. The attention is brought to observing what speakers do and how they do it. Topics are (or, topicality is) a pervasive feature of conversation: no one talks about nothing with anybody. There is always something people talk about, but the question to ask is, *how* do conversationalists talk about what they talk about? This question creates a discrepancy from more traditional linguistic theories, such as text linguistics, discourse analysis, or functionalism. Conversational topics need to be analyzed in terms of methods and resources, because it is enriching and it sheds new light on the concept of topic itself.

A major challenge was related to the existing terminology on topics, and the terms used in this book are not always satisfying. For instance, in Chapter 4, I have stated that I look at topics as conversational topics or as topic talk, thus investigating how interactants introduce, close, and shifts topics. This definition, however, appears to be circular: I do not want to define what a conversation is about and call this topic, but I analyze how topics are managed. How, then, shall I define a topic if not in the terms of "what is talked about"? It is helpful to declare from the beginning that the analytical focus is not about the definition of what the matter at stake is in the talk; that is I am not labeling sections in conversations based on their content. Instead, I describe how speakers collaboratively bring the conversation further by showing to their interlocutors what they are doing, such as by introducing and abandoning specific things to talk about while on or off topic. Maybe the term "topicality," as Maynard (1980) introduced it, would be more apt. This term relates semantically more to an action/activity sphere than does the term "topic," which is often used for labeling an entity. Because topic management is an underlying activity in all conversations, maybe the term "topicality" should be pushed forward when the analysis of conversational "content" is at stake. In sum, more empirical observations and reflections are needed to reach clearer concepts and terms.

8.2 Implications of This Study

After analyzing more and more data, I have become convinced that talking about topics in CA is easier when one works on L2 data. The mechanisms of introducing, closing, and changing topics are somehow more rudimental, and the linguistic resources are more limited, so some turns or silences gain more importance than they do in L1 conversations. For this reason, I hope that more attention will be paid to topic in the domain of CA-SLA: topics are an underlying feature of conversations; they are omnipresent and continuously adjusted by the interactants with every turn-at-talk. This makes a clear-cut analysis of this conversational aspect more difficult, but looking at how L2 speakers present and treat what they hold to be a conversational topic makes it clearer for the researcher too.

The most important question when it comes to implications for all applied linguistics research is the question of applicability and usefulness to the world of practice. For me, the question related to the usefulness of my research is omnipresent. However, the call for such reflexivity is still weak (but see Antaki, 2011; Grujicic-Alatriste, 2015; Paltridge, 2014), and more work needs to be undertaken to reach the goal of better information exchange between the world of research and the world of practice. I will now discuss two possible applications of CA-SLA research outputs.

First, the pedagogical universe could profit a lot from CA-SLA (Wong & Waring, 2010; Eskildsen & Majlesi, 2018; Hall, 2019; Salaberry & Kunitz, 2019). My analyses of conversational topics in L2 interactions, for instance, have considered several intertwined features of conversation, namely the sequential structure, the L2 speaker's participation, and the development of the L2 speaker's interactional competence, i.e. how they change their way of participating in conversations over time. Therefore, I believe that CA-SLA investigations can contribute in several ways to a better understanding of the process of L2 language learning.

During a recent interview, Joan K. Hall was asked why it is that CA-SLA research results are not widespread outside the research field. I report here Hall's answer to this question, and I then build on it to discuss the usefulness of CA-SLA research outcomes in other disciplines:

> There are many reasons why there is a disconnect between the research we do on L2 teaching and learning and pedagogical materials. One is that at least in the U.S., academics are rewarded more for publishing research studies and far less for publishing pedagogical materials. So those who are writing the materials are usually not those who are doing the research. A second reason is that we do not make our research easily interpreted by others, outside the field. Just take the example of the conflated use of interactional competence. As I noted earlier, you'll often read in studies "learners use their interactional competence to develop their interactional competence." While we researchers may understand what this is meant to state, those unfamiliar with the different meanings in terms very likely do not. . . . A third reason has to do with the constraints of state-mandated curriculum standards, at least in the United States. . . . Textbooks are written to meet the standards, regardless of whether the standards reflect current understandings of language and learning. Making changes to the standards can take a very long time.
> (Malabarba & Hall, 2017: 401)

So first, the world of research and the world of material creation and implementation are somehow divided by funding, prices, and public acknowledgment. This surely does not support the contact between the two sides. Second, it is true also that in language pedagogy, research is done on several matters, such as the definition of (linguistic) competence in itself (recent studies among others in the Swiss and European areas include Bronckart et al., 2005; Lüdi, 2006; Pekarek Doehler, 2003, 2009). However, as it is pointed out also by Hall in her answer, language pedagogy has to deal with more practical issues, such as the identification and applicability of linguistic curricula in schools and the evaluation of linguistic competences (see for example the documents of the European National Council, and the recent studies by Bachman & Palmer, 2010; Lenz & Berthelé, 2010; Pekarek Doehler, 2007). Bridging CA-SLA and the real world still seems to be difficult, probably due to the technical and detailed analyses contained in CA-SLA studies. Perhaps in this sense, a reflection on the terms used can be fruitful, as is wished for in the recent paper by Hall (2018). Making a clearer difference between a generic L2 interactional competence (Eskildsen, 2018) and L2 interactional repertoires leads to improve the readability and understandability of CA-SLA research outcomes also for scholars of other, related disciplines, such as education, psychology, and sociology.

In fact, CA has some similarities to other approaches, such as to discursive psychology (henceforth DP). De Ruiter & Albert (2017) highlight, for example, that both CA and DP are committed to the use of empirical, non-elicited data and to a general skepticism toward introspection and folk beliefs as source of information for understanding data and human conduct. The authors call for more collaboration and propose, for instance, to use CA analytical methods as starting point for psychological analyses. In contrast, they suggest adopting CA methodological tools for analyzing interactions in more experimental settings.

Although it is difficult to directly integrate CA-SLA studies into other domains, such as language pedagogy or DP, it is not impossible to use their analytical results as a basis for approaching the process of L2 learning in a different way. Especially the attention paid to the management of the relationship with one's interlocutors, the documentation of changes in the way an L2 speaker accomplishes one and the same action over time, and finally the changing way of participating in conversation are all aspects of an increased L2 interactional competence. This competence, CA-SLA researchers argue (see for instance the studies by Brouwer, 2013; Firth & Wagner, 1997; Hall, 1995, 2018; Hall et al., 2011; Hellermann, 2008; Huth & Taleghani-Nikazm, 2006; Kasper & Wagner, 2011; Pekarek Doehler, 2005, 2006, 2013), should become more central when the pedagogy specialists fix the linguistic curricula and the references for evaluating the L2 level of a speaker. In an interesting paper, Waring (2018) proposes an example of what the teaching of interactional competence could look like. Her example stems from a class for English as a second language, and it is built on a transcript that is used as basis for showing to the learners what actually happens in a normal conversation. Kim's (2017) study of topic introduction has shown what changes longitudinally in the way topics are proposed in conversation by two Japanese learners of English. Her final claim opens up in the same direction, with the author's suggestion:

> mapping this use of grammatical resources onto appropriate marking of one's epistemic stance according to interactional dynamics in topic initiation has not been part of the existing English curriculum. This can be incorporated as part of explicit teaching points in curriculum for English conversation.
>
> (Kim, 2017: 99)

First, steps are taken for bridging the world of research with the world of practice, specifically in the domains of education and psychology, but a lot of work still needs to be done in this respect.

Similarly, CA-SLA research results can contribute to a better understanding of what happens in some professional domains that explicitly deal with L2 learning issues. The case of au pairs' employment is exemplary in this sense. Generally speaking, spending some time abroad is the best opportunity for learning a new language. There are several papers that have dealt with the learning context of study abroad (Cook, 2014; Greer, 2018; König, 2013, 2014, 2018; Masuda, 2011; Pekarek Doehler & Pochon-Berger, 2011, 2015; Pekarek Doehler & Berger, 2018; Taguchi, 2015). However, not all the contexts of a study abroad experience are similar. In many cases, the study abroad experience takes place at university, such as during an exchange period. In this case, the daily life of the L2 speakers is organized differently from the life of an au pair.

At the beginning of this book, I discussed the specificities of this experience abroad and defined the learning context as a hybrid one. By this, I mean that when an au pair arrives in a host family and stays there for a longer sojourn, two social traits arise: formal (because of the professional relationship between the subjects) and informal (because of the familiar setting). CA-SLA studies have shown that these formal traits are overtly addressed by the interactants themselves during their interactions and are therefore made relevant only at some specific interactional moments (Pekarek Doehler &Pochon-Berger, 2018; König, 2013; Pochon-Berger et al., 2015; Wagner, 2015).

These investigations reveal the undergoing social processes that characterize this particular social relationship and the results of their studies can be useful to all the participants. Pochon-Berger et al. (2015) presents some practical steps for narrowing the gap between the research and the professional world, such as the implementation of consultations for host families, agencies, and future au pairs by the researchers. This is an attempt to popularize the research results in the CA-SLA domain and to show that a clear analysis of everyday talk can be useful to better understand and organize daily activities in families (more steps in this direction are presented in König, forthcoming). Similar reflections are

156 *Conclusion(s)*

found in a growing body of research on L2 learning "in the wild," i.e. in papers that show how the process of L2 acquisition takes place on a daily basis in a vast array of contexts, such as in service encounters, at work, or during everyday social encounters (Eskildsen, 2018a; Eskildsen & Theodórsdóttir, 2017; Hellermann et al., 2019; Svennevig, 2018; Theodórsdóttir, 2011a, 2011b; Theodórsdóttir & Eskildsen, 2011). The step that still seems more difficult to make is to contact the stakeholders and show them how useful CA-SLA research results are for professional practice. In this sense, I hope to see more discussions and more convergence between research and practice coming from both sides—because a collaboration between both worlds can succeed only if the willingness to try is bidirectional.

To conclude, in this study, I set out to investigate the development of interactional competence in French L2 through the study of topic management. Specifically, I have investigated the actions of topic introduction and of topic closure. My results show that topic management is a good starting point for the investigation of L2 interactional competence and its development over time. In fact, the au pairs of my study have shown a longitudinal diversification of the resources and the practices implemented for participating in conversation as far as topical issues are concerned. These findings have been shown to have important theoretical implications for the study of L2 interactional competence. One implication is that they can also be useful for practical purposes in different working and teaching domains.

References

Antaki, C. (2011). Six kinds of applied conversation analysis. In C. Antaki (Ed.), *Applied conversation analysis: Intervention and change in institutional talk* (pp. 1–14). New York: Palgrave Macmillan.

Bachman, L. F., & Palmer, A. S. (2010). *Language assessment in practice*. Oxford: Oxford University Press.

Bronckart, J.-P., Bulea, E., & Puliot, M. (2005). *Repenser l'enseignement des langues: Comment identifier et exploiter les compétences?*. Lille: Presses du Septentrion.

Brouwer, C. E. (2013). Conversation analysis methodology in second language studies. In C. A. Chapelle (Ed.), *The encyclopedia of applied linguistics*. Chichester: Wiley-Blackwell Publishing.

Cook, H. M. (2014). Language socialization and stance-taking practices. In A. Duranti, E. Ochs, & B. B. Schieffelin (Eds.), *The handbook of language socialization* (pp. 296–321). Malden and Oxford: Wiley Blackwell.

de Ruiter, J. P., & Albert, S. (2017). An appeal for a methodological fusion of conversation analysis and experimental psychology. *Research on Language and Social Interaction, 50*(1), 90–107. DOI:10.1080/08351813.2017.1262050

Eskildsen, S. W. (2018). Building a semiotic repertoire for social action: Interactional competence as biographical discovery. *Classroom Discourse, 9*(1), 68–76. DOI:10.1080/19463014.2018.1437052

Eskildsen, S. W. (2018a). 'We're learning a lot of new words': Encountering new L2 vocabulary outside of class. *The Modern Language Journal*, *102*(Supplement 2018), 46–63. DOI:10.1111/modl.12451

Eskildsen, S. W., & Majlesi, A. R. (2018). Learnables and teachables in second language talk: Advancing a social reconceptualization of central SLA tenets. Introduction to the Special Issue. *The Modern Language Journal*, *102*, Supplement 2018, 3–10.

Eskildsen, S. W., & Theodórsdóttir, G. (2017). Constructing L2 learning spaces: Ways to achieve learning inside and outside the Classroom. *Applied Linguistics*, *38*(2), 148–164.

Firth, A., & Wagner, J. (1997). On discourse, communication and some fundamental concepts in SLA research. *The Modern Language Journal*, *81*(3), 285–300.

Greer, T. (2018). Learning to say grace. *Social Interaction: Video-Based Studies of Human Sociality*, *1*(1). Retrieved from https://tidsskrift.dk/socialinteraction/article/view/105499/154290

Grujicic-Alatriste, L. (Ed.) (2015). *Linking discourse studies to professional practice*. Bristol: Multilingual Matters.

Hall, J. K. (1995). 'Aw, man, where you goin'?': Classroom interaction and the development of L2 interactional competence. *Issues in Applied Linguistics*, *6*(2), 37–62.

Hall, J. K. (2018). From L2 interactional competence to L2 interactional repertoires: Reconceptualizing the objects of L2 learning. *Classroom Discourse*, *8*(1), 25–39.

Hall, J. K. (2019). *Essentials of SLA for L2 teachers*. New York: Routledge.

Hall, J. K., Hellermann, J., & Pekarek Doehler, S. (Eds.) (2011). *L2 interactional competence and development*. Clevedon: Multilingual Matters.

Hellermann, J. (2008). *Social actions for classroom language learning*. Clevedon: Multilingual Matters.

Hellermann, J., Eskildsen, S., Pekarek-Doehler, S., & Piirainen-Marsh, A. (Eds.) (2019). *Conversation analytic research on learning-in-action: The complex ecology of second language interaction 'in the wild'*. Berlin: Springer.

Huth, T., & Taleghani-Nikazm, C. (2006). How can insights from conversation analysis be directly applied to teaching L2 pragmatics? *Language Teaching Research*, *10*(1), 53–79.

Kasper, G., & Wagner, J. (2011). A conversation-analytic approach to second language acquisition. In D. Atkinson (Ed.), *Alternative approaches to second language acquisition* (pp. 117–142). London and New York: Routledge.

Kim, Y. (2017). Topic initiation in conversation-for-learning: Developmental and pedagogical perspectives. *English Teaching*, *72*(1), 73–103. DOI:10.15858/engtea.72.1.201703.73

König, C. (2013). Topic management in French L2: A longitudinal conversation analytic approach (pp. 226–250). *EUROSLA Yearbook 13*. Amsterdam/Philadelphia: John Benjamins Publishing Company.

König, C. (2014). Competenza interazionale in francese L2: l'esempio della 'parola ripresa' nella conversazione familiare. *Linguistica e Filologia*, *34*, 135–165.

König, C. (2018). Französischlernen mit Kindern. Reparatursequenzen im Alltagsleben von Au pair Mädchen. In G. Albert & S. Diao-Klaeger (Hgs.), *Mündlicher Sprachgebrauch zwischen Normorientierung und pragmatischen Spielräumen* (pp. 45–64). Tübingen: Stauffenburg Verlag.

König, C. (forthcoming). Disseminating CA-SLA research outputs: An essay in the professional world of au pair girls. In L. Grujicic-Alatriste (Ed.), *Language research in multilingual settings: Doing knowledge dissemination at the sites of practice*. London: Palgrave Macmillan.

Lenz, P., & Berthelé, R. (2010). Prise en compte des compétences plurilingue et interculturelle dans l'évaluation. Document de réflexion préparé pour le Forum politique 'Le droit des apprenants à la qualité et l'équité en éducation—Le rôle des compétences linguistiques et interculturelles'. Geneva. https://www.unil.ch/files/live/sites/magicc/files/shared/Ressources/Assessment2010_Lenz_FRrev.pdf

Lüdi, G. (2006). Multilingual repertoires and the consequences for linguistic theory. In K. Bührig & J. D. ten Thije (Eds.), *Beyond misunderstanding: Linguistic analyses of intercultural communication* (pp. 11–42). New York and Amsterdam: John Benjamins Publishing Company.

Malabarba, T., & Hall, J. K. (2017). Interaction and second language acquisition research: Interview with Joan Kelly Hall. *Calidoscópio*, 15(2), 399–403. DOI:10.4013/cld.2017.152.16

Markee, N. P. P. (2005). Conversation analysis for second language acquisition. In E. Hinkel (Ed.), *Handbook of research in second language teaching and learning* (pp. 355–374). Mahwah: NJ: Lawrence Erlbaum Associates.

Masuda, K. (2011). Acquiring interactional competence in a study abroad context: Japanese language learners' use of the interactional particle ne. *The Modern Language Journal*, 95(4), 519–540.

Maynard, D. W. (1980). Placement of topic changes in conversation. *Semiotica*, 30, 263–290.

Paltridge, B. (2014). What motivates applied linguistics research? *AILA Review*, 27(2014), 98–104. DOI:10.1075/aila.27.05pal

Pekarek Doehler, S. (2003). Représentations sociales et apprentissage: situer les représentations sociales dans les activités pratiques. In F. Regnard & E. Cramer (Eds.), *Apprendre et enseigner la musique: représentations croisées*. Paris: L'Harmattan.

Pekarek Doehler, S. (2005). De la nature située des compétences en langue. In J. P. Bronckart, E. Bulea, & M. Puliot (Eds.), *Repenser l'eneseignement des langues: Comment identifier et exploiter les compétences* (pp. 41–68). Villeneuve d'Arc: Presses Universitaires du Septentrion. Retrieved from https://gemma.unine.ch/sites/islc/CLA/Documents%20CLA/Biblioth%C3%A8que%20PDF%20du%20CLA/Pekarek%20Doehler_2005a.pdf

Pekarek Doehler, S. (2006). Compétence et langage en action. *Bulletin Suisse de Linguistique Appliquée*, 84, 9–45.

Pekarek Doehler, S. (2007). L'évaluation des compétences: mythes du langage et défis pour la recherche. *Cahiers de l'ILSL*, 23, 125–136.

Pekarek Doehler, S. (2009). Démythifier les compétences: vers une pratique écologique d'évaluation. In O. Galatanu, M. Pierrard, & D. Van Raemdonck (Eds.), *Construction du sens et acquisition de la signification linguistique dans l'interaction* (pp. 19–38). Bern: Peter Lang.

Pekarek Doehler, S. (2013). Conversation analysis and second language acquisition. In C. A. Chapelle (Ed.), *The encyclopedia of applied linguistics* (pp. 1–8). Blackwell Publishing. DOI:10.1002/9781405198431.wbeal0217

Pekarek Doehler, S., & Pochon-Berger, E. (2011). Developing 'methods' for interaction: A cross-sectional study of disagreement sequences in French L2. In J. K.

Hall, J. Hellermann, & S. Pekarek Doehler (Eds.), *L2 interactional competence and development* (pp. 206–243). Clevedon: Multilingual Matters.

Pekarek Doehler, S., & Pochon-Berger, E. (2015). The development of L2 interactional competence: Evidence from turn-taking organization, sequence organization, repair organization and preference organization. In T. Cadierno & S. Eskildsen (Eds.), *Usage-based perspectives on second language learning* (pp. 233–267). Berlin: Mouton de Gruyter.

Pekarek Doehler, S., & Pochon-Berger, E. (2018). L2 interactional competence as increased ability for context-sensitive conduct: A longitudinal study of story-openings. *Applied Linguistics*, 39(4), 555–578. DOI:10.1093/applin/amw021

Pochon-Berger, E., Pekarek Doehler, S., & König, C. (2015). Family conversational storytelling at the margins of the workplace: The case of au pair girls. In L. Grujicic-Alatriste (Ed.), *Linking discourse studies to professional practice* (pp. 86–108). Bristol: Multilingual Matters.

Salaberry, M. R., & Kunitz, S. (2019). *Teaching and testing L2 interactional competence bridging theory and practice*. New York: Routledge.

Sidnell, J. (2010). *Conversation analysis: An introduction*. London: Wiley Blackwell.

Svennevig, J. (2018). 'What's it called in Norwegian?' Acquiring L2 vocabulary in the workplace. *Journal of Pragmatics*, 126, 68–77.

Taguchi, N. (2015). *Developing interactional competence in a Japanese study abroad context*. Bristol: Multilingual Matters.

Theodórsdóttir, G. (2011a). Language learning activities in everyday situations: Insisting on TCU completion in second language talk. In G. Palotti & J. Wagner (Eds.), *L2 learning as a social practice: Conversation-analytic perspectives*. Honolulu, Hawaii: University of Hawaii at Manoa, National Foreign Language Resource Center.

Theodórsdóttir, G. (2011b). Second language interaction for business and learning. In J. K. Hall, J. Hellermann, & S. Pekarek-Doehler (Eds.), *L2 interactional competence and development*. New York: Multilingual Matters.

Theodórsdóttir, G., & Eskildsen, S. W. (2011). Achieving intersubjectivity and doing learning: The use of English as a lingua franca in Icelandic L2. *Nordand*, 6, 59–85.

Wagner, J. (2015). Designing for language learning in the wild: Creating social infrastructures for second language learning. In T. Cadierno & S. W. Eskildsen (Eds.), *Usage-based perspectives on second language learning* (pp. 75–104). Berlin: Mouton de Gruyter.

Waring, H. Z. (2018). Teaching L2 interactional competence: Problems and possibilities. *Classroom Discourse*, 9(1), 57–67. DOI:10.1080/19463014.2018.1434082

Wong, J., & Waring, H. Z. (2010). *Conversation analysis and second language pedagogy. A guide for ESL/EFL teachers*. New York: Routledge.

Appendix I
Transcription Conventions

Please note that the transcriptions in French have three lines. The first line is in Courier New and is the actual transcription. The second line is in Times New Roman italics and contains the grammatical translation. The third line is in Times New Roman and contains the linguistic translation.

.	Final falling intonation
?	Final rising intonation
,	Continuative intonation
bla:::	Vocal prolongation
(bla)	Unclear segment
(xx)	Incomprehensible segment
BLA	High voice volume
bla	Low voice volume
↑bla	High pitch
>bla<	Faster speech speed
<bla>	Slower speech speed
.h .hh .hhh	In-breath
h. hh. hhh.	Out-breath
=	Latching
(non;mon)	Uncertain segment for which possibilities are given
+ bla ((comment))+	Comment
[	Overlap
&	Turn continuation
(.) (. .) (. . .) (2.5)	Pauses
INTERJ	Interjection
DIR	Direct object
IND	Indirect object
SUBJ	Subject
NEG	Negation
DET	Determinate
pl—sg, M - F	Plural—singular, masculine - feminine
1. 2. 3.	1st, 2nd, or 3rd person
INF	Infinite (for verbs)

Index

ability/abilities 31, 47, 48–49, 57, 69, 97, 132, 135, 137, 138, 140, 151
aboutness 21
action/s: accomplishment of 47, 80, 131, 142; coordination 49; social 4, 5, 8, 34, 46, 64, 137–138, 144
activity/activities: interactional 12, 138; language-related 50; social 50, 57; type 65, 146
affiliation 6–7, 29, 30, 34, 92, 116; affiliative response 103
agenda 26, 70, 73, 98, 141, 146
alignment 6–7, 34, 73, 89, 92, 98, 103, 112, 114, 116, 121, 136
anaphora 22, 58, 63–65
applicability 152, 154
asymmetries: authority and epistemic 12, 25–26, 70, 73; linguistic 12

CA analytical methods 154
caregiver 12, 141
CA-SLA i, 2–3, 13, 35–36, 45–48, 51, 53–58, 67, 132, 134, 138, 150, 153–156, 158
change driven 117
closing: sequence/s 23, 67, 72–75, 87, 114, 116, 119, 120, 122, 124, 130–131, 146; turns-at-talk 117, 142, 146–147
closing implicative: context/s 89, 142; environment 72, 97–98, 112, 114–116, 119, 124, 132, 137, 139, 143; expressions 130–131, 143; items 124; laughter 34; turn/s 33, 91, 97, 119, 121–122, 128, 130–131, 139, 143
collection 9, 56, 67, 93, 98–99, 134, 139, 142, 151
communicative project 71, 84, 86, 98

community: discourses 50; linguistic and cultural 50; of practice 57–58
competence: communicative 49–50; distributed 51; interactional 2–3, 9–10, 13, 43, 45, 47–49, 51–58, 79–80, 97, 99, 106, 131–138, 141, 143–144, 146–147, 150–151, 153–154, 156; procedural 52
context/s: family 54, 70, 84; hybrid learning 13; informal 53–54; interactional 4, 11, 49, 52, 70, 142, 146; learning 13, 52, 145, 155; -sensitive 25, 140, 151; study abroad 52
conversation/s: analysis 1–2, 4, 8, 17, 43; everyday 13, 26, 46, 137–138, 146; family 5, 34, 46, 57; -for-learning settings 70; for second language acquisition i, 43; structural organization of 4
conversational: activity/activities 47, 69, 140; practice 35
course/s of action 25, 51, 82

DP 154
discourse: analysis 1, 17–18, 20; marker/s (*see* marker/s)
discursive psychology 154
deictic: expression/s 64; means 66
deixis 63, 66
disalignment 73, 114, 130
dislocation/s 21–22, 32, 64–69, 104

emic perspective 1, 9, 46, 56, 151
epistemic(s): access 34, 36–37, 73; access and primacy 36; authority 35–36; positioning 35; stance 36, 114; status 36
everyday: conversations 13, 26, 46, 137–138, 146; interactional data 70;

interactions 2, 34, 54, 63, 69–70, 150; institutional interactions 34; talk 70–71, 155; talk-in-interaction 1, 7, 43, 46

final statement 23, 89, 116, 120–121, 128–129
formulaic language 142–143
French: L1 63, 66, 69; L1 and L2 interactions 63; L2 2, 9–10, 13, 21, 36–37, 54–55, 57, 66, 67–69, 71, 79–80, 83, 117, 124, 130–132, 134–135, 137–138, 143, 156; L2 interactions 36

grammar in interaction 8

host-family/families 2, 5, 9–13, 43, 53, 56, 69, 79–80, 89, 99, 110, 127, 132, 134, 141, 143, 145–147, 151, 155

identities 36, 45
information structure 21, 64–65, 69, 80
interactional: activities (*see* activities); linguistics 8–9, 75
interactional competence: interactional repertoires 53, 138, 140, 154; teaching of 154; *see also* competence
intersubjectivity 45–47, 49, 53–54, 72, 92, 96, 138

joint laughter 72, 114
joint topic closure 130

knowledge asymmetry *see* asymmetries

L2: acquisition 2, 20, 43, 55, 156; daily use 51; developmental level 22; interactions 34, 36, 63, 153; learning 2, 12–13, 43, 45–46, 53–58, 131, 138, 140, 154–156; proficiency level 9–10, 75, 106, 132, 135, 139, 141, 143; talk-in-interaction 49, 51–53, 58, 67, 74, 138
L2 interactional competence 2–3, 10, 13, 15, 45–46, 48, 52–55, 57–59, 79, 97, 99, 106, 131–132, 134–141, 143–144, 146–147, 154, 156; development of 2, 51–52, 57, 97, 132, 134, 138, 140–141, 143, 151,

156; nature of 2, 99, 134, 136, 138, 144, 147, 151; stable 147; in the wild 13, 53
L2 interactional repertoires *see* interactional competence
language: language-in-use 4; pedagogy 153–154; problems 55; socialization 58; switching 54
learnables 54
learning: observe and trace 45; process 2, 12–13, 43, 46, 48, 50, 54, 131, 140, 145
longitudinal: changes 130, 143, 146; data 37, 79, 99, 117, 135; design 2, 134, 141, 150; development of L2 interactional competence 57; investigations 2, 55, 69, 134, 141, 151; study/studies i, 9, 13, 43, 55–56, 58

management of intersubjectivity *see* intersubjectivity
marker/s: discourse 26, 71, 84, 97; disjunctive 102; hesitation 71, 82, 84, 86, 89, 119–121; misplacement 67, 69, 71, 83, 86–87, 98, 139, 141, 150; opposition 82, 104
mentionables 24, 107
metalinguistic question 96, 126

narratives 21, 30, 35–36
naturally occurring: conversations 4; data 4; interactions 4, 46

participation in topic closure 124, 130, 143, 147
power relationship 70
practice/s: interactive 51; oral 50; social 57
Prague: school 17–18; circle 17
preference 7, 63, 65, 116; organization of 6–7, 64
procedural information 29, 33, 66
procedure/s 4, 52, 56
proficiency level: ESL 74; L2 9–10, 75, 106, 135, 135, 139, 141, 143
progressivity 29, 33, 80, 83, 87
projectability 29–30

real-life data 9
recipient design 13, 36, 87, 98, 138, 140, 145, 151
reference: establishing 64; establishment of 64; multiple

104, 140; personal 63; referential expressions 104; referential process 64; shift 100
response/s 6–7, 25, 27, 30, 32, 55–57, 70, 72, 84, 87, 89, 91, 95, 101, 103–106, 108, 112, 115–116, 124, 126, 130
rheme 18

second language acquisition 17, 20, 43
sequence/s: boundaries 74, 136; organization 6, 57, 64–65, 67; side sequence 23, 74, 95
sequential: analysis 75, 80, 110, 117; organization 33, 86, 97; progression 80, 83
socialization 2, 50, 53–54, 58
social nature of L2 learning 55
storytelling/s 7, 12, 34–36, 49, 51, 54, 58, 74, 86, 112, 131
strategies i, 21–22, 63, 66, 70, 102, 134, 140, 151
systematic procedures *see* procedure/s

text linguistics 17
theme 17–18
topic/s: boundaries 23, 27, 70–71, 136; change 23–25, 67, 83, 95, 114, 150; conversational i, 2, 12–13, 27, 34–37, 52, 58, 63–67, 69–71, 79, 83–85, 87, 89, 91, 95–99, 104, 106–108, 110, 116–117, 119, 124, 131, 135–142, 144–145, 150–153; closure 2–3, 12–13, 25, 58, 63, 67, 71–72, 74–75, 110, 113–114, 117, 120, 122, 124–125, 127–128, 130–132, 134–138, 142–143, 146–147, 151, 156; (dis)continuity 21, 31, 39; interactional 66–67, 100; introduction 2–3, 12–13, 27–28, 36, 57–58, 63, 66–67, 70, 75, 79–80, 83, 85, 87–88, 90, 92–93, 96–99, 116–117, 131, 134–141, 144–145, 147, 150–151, 154, 156; management 1–2, 6, 13, 22, 34, 36–37, 57–58, 63–65, 67, 69, 99, 134, 136–138, 151–152, 156; marking 18, 21; progression 23, 25, 27, 99; shift 24, 69, 79, 99–102, 104, 106–108, 135, 139–140; talk 22, 74, 152; topic-comment structure 21
topical: backlinking 54, 67, 69, 99, 135; disjunctions 27; line 26, 33, 66, 140–141; progression 25, 27, 71, 80, 151; progressivity 80, 83; reorientation 116; sequence 36, 79, 83, 145; talk 24–27, 29, 33, 36, 83
topicality 1, 23, 29, 151–152
topicalization 29–30
topicalizer 27, 30, 112, 119, 139, 142
turn/s: architecture 13, 85, 87, 97, 121; construction 9, 65, 80, 87, 91, 96; design 36, 104; taking 5–6, 8, 25, 52, 57, 67, 69–70, 121, 124, 130

word search sequences 54
workplace 13, 46

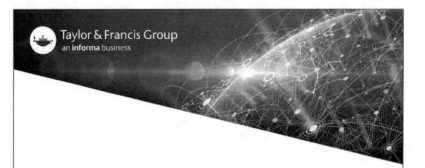